DATE DUE

THOMAS JEFFERSON

"Negro President"

TIMOTHY PICKERING

"Negro President"

Jefferson and the Slave Power

Garry Wills

Houghton Mifflin Company
BOSTON • NEW YORK
2003

For information about permission to reproduce selections
from this book, write to Permissions, Houghton Mifflin Company,
215 Park Avenue South, New York, New York 10003.

Visit our Web site: www.houghtonmifflinbooks.com.

Library of Congress Cataloging-in-Publication Data is available.

ISBN 0-618-34398-9

PRINTED IN THE UNITED STATES OF AMERICA

Book design by Robert Overholtzer

QUM 10 9 8 7 6 5 4 3 2 1

Frontispiece: Portrait of Thomas Jefferson by Thomas Scully, 1821,
courtesy of the American Philosophical Society. Portrait of
Timothy Pickering by Charles Willson Peale, from life, 1792–1793,
courtesy of Independence National Historical Park.

To Lydia

WHO KNOWS SO MUCH MORE
ABOUT BOOKS THAN I DO

Contents

12. 1808: Pickering and Governor Sullivan   159
13. 1808: Pickering and J. Q. Adams   171
14. 1809–1815: Pickering and Madison   182

IV. THE PICKERING LEGACY   195

15. J. Q. Adams: The Federal (Slave) District   200
16. J. Q. Adams: Petition Battles   214
    Epilogue: Farewell to Pickering   226

    Notes   233
    Acknowledgments   259
    Index   260

Key to Brief Citations

B   Burr: Mary-Jo Kline et al., editors, *Political Correspondence and Public Papers of Aaron Burr* (Princeton University Press, 1963)

C   Gerard H. Clarfield, *Timothy Pickering and the American Republic* (University of Pittsburgh Press, 1980)

D   Documents: Henry Adams, *Documents Relating to New-England Federalism, 1800–1815* (Little, Brown, 1905)

F   Max Farrand, editor, *The Records of the Federal Convention of 1787* (Yale University Press, 1966)

H   Gaillard Hunt, editor, *Journals of the Continental Congress, 1774–1789* (Government Printing Office, 1904–1937)

J   Jefferson: Julian P. Boyd et al., editors, *The Papers of Thomas Jefferson* (Princeton University Press, 1950–)

JQ   John Quincy Adams, Diary, by volume in the Massachusetts Historical Society

M   Madison: William T. Hutchison et al., editors, *The Papers of James Madison* (University Presses of Chicago and Virginia, 1962–)

P   The Papers of Timothy Pickering, by volume (and microfilm reel) in the Massachusetts Historical Society

PM   Plumer *Memorandum:* Everett Somerville Brown, editor, *William Plumer's Memorandum of Proceedings in the United States Senate, 1803–1807* (Macmillan, 1923)

Prologue: Coming to Terms with Jefferson

I HAVE ADMIRED Jefferson all my life, and still do — though some may question that statement after reading this book. His labors to guarantee freedom of religion would in themselves be enough to maintain his place in my private pantheon. But there is much else I revere in him. A quarter of a century ago, I published a book praising him as an Enlightenment philosopher.[1] A year ago, I published a book praising him as an artist.[2] In the interval between those two I have served on the board of advisers to the Jefferson International Center at Charlottesville and the scholars' advisory group for his friend Madison's home, Montpelier. I have also spoken and written for fundraisers benefiting his two homes, Monticello and Poplar Forest, his university at Charlottesville, and the publication project of his papers. Along the way I have written review-articles that looked at different aspects of his life.[3] But I have never devoted an entire book to one deadly part of his politics — the protection and extension of slavery through the three-fifths clause in the Constitution.

This book depends on, and wants to join, modern historians' general and growing labor to grasp the pervasiveness of slavery's effects on our early history. I do *not* mean for it to join an unfortunate recent trend toward Jefferson-bashing. I disagree with those who would diminish his great achievement, the Declaration of Independence.[4] Or those who call him more a friend to despotism than to freedom.[5] Or those who would reduce his whole life to one affair with a slave. My Jefferson is a giant, but a giant trammeled in a net, and obliged (he thought) to keep repairing and strengthening the coils of that net.

One of the most important elements in this self-imprisoning purchase upon power was the three-fifths clause of the Constitution. It was with the help of that clause that he won his election in 1800. My recognizing that fact does not mean that I would have preferred to have John Adams win. Like Henry Adams, I think Jefferson was a better president than either of Adams's own forebears.[6] Jefferson had a national vision that the Federalists lacked. In one of the many ironies studied by Henry Adams, the states'-rights school imposed a national system on this continent. The southern regionalists realized, as the northern ones never did, that they had to recruit other areas to the protection of their own turf. The South tended its stake in slavery when it looked west; but at least it did look west, and forged a continental system in the process, while the Federalists were more concerned with purifying themselves at home. The Federalists, by righteously defining themselves as the party of the few, guaranteed their own demise.[7]

Yet this does not make Republicans "pure" democrats. They blended a paradoxical and insidious populism with the holding of slaves. Though everyone recognizes that Jefferson depended on slaves for his economic existence, fewer reflect that he depended on them for his political existence. Yet the latter was the all-important guardian of the former. Like other southerners, Jefferson had to take every political step he could to prevent challenges to the slave system. That is why southerners made sure that slavery was embedded in the very legislative process of the nation, as that was created by the Constitution — they made the three-fifths "representation" of slaves in the national legislature a non-negotiable condition for their joining the Union (see Chapter 3 below). This had nothing to do, necessarily, with approval of slavery in itself — only with the political use of it to fend off challenges to the southern economic base. One could feel revulsion against slavery as an institution, yet expend great energy in buttressing it — George Washington freed his own slaves at his wife's death, but labored mightily to place the national capital in territory where it would be populated with slaves (see Chapter 15 below).

In this book, then, I shall neglect Jefferson's many other claims on our admiration and gratitude — material I shall be returning to in my next book. Here I concentrate solely on his role as a protector and extender of the slave system. To highlight that aspect of the man, I review the trenchant criticisms of him voiced by one of his most vociferous congressional critics, Timothy Pickering of Massachusetts. Pickering is, for my purposes, a useful anti-Jefferson, a kind of mirror image in reversal. My concentration on just one aspect of Pickering's career, taken from a long and controversial public life, does not mean that I wish Pickering had prevailed over Jefferson, any more than I wish that John Adams had won in 1800. Pickering is Jefferson's critic, not his equal. On one point at issue between them, the slave system, Pickering is seen at his most creditable, and Jefferson at his least creditable. Their conflict clarifies what was at stake in the preservation of the slave system.

That system ruled the South. It cowed and silenced the North. Pickering could see the evil, but could do little about it, because of the very power he was denouncing. Jefferson felt he had no choice but to defend the evil. There was no large-scale political career open to southerners who refused to defend it.[8] That is the tragedy of Jefferson, and of the nation. We may admit that he was trapped in the system — which is all the more reason for deploring the trap.

Introduction: The Three-Fifths Clause

> The election of Mr. Jefferson to the presidency was, upon sectional
> feelings, the triumph of the South over the North — of the slave repre-
> sentation over the purely free.
>
> — John Quincy Adams

WHAT DID Thomas Jefferson's Federalist critics mean, after 1800, when they called him the "Negro President"? A
person first encountering the term might, in the not too
distant past, have thought it referred to Jefferson's private life at
Monticello. In those hagiographical days, calling him a "Negro president" might have been interpreted to mean that he was a *pro*-Negro
president, an *ami des noirs* who sympathized with the plight of
slaves, though he could not do much about it.[1] That was the line I
heard when I first visited Monticello more than forty years ago.
More recently still, the term might be taken to mean that he loved
his own slave Sally Hemings, or exploited her, or both. But those
first calling him the "Negro President" were not prying into his private life. They were challenging his public boast that the election of
1800 was a "Second Revolution" based on the expressed will of a
popular majority. It was no such thing, they argued. In terms of the
number of actual votes cast, John Adams was re-elected. The Second Revolution never occurred.

Jefferson's Election

If real votes alone had been counted, Adams would have been re-turned to office. But, of course, the "vote" did not depend solely on voters. Though Jefferson, admittedly, received eight more votes than Adams in the Electoral College, at least twelve of his votes were not based on the citizenry that could express its will but on the blacks owned by southern masters.[2] A bargain had been struck at the Constitutional Convention — one of the famous compromises on which the document was formed, this one intended to secure ratification in the South. The negotiated agreement decreed that each slave held in the United States would count as three-fifths of a person — the so-called federal ratio — for establishing the represen-tation of a state in the House of Representatives (and consequently in the Electoral College, which was based on the House and Senate numbers for each state in Congress).

It galled the Federalists that Jefferson hailed his 1800 victory as a triumph of democracy and majority rule when, as the *Mercury and New-England Palladium* of Boston said (January 20, 1801), he had made his "ride into the temple of Liberty on the shoulders of slaves." He was president only because of "somber" or "sable" non-votes, and the *Columbian Centinel* noted (December 24, 1800) that the half-million slaves affecting the outcome had no more will in the matter than "New England horses, cows, and oxen."[3] Timothy Pickering, the former secretary of state under Washington and Ad-ams, coined the term "Negro President" and made it current among his Federalist allies — along with references to Negro electors, Negro voters, and Negro congressmen.[4] Senator William Plumer of New Hampshire wrote that "the Negro votes made Mr. Jefferson presi-dent."[5] He felt that "Negro electors exceed those of four states, and their representatives are equal to those of six states" (PM 67).

Even four years before the 1800 election, New Englanders had feared that Jefferson might win on his first try for the presidency, but only because of the "Negro electors." Connecticut governor Oli-ver Wolcott said then that the country would not submit to election "by a Negro representation only," and papers in his state predicted that such an event might prompt the North to secede from the

Union.[6] When their fears were confirmed by the outcome in 1800, Pickering faced the 1804 contest with a dread premonition:

> Without a separation, can those [New England] states ever rid them- selves of Negro Presidents and Negro Congresses, and regain their just weight in the political balance? At this moment, the slaves of the middle and southern states have fifteen representatives in Congress, and they will appoint that number of electors of the next president and vice president; and the number of slaves is continuously increas- ing. (P 14.101)

The Federalists predicted that this Negro "representation" would increase year by year so long as the federal ratio were retained. This prospect is what they meant by "the slave power." They did not mean the power that plantation owners exerted over their black slaves, or the power slaves might someday use in retaliation. They meant the power that slave states wielded over non-slave states. The Federalists said that the plantation men were *their* masters. As Wil- liam Plumer wrote in a public appeal to his New Hampshire con- stituents:

> Every five of the Negro slaves are accounted equal to three of you . . . Those slaves have no voice in the elections; they are mere property; yet a planter possessing a hundred of them may be considered as having sixty votes, while one of you who has equal or greater prop- erty is confined to a single vote.[7]

Though the election of 1800 is one of the most thoroughly stud- ied events in our history, few treatments of it even mention the fact that Jefferson won it by the slave count. It is called the first modern election, because political parties contested it. People de- bate whether it earns Jefferson's own title for it, the "Second Revolu- tion." But Jefferson's ascendancy is most frequently hailed as a tri- umph for the stability of the young constitutional system, since the incumbent was ousted without violence: "Above all, the election demonstrated that control of the vast political power of the na- tional government could pass peacefully from one political party to another."[8]

The election is studied, as well, because it was deflected to the

House of Representatives for decision, since the two Republican candidates, Jefferson and Burr, received a tie vote in the Electoral College. That tie led to one of the earliest constitutional readjustments after the adoption of the Bill of Rights — the Twelfth Amendment, which established a separate vote for the vice presidency. The election can also be treated as a clash between the personalities of Jefferson and Burr, or between Jefferson and Adams. These are all interesting aspects of the event. But they are not enough, in themselves, to explain the odd neglect of the fact that this was an election where the federal ratio made the margin of difference.

Two authors have written books on the election of 1800 without a single reference to the votes given Jefferson by the slave bonus.[9] A fine symposium on the election, rated in its own pages as "the best new scholarship on the politics of 1800," has in its sixteen major essays only three glancing mentions of the federal ratio.[10] Respected biographers of the principals in the affair — Adams, Jefferson, and Burr — also fail to mention the boost given Jefferson by the three-fifths clause, or they refer to it only peripherally, as if it were unimportant.[11] To judge by the mass of things written on the election, Jefferson's debt to the federal ratio must be one of the great non-events of our past.

Yet for Federalists the slave count was not a subsidiary concern; it was at the very core of sectional division in the country. Josiah Quincy, who became the president of Harvard, always maintained that "the slave representation is the cause of all the difficulties we labor under."[12] Fisher Ames called it a flaw in the Constitution that, "instead of *ap*portioning, *dis*proportions representatives to numbers [of citizens]."[13] For such men, the ratio was even more pernicious in its consequences than the clauses in the Constitution that recognized the legitimacy of the slave trade for the next twenty years (Article I, Section 9) or that imposed a fugitive slave law on the states (Article IV, Section 2). The federal ratio undermined the very possibility of debating or changing the status of slaves — as the gag rules of the 1830s and 1840s would demonstrate. It gave a key electoral tool for maintaining slavery against a majority of white voters. The federal ratio was such an irritant to the Federalists that one man's gibe at Jefferson's children by Sally Hemings was seen as swelling the ratio. Five children by her would give him three extra votes.

> Great men can never lack supporters
> Who manufacture their own voters.[14]

Reach of the Three-Fifths Clause

Why is the impact of the federal ratio so little known? The first reaction of many people when told about its role in Jefferson's election is to ask why they never heard of it before. There are several explanations for this, all contained within the fact that through much of our history Americans have shied away from slavery as too divisive or hot an issue, leading to a great national amnesia about its impact and reach. More particularly, the force of the three-fifths clause is neglected because it "only" affected one presidential election, Jefferson's — though Paul Finkelman suggests that it may have deprived John Quincy Adams of a majority in the contested election of 1824.[15] The federal ratio is neglected, as well, because dire predictions of southern majorities in the Congress never came true, even with the benefit of the slave count, since immigration was heavier in the North during the early nineteenth century.

But the power of the South was not measured solely in terms of an overall majority. On crucial matters, when several factions were contending, the federal ratio gave the South a voting majority. Without the federal ratio as the deciding factor in House votes, slavery would have been excluded from Missouri (see Chapter 14 below), Jackson's Indian removal policy would have failed (see Chapter 16), the 1840 gag rule would not have been imposed (Chapter 16), the Wilmot Proviso would have banned slavery in territories won from Mexico (Chapter 16), the Kansas-Nebraska Bill would have failed (Chapter 16). Other votes were close enough to afford opposition to the South a better chance, if the federal ratio had not been counted into the calculations from the outset. Elections to key congressional posts were affected continually by the federal ratio, with the result that southerners held "the Speaker's office for 79 percent of the time [before 1824], Ways and Means for 92 percent."[16]

Leonard Richards shows another pervasive influence of the three-fifths clause. Even when it did not affect the outcome of congressional votes, it dominated Democratic caucus and convention votes, since the South had a larger majority there than in the total body. The federal ratio guaranteed that Democratic presidential nominations would be friendly to the slave interest. When control of the caucus seemed to be slipping from southern hands, a two-thirds requirement for nominating candidates was installed, to give them power to veto unacceptable men. The federal ratio was, therefore, just the starting point for seizing and solidifying positions of influence in the government. It was a force supplemented by other maneuvers. It gave the South a permanent head start for all its political activities.

> The slave states always had one-third more seats in Congress than their free population warranted — forty-seven seats instead of thirty-three in 1793, seventy-six instead of fifty-nine in 1812, and ninety-eight instead of seventy-three in 1833 . . . The Deep South also imported more slaves from Africa in the twenty years from 1788 to 1808 (the year the international slave trade was legally banned) than in any other twenty-year period . . . the three-fifths rule would also play a decisive role in every political caucus and every political convention.[17]

The federal ratio, and its ripple of side effects, had a great deal to do with the fact that for over half a century, right up to the Civil War, the management of government was disproportionately controlled by the South.

> In the sixty-two years between Washington's election and the Compromise of 1850, for example, slaveholders controlled the presidency for fifty years, the Speaker's chair for forty-one years, and the chairmanship of House Ways and Means [the most important committee] for forty-two years. The only men to be reelected president — Washington, Jefferson, Madison, Monroe, and Jackson — were all slaveholders. The men who sat in the Speaker's chair the longest — Henry Clay, Andrew Stevenson, and Nathaniel Macon — were slaveholders. Eighteen out of thirty-one Supreme Court justices were slaveholders.[18]

Seven justices delivered the majority opinion in the Dred Scott decision, and a majority of them were slaveholders.[19] The lower courts, too, were stocked with pro-slavery men. Jefferson came into office complaining about a federal judiciary unbalanced in favor of Federalists; but that balance shifted to the other extreme over the next decades.[20]

Richard H. Brown states flatly: "From the inauguration of Washington until the Civil War, the South was in the saddle of national politics. This is the central fact in American political history to 1860."[21] Ten of the pre–Civil War presidents were slave owners themselves, and two of the postwar presidents had owned slaves earlier — Johnson and Grant. That means that over a quarter of the presidents in our history were slaveholders.[22] Even those who were not southerners had to temporize with the South. Northerners or westerners like Van Buren, Tyler, Polk, Clay, and Buchanan helped craft the gag laws protecting slavery in the District of Columbia (see Chapter 16 below). Tyler added a slave Texas, and Polk waged the war for slave territory taken from Mexico. It was a northerner who constructed the North-South alliance that protected slavery for decades: "Many scholars have long suspected that Van Buren and his colleagues purposely fashioned the Jackson coalition so that it protected slavery and southern interests."[23] Buchanan worked behind the scenes to keep Dred Scott a slave.[24] Even John Quincy Adams had to settle for a southern cabinet, led by the slaveholding Clay, to deal with a Jacksonian Congress. (For Adams's compromises with slavery before he entered Congress in 1831, see Chapter 15 below.)

Control of the presidency rested on the slave power's deep roots in the patronage and court systems of the Jeffersonian party. A survey of the highest federal office holders in this time showed that half of them were southerners, though the North had almost twice the free population of the South.[25] Southerners held 57 percent of the high civil-service posts under Adams, 56 percent under Jefferson, 57 percent under Jackson.[26] And this imbalance was not merely a matter of quantity. It had to do with quality as well, since the South promoted strong, even extreme, proponents of slavery to office while keeping critics of slavery, even of the mildest sort, from among the northerners winning confirmation.[27] In many ways, direct and indirect, this reflected the advantage given by the federal ratio. In 1843, Adams told the House of Representatives, "Your country is no longer a democracy, it is not even a republic — it is a government of two or three thousand holders of slaves, to the utter exclusion of the remaining part."[28] An abolitionist would point out, in the 1850s, that six slave states, taken together, had a free population with 199 fewer people than Pennsylvania alone — which meant that the people in those states had twelve senators to the Pennsylvanians' two.[29]

The importance of protecting the South's extra congressional votes became clear as early as 1792, in one of the first major battles under the Constitution, provoking the first presidential veto in our history. Initially, representation in the House had to be assigned by estimate, since there was no census to work from. But when the first census was taken in 1790, Congress tried to come up with truer figures. To set the total number of House seats, it divided the aggregate population of the nation by 30,000, the constitutional number for each representative. Then it assigned seats for each state proportionally, rounding figures for single seats up or down to the nearest 30,000, and sent the bill to Washington for his signature. Jefferson saw that Congress's act would add six seats to the North, and only two to the South — thus cutting into the extra margin given by counting slaves. He insisted that each state must be counted separately, with no extra seats for any fraction above the 30,000 divisor (J 23.370–77). This left the total number of seats eight fewer than the general population would warrant, but removed the four new seats from the North. The Virginians in the cabinet, Jefferson and Edmund Randolph, working with Madison in the Congress, jointly drafted Washington's veto, which Hamilton had urged the president not to cast. When Washington objected to Jefferson that his veto would appear like a sectional move favoring the South, Jefferson said that the soundness of his own argument should be relied on, not the appearance of equity.[30]

The size of the slave representation was at issue in each of Jefferson's expansions of what he called "the empire of liberty" — the survey of the West, his purchase of Louisiana, his attempt to add the Floridas and Cuba to America, his support for slavery in Missouri and beyond, even his panic over Burr's detaching part of the Southwest from the Union. (For Burr and the federal ratio, see Chapter 9 below.) In all these matters, the importance of the federal ratio has been overlooked, largely because historians have not listened to the objections raised on its basis by Federalist critics like Timothy Pickering. Each new addition to the plantation region became for them a flash point in the concern over the federal ratio, several times prompting moves to amend the Constitution by its repeal.

People neglect this aspect when discussing the way Jefferson changed his stand on slavery in the territories between 1784, when there was no three-fifths representation, and 1820, when there was (see Chapter 1 below). Even Jefferson's drive to open as soon as possible the University of Virginia was meant to provide educated defenders for the extension of slavery westward, to keep good southerners away from Harvard or Yale, where men were taught "the sacred principle of our holy alliance of 'restrictionism.'"[31] As David Brion Davis puts it, "When the chips were down, as in the Missouri crisis, he threw his weight behind slavery's expansion."[32]

This had less to do with theories about slavery than with the concrete advantage the three-fifths clause gave to any added slave territory. Michael Zuckerman attributes Jefferson's plantation imperialism to a more or less subconscious "Negrophobia."[33] It is more plausible, as well as more respectful, to see it as based on a simple political and economic calculus. The Constitution rewarded too well any new slave territories for him to throw away this advantage given to "agrarian virtue." Even an argument used against taking the federal ratio too seriously shows how crucial it was. We are told that the North almost always had a majority of seats in Congress. But that just made the South more anxious to gain the territory that would make the federal ratio give them a majority — as it made the North more wary of letting that happen.

What Was the Slave Power?

The fear of a "slave power" has been dismissed as alarmist by those who think the term refers always to a slave owners' *conspiracy*. For a long time historians were frightened away from reference to a slave power by a long and influential article written by Chauncey Bou-

cher in 1921, "*In re* That Aggressive Slavocracy."[34] The key word in
that defense of Boucher's beloved South was "aggressive." Boucher
said that the South did not take unified and secret actions to deprive northerners of their liberties, as some conspiratorialists had
claimed. Its actions were scattered, defensive, uncoordinated, and
far from secret. Boucher denied, in Russel Nye's words, that there
was "a secret and highly organized group with conscious aims of
imposing restrictions upon traditional liberties."[35]

Some people did fear and denounce such a conspiracy. The most
famous of these was Abraham Lincoln, who in his "House Divided" speech said that Stephen Douglas and Roger Taney of
the Supreme Court had schemed with Presidents Pierce and Buchanan to bring about a second Dred Scott decision spreading slavery throughout the Union.[36] One problem with the conspiracy view
is that different men identified different conspirators with different
secret aims. David Brion Davis tried to overcome that problem by
saying there was a "paranoid style," rather than a unified thesis,
behind charges of a slave power conspiracy.[37] He was picking up
on Richard Hofstadter's concept of the paranoid style, formulated
to criticize those who believed there were Communist conspirers
in the federal government of the 1950s and 1960s. Davis explicitly compared conspiracy-mindedness like Lincoln's with Mc-
Carthyism.[38]

One of the effects of this line of argument was to continue the
marginalizing of abolitionists, an effort at which the South was very
effective. William Lloyd Garrison was the Ur-conspiratorialist in
this view. He thought even the Constitution a plot against freedom (a "covenant with death"). He went beyond a criticism of the
open concessions to southern demands — on the three-fifths clause,
the slave trade, and fugitive slaves — and found a pro-slavery slant
throughout the document. A claim that this was the conscious aim
of the framers cannot be sustained. But Paul Finkelman shows that
the South did find ways to use many clauses of the Constitution,
and many interpretations of it, to protect their slave property. The
concept of "state sovereignty" was just one of these tools. For southerners "states' rights" meant first and foremost the right to declare
that their slaveholding was no one else's business. Other constitu-

tional conveniences afforded them included the bans on taxing exports or interstate taxes, which favored the products of slave labor. Similarly, the guarantee of states against domestic insurrection, and the use of the militia for that purpose, put the federal government on the slave owners' side if their property should rebel. The "full faith and credit" clause made other states recognize all the South's legal provisions for slavery. And so on.[39]

Southerners did not foresee all possible uses of these clauses, and provide for their inclusion with that in mind, duping their northern counterparts in the process. But they were resourceful in turning each of them to their advantage when the occasion for doing so arose. That is what is really at issue. Most people, when they referred to the slave power, were not thinking of a conscious conspiracy with secret goals and instruments. They were talking about the slave *interest,* and the way that powerful interest prompted people to defensive measures, whether short-term or long-range. John Quincy Adams got it right in 1820, when he saw his own former vice president, John Calhoun, defending the extension of slavery into the West: "It is a contemplation not very creditable to human nature that the cement of common interest produced by slavery is strong and more solid than that of unmingled freedom."[40] When, in this book, I talk about the slave power, I will mean the political efforts exerted to protect and expand slavery. This took many forms, but almost all of them depended in some way on the three-fifths clause, since that permeated the process of representative government. It was a potential factor in situations long before it became actual — for instance, in the maneuvering to add new slave territories. The series of antebellum compromises aimed at holding the nation together addressed the balance of power that would result from adding or blocking states with the three-fifths advantage.

One of the great achievements of the slave power was to use its political clout to silence opposition. Freehling calls this its blackmail power over the northern Democrats who needed the southern part of their coalition. The price of this bargain was that slavery be ignored as an issue in the North. The Democrats there were able to marginalize abolitionists as "extremists," as disturbers of sectional harmony, as enemies of immigrant laborers (who did not want free black competition).[41] It was in the name of "law and order," ironically, that these northern Democrats encouraged the mobs that beat or intimidated abolitionists.[42] The result was that, even after the formal gag rules were defeated in Congress, there was a gentleman's agreement not to push the slavery issue in ways that would embarrass the South. Lincoln accurately described the general attitude toward slavery:

> You must not say anything about it in the free states *because it is not there.* You must not say anything about it in the slave states *because it is there.* You must not say anything about it in the pulpit, because that is religion and has nothing to do with it. You must not say anything about it in politics *because that will disturb the security of "my place."* There is no place to talk about it as being a wrong, although you say yourself it *is* a wrong [emphasis in original].[43]

Theodore Parker might have said, *De te fabula narratur,* "You're telling your own story," since Lincoln prudently avoided all open association with abolitionists like Parker.

But Parker agreed with Lincoln's description of the way the nation was made almost mute on the subject of slavery.

> It silences the great sects, Trinitarian, Unitarian, Nullitarian: the chief ministers of this American Church — threefold in denomination, one in nature — have naught to say against slavery. The Tract Society dare not rebuke "the sum of all villainies." The Bible Society has no "Word of God" for the slave, the "revealed religion" is not revealed to him. Writers of schoolbooks "remember the hand that feeds them," and venture no word against the national crime that threatens to become also the national ruin . . . The Democratic hands of America have sewed up her own mouth with an iron thread.[44]

Mark Twain looked back on the Missouri of his mother's day:

> She had never heard it [slavery] assailed in any pulpit but had heard it defended and sanctified in a thousand; her ears were familiar with Bible texts that approved it but if there were any that disapproved it they had not been quoted by her pastors; as far as her experiences went, the wise and the good and the holy were unanimous in the conviction that slavery was right.[45]

The national reticence continued long after the Civil War. It skewed the historiography of Reconstruction for decades. In the early twentieth century, it whitewashed the South in popular culture and at sites like Monticello and Mount Vernon. It entertained the absurd notion that the Civil War was not fought over slavery but over tariffs, or states' rights, or federal usurpation. It encouraged Edmund Wilson to romanticize the Ku Klux Klan.[46] In our time it has defended the Confederate Battle Flag as untainted by slavery. And it has kept the image of Jefferson relatively unclouded by the things he did to promote and protect and expand the slave power.

Luckily, things are changing. The fine works I have been citing by Paul Finkelman, Leonard Richards, Don Fehrenbacher, William Freehling, and others show that we are finally coming to grips with the vast octopus that was slavery, with the tentacles it spread through every part of our nation and its political life. No, I guess an octopus is not the right image. For that we should turn again to Theodore Parker:

> There is an old story told by the Hebrew rabbis, that before the flood there was an enormous giant called Gog. After the flood had got into the full tide of successful experiment, and every man was drowned except those taken into the ark, Gog came striding along after Noah, feeling his way with a cane as long as the mast of the *Great Republic*. The water had only come up to his girdle; it was then over the hill tops and was still rising — raining night and day. The giant hailed the Patriarch. Noah put his head out of the window and said, "Who is there?" "It is I," said Gog. "Take us in; it is wet outside." "No," said Noah, "you're too big; no room. Besides, you're a bad character. You would be a very dangerous passenger, and would make trouble in the ark. I shall not take you in. You may get on top if you like." And he clapped to the window. "Go to thunder," said Gog. "I will ride, after all." And he strode after him, wading through the waters; and mounting on the starboard side, steered it just as he pleased, and made it rough weather inside. Now, in making the Constitution, we did not care to take in slavery in express terms. It looked ugly. We allowed it to get on the top astride, and it steers us just where it pleases.[47]

[1]

Before 1800

Timothy Pickering served in the Washington and Adams administrations with Jefferson, before becoming his harsh critic in the Congress. He was Washington's secretary of war while Jefferson was his secretary of state. He was secretary of state under John Adams while Jefferson was the vice president. They did not directly engage each other in those early roles, though their views were dramatically different, on two points especially — on slavery in the Northwest Territory, and on the Haitian revolution. A look at those two issues helps explain Pickering's deeply antagonistic stance toward Jefferson in and after the 1800 election.

Despite a few points of similarity in their background, the two men were far apart in political philosophy. Both were the sons of farmers they deeply respected, and both were Enlightenment deists (P 5.9). Each, moreover, was a supporter of the Revolution — though Pickering, unlike Jefferson, fought in it. They were early admirers of General Washington, but became disillusioned with him. Pickering was a critic of aristocracy, and of institutions that prolonged it. He wrote: "When all existing entails shall be broken, and future ones forbidden, we may make ourselves easy about aristocratic ambition. Great accumulations of wealth will then be rare, of short continuance, and consequently never dangerous" (P 5.413).

Yet that is about all that can be said of his convergence with Jefferson. After that, all is divergence. Pickering was the son of an abolitionist, whose hatred for slavery he maintained. He was also a northern friend of commerce who thought "agrarian virtue" a code word for plantation economies, and Virginia "luxury" a betrayal of republican values. There could be little sympathy between the two men.

1

Pickering vs. Jefferson: The Northwest

The only really competent prize-fighter [against John Adams] was old
Tim Pickering, whom I regard as a stunning writer and critic. Against
him I find it difficult to stand up. A good life of Pickering would be my
ideal of a task.

— Henry Adams to Charles Francis Adams, Jr.[1]

You have now pretty well completed the story of Boston Federalism.
Only Tim Pickering remains, and I much wish you would do him.

— Henry Adams to Samuel Eliot Morison[2]

TIMOTHY PICKERING has been no favorite of American
historians, who only dimly remembered him — as an enforcer of the Sedition Act and John Adams's disloyal secretary of state — until 1877, when Henry Adams brought him back
into prominence as the man who attempted a New England secession in 1804.[3] The only full defense of Pickering, published a century
and a half ago in four large volumes, was a partisan hodgepodge of
materials assembled by his son and a collaborator.[4] The best-known
recent books about him are two volumes written by Gerard H.
Clarfield, and Clarfield considers Pickering a fanatic.[5] It puzzles
me that some people spend their scholarly lives concentrating on a
person they despise. Perhaps that makes sense if the person is a

great moral threat or scourge of history, sympathy with whom could be morally dangerous — a Hitler, say, or a Stalin. But *Timothy Pickering?*

Two fine doctoral dissertations take a more balanced approach to Pickering than Clarfield does, but both end their account before Pickering's twelve-year service in Congress, when he carried on his campaign against Jefferson, and that is the time my book concentrates on.[6] The only sympathetic treatment of Pickering written in the twentieth century was a series of three articles by Hervey Putnam Prentiss, who exaggerated his influence on New England Federalists.[7] This is not a promising record for a man who might throw some light for us on the problem of Jefferson and the slave power.

Nonetheless, it is hard to see how a man so vilified (when not forgotten) could have been called to the range of positions he held in the formative period of our country — leader of the Salem militia in the Revolution, adjutant general in Washington's army, member of the congressionally appointed War Board, quartermaster general of the army, Washington's special emissary to various Indian tribes, second postmaster general of the United States (after Samuel Osgood), second secretary of war (after Henry Knox), third secretary of state (after Jefferson and Edmund Randolph), later elected by the state of Massachusetts twice to the United States Senate and twice to the House of Representatives. Who is this man who combines such a distinguished résumé with a reputation so ragamuffin?

Pickering's Background

Pickering was born in 1745 to the man for whom he was named, a tough public nag whom he resembled, tall and cadaverous and humorless. The elder Timothy was deacon of the Third Presbyterian Church, a breakaway body from which he would eventually break away, always the keeper of strict doctrine while others backslid. An independent farmer in the merchant city of Salem, he was a loud abolitionist in a place whose harbor circulated about a hundred slaves through the city at any one time.[8] This elder Pickering, vociferous in city councils, sounded off as well in the Salem *Gazette* (soon to be his son's first forum). As local doggerel put it:

> T. Pickering is his name, a man that spends
> His time in wrangling for his dear self-ends.[9]

The son, with his plain puritan dress, was as ascetical as the father. They were if anything more scathing against aristocrats than Jefferson; and neither of them, unlike Jefferson, was ever mistaken for one. Henry Cabot Lodge rightly stressed the democratic instincts of the son, who wrote: "Having, from my earliest remembrance of reflections of the kind, looked on all mankind as possessing equal rights, I am wont not to make those distinctions between the high and the low which gave birth to the term *politeness*" (P 5.192).

Pickering's opposition to slavery was such that it dazzled a young family friend, William Lloyd Garrison. Pickering, says Linda Kerber, provided Garrison with a "father image," and some of the future abolitionist's earliest writings were defenses of Pickering.[10] The younger Pickering would, like his father, remain a farmer all his life, yet he moved in Salem's commercial circles, too, after marrying a shipmaster's daughter. Shortly after becoming a lawyer, he became the sole judge of Salem's maritime court (an extremely important position in that sailing town). When the Revolution came, he made his strongest break from his father, who remained a Loyalist. Young Timothy became a leader of the local committee of correspondence and colonel of the militia.

Clarfield thinks Pickering was too cautious a revolutionary, but most sensible men tried, as long as they could, to exhaust other means of resolving the conflict with England.[11] The Revolution began by alternating protestations of loyalty to the Crown with legalistic attacks on Parliament. That Pickering was not lagging behind his community is shown by the fact that he was elected and re-elected to Salem's civil and military leadership. His strict love of discipline made him write *An Easy Plan for a Militia* (1775), which became the standard Continental drill book, first in Massachusetts and then in Washington's Continental army, until it was replaced by the manual of Baron von Steuben. Pickering was criticized for getting his militia to Boston too late to fight the British troops retreating from Lexington and Concord; but he got them there. He went on to serve in Washington's Continental army, where his demanding nature was shocked by the laxity of some men in the ranks (P 5.53–54). His emphasis on discipline made Washington promote him to be his adjutant general (P 33.173).

Pickering criticized aspects of Washington's leadership — as did his prickly coevals in the army, Alexander Hamilton and Aaron Burr. But Congress valued his perfectionism and put him on the newly formed War Board, with Washington's approval (P 1.73). Congress then considered him successful enough in that role to give him the difficult post of quartermaster general, an appointment he held for over five years (1780–1785). In a situation that practically forced graft on men, he brought honesty and order to chaos, antagonizing some by his obsession with proper procedure. David Fischer writes: "Timothy Pickering . . . was a man of deep integrity; during the Revolution he was perhaps the only quartermaster general on the 'Patriot' side who did not profit privately from his office."[12] General Horatio Gates gave Pickering this wry compliment: "You have been an honest Q.M.G., and of course deserve to starve" (P 18.244).[13]

At the war's end, Pickering drafted the army's response to Washington's last orders to the troops. Clarfield thinks it was inappropriate to bring up the grievances of unpaid soldiers in such a place (C 83–84); but the officers accepted this draft, and Pickering was never one to drop a just complaint. Washington seems not to have been offended by Pickering, since his own report to Congress on the nation's future defense requirements drew extensively and verbatim on a draft that Pickering had prepared for him.[14]

Slavery in the Territories

As quartermaster, Pickering was deeply concerned with the pay of soldiers, the general finances of the army, and demobilization at the war's end. One of the recruiting devices of the war was the promise of land bonuses to veterans. Pickering pursued this idea by drawing up, in 1783, a model plan for a new state to be conferred on veterans, with land given them by the government in the Northwest Territory (P 53.134–58). This document would have a wide influence because it included the clause, "the total exclusion of slavery from the state to form an essential and irrevocable part of the Constitution." David McLean says this clause made Pickering "one of the first public men in any part of the world to propose concrete measures for limiting black slavery."[15]

That is a claim normally assigned to Thomas Jefferson, whose proposal for settling the Northwest Territory, submitted a year after Pickering's plan, would affirm that "after the year 1800 of the Christian era there shall be neither slavery nor involuntary servitude in any of the said states" (J 6.608). That clause, in David Brion Davis's eyes, earned for Jefferson the right to be called "one of the first statesmen in any part of the world to advocate concrete measures for restricting and eradicating Negro slavery."[16] But Jefferson's proposal was not only made a year later than Pickering's; it contained the self-defeating delay of emancipation until 1800 — which would have allowed sixteen years for slavery to become irremovably entrenched in the life of the settlers. Pickering pointed out this flaw in urging members of Congress to remove it:

> To suffer the continuance of slaves till they can be gradually emancipated in states already overrun with them may be pardonable because unavoidable without hazarding greater evils; but to introduce them into countries where none now exist — countries which have been talked of, which we have boasted of, as asylums to the oppressed of the earth — can never be forgiven. For God's sake, then, let one more effort be made to prevent so terrible a calamity. (P 5.551)

In other words, Pickering saw at once what modern historians agree on, including Paul Finkelman:

> By 1800 some of the territories probably would have had large slave populations and politically powerful masters who would have worked to undermine the Ordinance of 1784 had it included Jefferson's prohibition. With no enforcement clause, it is almost impossible to imagine a territorial or state legislature voluntarily ending slavery after the institution had been allowed to grow until 1800.[17]

Even though the anti-slavery clause in Jefferson's draft would have been ineffectual, it was removed from the Ordinance that passed in 1784. Southern states, including Jefferson's own Virginia, voted it down. Pickering urged members of the Continental Congress to resurrect the clause, but without the grace period until 1800. He worked through House members from his own Massachusetts, Elbridge Gerry and Rufus King. Gerry knew of Pickering's 1783 plan for excluding slavery, and conveyed ideas from it to King (P 18.225). Pickering supplied King with ammunition drawn from Jefferson's own Declaration of Independence:

> Congress once made this important declaration: "That all men are created equal, that they are endowed by their creator with certain unalienable rights; that among these are life, liberty, and the pursuit of happiness" — and these truths were held to be self-evident. Nevertheless, a proposition for preventing a violation of these truths — in a country yet unsettled, and from which such violation might easily have been excluded — did not obtain. What pretence (argument there could be none) could be offered for its rejection? (P 5.352)

King was impressed by Pickering's arguments, calling them "so just that it would be impossible to differ from them" (P 18.226), and he proposed legislation to exclude slavery from the Northwest Territory. This did not pass in 1785, but the subject came up again when the Ordinance of 1787 was being debated. King was away from Congress, attending the Constitutional Convention, but his replacement, Nathan Dane, acted for him in introducing the ban on slavery, and this time it passed.[18]

Though Jefferson was in Paris in 1787, the anti-slavery provision in the Ordinance of that year is normally called a triumph for his 1784 proposal. Actually, the more immediate action for it, from Gerry and King and Dane, went back to Pickering's 1783 plan, which had no extension until 1800. Pickering deserves as much if not more of the credit that is usually given to Jefferson. King readily acknowledged this.[19] The victory, no matter to whom it belonged, proved to be a pyrrhic one. The clause was generally ignored in the territories, with the acquiescence of President Washington and Secretary of

State Jefferson.[20] In fact, a 1789 congressional committee, in which James Madison served, explicitly authorized the territories to protect slave property, "anything in the said Ordinance to the contrary notwithstanding."[21]

Thus the status of slaves in the territories had to be fought out and refought, decade by decade, in clashes over Louisiana, the Floridas, Texas, California, Missouri, Kansas, and Nebraska. Pickering was consistently on the side of excluding slavery. But in 1820, when the Missouri Compromise said that slavery was congressionally banned north of Missouri, Jefferson, in great agitation, denied that Congress had or could have any such power: "To regulate the condition of the different descriptions of men composing a state . . . is certainly the exclusive right of every state, which nothing in the Constitution has taken from them and given to the general government."[22] If Congress has no right to exclude slavery in any place where the inhabitants desire it, why did he say it had that right in 1784, when he drafted his Ordinance? Apologists for Jefferson have puzzled over this matter for years.

Of course, one can say that the Constitution was not the law of the land in 1784, so what was "in the Constitution" was not at issue then. But this leads to the absurd inference that Jefferson thought Congress under the Articles could ban slavery because it then had more power than would be granted it under the Constitution. (Actually, the Constitution was made necessary by Congress's *lack* of power.) Yet the difference between the Articles and the Constitution is the clue we should follow on this matter. Jefferson could ban slavery in the Northwest Territory under the Articles without any penalty to southern representation. Each state then had only one vote in Congress, so holding or not holding slaves did not affect its representation. All that changed with the three-fifths clause. By 1820, Jefferson had experienced the importance of adding slave states, with the swollen power given them by the "representation" of slaves. He valued the addition of Louisiana and the Floridas — and potentially of Cuba — for the very reasons that Pickering opposed them, for the added power they gave the "agrarian interest."

The first clash of ideas between Pickering and Jefferson had to do with the consistency of Pickering's thinking on the matter of slaves in the Northwest, as opposed to Jefferson's shifting standards on the matter as he felt compelled to defend southern interests. The different attitudes the two men adopted toward the Northwest were affected, as well, by the fact that Pickering had long and close engagement with the area, and Jefferson had none. Despite Jefferson's interest in the frontier, exhibited in his commissioning of the Lewis and Clark expedition, he did not himself explore or live in the West. Pickering, by contrast, lived and worked in the contested Wyoming Valley area of western Pennsylvania and penetrated deep into Indian territory on diplomatic missions.

Wyoming Valley

The Wyoming Valley was a southern extension of the Susquehanna Valley that had been purchased (fraudulently) from Indians in 1754 by the Connecticut-based Susquehanna Company. Settlers from Connecticut defended their land against British and Indian forces during the Revolution. But the valley was also claimed by Pennsylvania as part of its western extension. In 1782, the contending states — Connecticut and Pennsylvania — took their respective claims to the Continental Congress. Since there was no federal judiciary under the Articles of Confederation, resort was had — for the first and only time — to the clumsy arbitration procedure spelled out in Article IX. Each state chose from a pool of arbiters, who met in Trenton and awarded the area to Pennsylvania.[23] What, then, was to be done with the Connecticut settlers who had long held land in the area? Were they simply to be ousted and sent north? The Susquehanna Company refused to give up its holdings, and it prodded the Connecticut legislature to back up its claims. There was a movement to break away from *both* Connecticut and Pennsylvania, to set up a new state, Westmoreland, as "the Fourteenth Commonwealth." Oliver Ellsworth, the Connecticut leader, even wrote a constitution for the new state, and Ethan Allen's Green Mountain Boys came down to defend it. Merrill Jensen calls this "by all odds the most serious and violent statehood movement" occurring under the Articles of Confederation.[24]

At the end of the Revolution, Pickering did not want to return to his father's farm near Salem. As quartermaster of the army, he had worked out of Philadelphia, becoming the associate of members of Congress and a friend of such prominent Philadelphians as Benjamin Rush, James Wilson, Robert Morris, and others. He decided to follow their example and speculate in western lands. But unlike them he meant to go and work his farms. This suited the speculators, who wanted a man who could bring peace to the area where "Yankees" and "Pennamites" were squabbling over the same pieces of land. This would solidify Pennsylvanians' holdings and make people less wary of settling on disputed turf. In 1786, the Pennsylvania Executive Council, under its president Benjamin Franklin, made the contested area a new county, Luzerne, and equipped Pickering with all the offices he might need to pacify the region — as Prothonotary of the Court of Common Pleas, Clerk of the Court of Quarter Sessions, Clerk of the Orphans' Court, Judge of the Court of Common Pleas, Recorder of Deeds, and Register of the Probate of Wills.[25]

Pickering realized at once that he must fight on three fronts, with the Connecticut settlers, with Pennsylvanians trying to wrest their farms from those settlers, and with the legislature in Philadelphia, which was disposed to favor the latter over the former. He formed an alliance with the moderate wing of the Connecticut settlers, led by Zebulon Butler. These people were willing to accept Pennsylvania's jurisdiction if it would confirm their possession of lands cultivated before the Trenton decision. Pickering backed such moderates against radical representatives of the Susquehanna Company, led by John Franklin (no relative of Benjamin Franklin, who was now negotiating with Connecticut to end the two states' conflict). Pickering called for the election of county officers under Pennsylvania. John Franklin threatened to prevent the elections by force. Pickering made Zebulon Butler the head of a militia to guarantee peaceful conduct of the voting, and received from Philadelphia a warrant for Franklin's arrest as an insurrectionary. He personally assisted in the arrest and sent Franklin to prison in the capital.[26]

In the rough frontier conditions of Wyoming, Pickering's life was routinely threatened, and one feckless attempt had already been made to kidnap or kill him. But the imprisonment of John Franklin led to more effectual steps. Pickering was seized by men in blackface and taken to the woods, where his captors threatened they would kill him if Franklin were not released. Pickering stayed cool and determined, engaging his captors in talk of crops, writing a cryptic diary of his ordeal in tiny script on a single folded sheet of paper (now preserved at the Massachusetts Historical Society, P 58.45–46). When the kidnapers demanded that he write a letter pleading for Franklin's release, he refused.[27] After nineteen days, when it was clear that Franklin was not going to be surrendered, his captors let Pickering go.

Negotiating between the two parties on the frontier was only part of Pickering's task. He had to journey back to Philadelphia to plead for the Connecticut settlers who had established and worked their farms before the Trenton decision. He asked that these old settlers be confirmed in their title, and that Pennamite claimants to the same holdings be compensated with other land. This was achieved in the Confirming Act of 1787. Meanwhile, Pickering was elected as a delegate to the constitutional ratifying convention in Philadelphia, where he supported his friend James Wilson in the work of making Pennsylvania the first major state to ratify the Constitution. In the convention, Pickering called for the opponents of Wilson to present their objections in order, not randomly.[28]

Despite Pickering's good relations with leading men in Philadelphia, opponents of the Confirming Act were not willing to allow the Connecticut claims to stand, even under Pennsylvania jurisdiction. There were too many Pennsylvanians poised to swoop down on the cultivated land of the Yankees. Their lobbyists achieved a suspension of the Confirming Act in 1788 and its repeal in 1790. Pickering pleaded with the legislators not to go back on their pledges to the longtime settlers, but to no avail. His own position was undermined in the valley, where his political work had kept him from development of his land. He looked now to the new government under the Constitution he had helped ratify, hoping for a federal office.

Though Pickering was unable to maintain the Confirming Act, individual claims would be adjudicated under Pennsylvania law.

The Susquehanna Company's power had been broken through his endeavors. He finally made implementation of the Trenton decision possible. He set up the militia, held regular elections, despite the continual threats of violence, and made the region irreversibly Pennsylvanian. It is ironic that the man who would later be vilified as a separatist, one sponsoring secession, helped block the break-away effort of "Westmoreland."

Indian Diplomacy

The office Pickering was hoping for under the new government was secretary of war. He thought his services on the War Board and as quartermaster general eminently qualified him. But the post went to his frequent wartime ally, General Henry Knox. The most imme-diate task of the secretary of war was to pacify or conquer western Indians in regions where borders were still uncertain between Brit-ish and American territory. Joseph Brant, the famous Mohawk chief who had fought with the British during the war, was opposing American intrusions westward, and he had sympathizers in the eastern tribes most affected by these encroachments. There had been a flare-up of angry threats after two Seneca warriors were killed by American settlers. Knox, who was aware of Pickering's successful frontier diplomacy in the Wyoming Valley, suggested to President Washington that he be sent in 1790 on a peace mission to the Senecas.

Pickering, the rigid disciplinarian, had a hard time at first adjust-ing to the dilatory ways of Indian representatives, who arrived late at the conference, drank heavily, and engaged in time-wasting cere-monies. But he rapidly developed a sympathy for their claims, as he had for the Connecticut farmers in Wyoming. His moralism was outraged by white mistreatment of the Indians (P 61.119). He criticized those swindling them out of their land and rebuked the western armies destroying their villages (P 35.109–10). When he was offered the post of quartermaster general for those armies, he re-jected it (C 120). Even so severe a critic of Pickering as Gerard Clarfield admits that his work with the Indians "transformed him into a staunch and influential advocate of the rights of native Americans" (C 117).

> Pickering had stumbled on a moral issue that he could not ignore. From that moment on, in the conflict between the rights of Indians and the pressures of expansion, he took his stand with the native people . . . Of all the figures involved in diplomacy with the Iroquois at this time, Pickering showed not only the best motives but also the soundest conception of policy. (C 119, 124)

This can be contrasted with Jefferson's Indian policies, which prefigured Andrew Jackson's "Indian removals" of later time.[29]

Pickering's successful first negotiations with the Senecas received high praise from Henry Knox and President Washington. They lost little time, therefore, in sending him on a more ticklish mission. The Six Nations, unhappy with American seizures of land, were considering an alliance with the pro-British tribes to the west. Pickering was to form a new treaty with the Nations that would bind them to the American side. He resisted his instructions for this mission, which included recruiting the Indians to fight their brothers to the west. He said that the most to be gained was the Nations' neutrality, and that could be accomplished only by redressing their wrongs. When he could not get the instructions changed, he simply ignored them. He also beat off the effort of his friend Robert Morris to purchase more Indian land at the treaty conference.

At the meeting, Pickering ran into stiff resistance from an Iroquois chief named Red Jacket (P 60.96–98). Though he could not form a useful treaty, he left assured of the Indians' neutrality, and extended an offer that they send leading men to see the president in Philadelphia, to confer on the improvement of their land and to win subsidies for their peaceful activities. President Washington, pleased with Pickering's second mission, rewarded him by making him postmaster general. This was another office with large patronage and temptations to graft. But Pickering was as righteous as ever, and as efficient. He set up the early postal stages and teams of relay riders. Instead of granting lucrative posts to favored people, he drove hard bargains with those to whom he awarded contracts

(C 130). He also offended some by employing freed blacks in the mail, and defended himself to one critic with the words: "If you admitted a Negro to be a *man,* the difficulty would cease."[30]

Despite the cares of Pickering's new office, Washington soon needed him once more. Pickering's earlier invitation to the chiefs for a visit in Philadelphia had been ignored by the administration. But late in 1791 General Arthur St. Clair's troops suffered a defeat in the West, and new Indian militance threatened to move the Six Nations from their neutral posture to a more hostile one. At this point, Washington asked Pickering to summon the chiefs after all. Pickering included an invitation to Joseph Brant, who was trying to dissuade the chiefs from moving onto the white man's turf. Sixty chiefs and braves — but not Brant — showed up on March 14, 1792. Pickering, to his own surprise and that of the invited Indians, was at first excluded from the ceremonies. But when Pickering protested this to Washington (P 62.11–12), he was put in charge of the conference. After a satisfactory conclusion to the event, Brant did indeed show up, traveling in great style and negotiating separately, as befitted his dignity. He refused attempts to recruit him for hostile actions against the British, but promised to work for better relations with the American government.[31]

Brant went as a conciliator to a meeting of all the tribes planned for that summer, and Pickering was engaged a fourth time to deal with the Indians at that conference (P 59.38–39). He led a commission of three empowered to make peace — the Iroquois themselves had requested his presence (C 138). For six weeks, the commissioners were stalled at Niagara by British agents trying to manipulate the conference, but Brant brought a party of fifty or so Indians to confer with the three Americans at Niagara. Brant was shrewdly playing them off against the British. With Brant's encouragement, the three commissioners sailed for Detroit, to meet with the larger Indian body.[32] But there they received a non-negotiable demand that the United States recognize the Ohio River as a bar to farther expansion. Knowing they could not get that pledge honored in Philadelphia, the commissioners had to return without having reached any agreement at all.

By the next summer (1794), the Six Nations were again restive, and Pickering was again sent to pacify them. At the meeting, held at Canandaigua, Brant sent a British emissary to represent him, but Pickering demanded his expulsion as a spy. Once again Pickering solicited expressions of Indian grievance and considered some of them well founded. He retroceded many acres of land to the Senecas. He tripled the funds given to Indians who would settle peaceably. "The agreements that Pickering signed in 1794 were extraordinarily generous ... [and] represent the consummation of the creative aspect of Timothy Pickering's career as an Indian diplomat" (C 152).

After his return to Philadelphia, Pickering was appointed secretary of war. Knox was retiring, and Pickering — from a combination of his negotiations in the Wyoming Valley and at various Indian council fires — knew as much about troubled frontier conditions as any civilian leader in high position. In his new post, he continued his enlightened policies toward the Indians. Urging the American negotiators to seek "peace and not increase of territory," he concluded the Greenville Treaty of 1795, ending the war waged by General Anthony Wayne and providing that new Indian lands be purchased, not seized.[33]

While talks on this treaty were pending, the conflict over the ratification of the Jay Treaty racked the nation. The nascent Republican party opposed it as a surrender to the British by the trading interests of New England, but Pickering saw one crucial advantage in it — it finally settled the disputed boundaries with England in the West, making the Greenville Treaty possible, for Indians to settle in peace without British interference. Up to this point, Pickering had been a Francophile. Not only did he resent the British troops he fought against in the war, and the British agents who had stirred up trouble in the West. He also hailed the French Revolution as the legitimate heir to America's revolution — he even approved of the execution of King Louis XVI and Marie Antoinette (C 154). But after he saw the tactics used by Jefferson and Madison to sabotage the treaty, he swung violently against the pro-French party in America. Madison, who had framed the Constitution to give the Senate sole power over the ratifying of treaties, was now using his House seat to rescind the Jay Treaty. He had the approval of Jefferson in this (J 8.200). Disagreement over this would lead to Pickering's violent anti-French stance as secretary of state, when he and Jefferson were on opposite sides with regard to the Sedition Act — but also with regard to revolution in Saint Domingue.

2

Pickering vs. Jefferson: Toussaint

A CCORDING TO Gerald Clarfield, Pickering became secretary of state in 1795 by disgraceful means. And according to most historians, he left the office disgracefully five years later. On the first date, the incumbent secretary of state, Edmund Randolph, a holdout against the Jay Treaty, was falsely accused of taking French bribes, and Pickering was one of his harshest accusers — Clarfield claims, in fact, that he fabricated evidence against Randolph.[1] The British minister in America, wanting to discredit French opposition to the Jay Treaty, gave Oliver Wolcott, the secretary of the treasury, an intercepted message of the French minister that ambiguously indicated Randolph had schemed with the French against his own government. Wolcott, who knew no French, turned the document over to Pickering, whose translation of the document made its possibly compromising language seem more culpable. It has been said that Pickering did this deliberately; but when Randolph answered the charges against him, he produced a translation that was fully as compromising — which shows that the mistakes were natural, not malevolent.[2] And the charge against Randolph was not self-evidently false. Even Madison, Randolph's supporter, admitted that his critics had "strictures of sufficient ingenuity and plausibility" (M 16.182).

Pickering's foes say that he ruined Randolph for two reasons —
to remove an opponent to the Jay Treaty, and to take his place as
secretary of state. But a) Washington was already prepared, following the majority of his cabinet and the solicited advice of Hamilton, to sign the treaty without resubmitting it to the Senate, and b)
it was unlikely that he would choose Pickering to replace Randolph.
As it turned out, he made Pickering the acting secretary of state
while he tried to find someone less prickly and more deferential
to him for a permanent appointment. It was only after five other
men had turned Washington down, and after he had overridden
Pickering's bruised ego at this show of distrust, that Washington
made Pickering the third secretary of state.

The claim that Pickering fooled Washington into jettisoning
Randolph, his Virginia comrade-in-arms, was based on the old idea
that Washington was a dupe of his advisers.[3] A more recent treatment of the matter argues that Washington was less concerned
with Randolph's criticism of the Jay Treaty than with his indiscreet
revelations to the French minister of continued divisions in the cabinet, especially over responses to the Whiskey Rebellion a year earlier.[4] In any case, Washington based his decision on a number of factors, and was not a puppet whose strings were being pulled by
Pickering.

As secretary of war and then of state under Washington, Pickering
was deeply involved in the construction and deployment of the
great Joshua Humphrey–built frigates that would give America the
naval strength to deal with French privateers in the Caribbean and
Barbary pirates in Algiers. Perhaps impressed by that fact, John Adams made the mistake of keeping Pickering on as secretary of state
when he succeeded Washington. Pickering was now such a Francophobe that he urged Adams into the Quasi War with France in the
Caribbean and tried to sabotage Adams's efforts to end those hostil-
ities, forcing Adams to fire him in 1800.

But before that bitter breakup Pickering had one great achievement as secretary of state, one setting him far apart from Jefferson
— the response to rebellion in Saint Domingue.

Jefferson and Saint Domingue

Saint Domingue was the French-held western part of the island natives knew as Haiti but Columbus called Hispaniola. It was the richest colony in the Caribbean, supplying half the world's sugar and
coffee. To keep this river of products running, the island maintained
the densest slave population in the New World — 500,000 of them
in a small country the size of Maryland (as opposed to 700,000 in
the whole of the United States). Jamaica, the island with the second
highest slave population, had only half that number.[5] When the
French Revolution began in 1789, its energies swirled out from the
Parisian metropolis to all French holdings. At first the "free colored"
population (*gens du couleur*), who numbered 30,000, demanded
their political rights. But by 1791 the spirit of revolution had spread
to the slaves, who killed or drove out many of their plantation owners. The local white establishment in Saint Domingue, not trusting the revolutionary government in Paris, sent out pleas for help
to England and America, arguing that a successful black revolution would jeopardize slaveholdings in British-held Jamaica and
in the southern part of the United States. The British, who were at
war with France, took the opportunity to send an army as well as
provisions.

Both of President Washington's principal advisers, though they
differed on most things, agreed to send aid to the slaveholders of
Saint Domingue. Alexander Hamilton, the secretary of the treasury,
was an abolitionist; but he was also a Francophobe and Anglophile,
so collaborating with England against the French empire was something he could accept. Jefferson, as secretary of state, might have
been expected to oppose this, since he was a Francophile and Anglophobe. He was, besides, a foe of monarchy, a celebrator of revolution as well as of the rights of man. But he was also a plantation
owner, whose sympathies went instantly to the fellows of his caste.
The South was seething with rumors of black revolutionaries coming from Saint Domingue to stir up a rebellion. Jefferson passed on
one such rumor to the governor of South Carolina (J 21.614). He
wrote his son-in-law, Thomas Mann Randolph, that "sooner or

later all the whites will be expelled from all the West India islands"
(J 26.504).

The two cabinet members therefore arranged for three shipments of funds to the beleaguered white minority on the island. The
French minister in Philadelphia, Jean-Baptiste de Ternant, did not
want the United States to be seen as dealing directly with Saint
Domingue, as if it were a separate nation, so it was decided to report
that the aid came from France, subtracted from money the United
States owed France for its aid to the American Revolution.[6] Ternant
tried to limit and control these sums, since it was not clear that the
owners they were being sent to were adherents to the revolutionary
government in Paris. Jefferson felt the plight of the plantation owners more urgently than Ternant did, and wrote the American minister in France:

> It would be ridiculous in the present case to talk about diplomatic
> forms. There are situations when form must be dispensed with. A
> man attacked by assassins will call to those nearest him and will not
> think himself bound to silence till a magistrate may come to his aid.
> (J 22.331)

Other slaveholders also felt that sympathy with the slaveholders
should not wait on forms. The state of South Carolina sent thousands of dollars to them, and debated sending part of its militia.[7]
The federal government did not resent this intrusion of a state into
foreign affairs. President Washington was also a plantation owner,
and he had written that it was "lamentable to see such a spirit of
revolution among the blacks" of Saint Domingue.[8]

The progress of the slave revolt continued to frighten Jefferson:

> We receive with deep regret daily information of the progress of in-
> surrection and devastation in St. Domingo.[9] Nothing indicates as yet
> that the evil is at its height, and the materials as yet untouched but
> open to conflagration are immense. (J 23.26)

He went around Ternant to make a personal appeal to Lafayette for
more aid to the plantation owners: "What are you doing for your
colonies? They will be lost if not now effectually succored" (J 24.85).

When he resigned as secretary of state because of his disagreement with Hamilton's financial policy, he could no longer aid the plantation owners from the federal city; but he urged Monroe to have the governor of Virginia assume extraordinary executive powers to succor them:

> The situation of the St. Domingo fugitives (aristocrats as they are) calls aloud for pity and charity. Never was so deep a tragedy presented to the feelings of man. I deny the power of the general government to apply money to such a purpose [sic!], but I deny it with a bleeding heart. It belongs to the state governments. Pray urge ours to be liberal. The executive should hazard themselves more on such an occasion, and the legislative when it meets ought to approve and extend it. It will have a great effect in doing away [with] the impression of other disobligations toward France.[10]

The greatest tragedy ever presented to the feelings of man was not the plight of slaves but of their owners when dispossessed of them.

Pickering and Toussaint

On August 19, 1793, French authorities in Saint Domingue, trying to ride the whirlwind of black revolution, anticipated by a year the French Directory's abolition of slavery. This was done to recruit blacks to the resistance against British and Spanish invaders seeking to restore the white planters. In this effort the French had the services of a skilled organizer of black troops, Toussaint Breda. He was a former slave known at first by the name of the plantation (Breda) where he had grown up and worked as a coachman. The son of an African, he could still speak his father's native language and the Haitian patois, but he also knew French, and he took a revolutionary name in the 1790s — Toussaint Louverture ("The Beginning"). Though Toussaint was using the French alliance to train his native troops, he changed his tactics when England withdrew its invasion and the Spanish gave up their part of the island to France. Now he wanted trade and good relations with England and the United States, to build up his economic strength for throwing off

French control. England was hesitant to help a slave rebellion so near its own slave colony on Jamaica; but it would give limited trade rights if those could be controlled from London.

The United States, under President Adams and his secretary of state Pickering, was waging a running sea war with French privateers in the Caribbean, and offered to do business with Toussaint if he would betray his French masters by denying his ports to their privateers (P 10.440). Pickering was especially enthusiastic for this alliance. Not only would it hurt the hated French and protect American ships, but it would guarantee new-won freedoms for the ex-slaves. The British minister in America, Robert Liston, told his government that this is what Pickering had in mind from the outset.[11] Pickering was aware, as he wrote to Rufus King in France, that "the Negroes and people of color of St. Domingo believe that France [intends] to bring them back again to slavery" (P 10.615). Pickering took the position that Saint Domingue was already de facto independent of France, so embargoes on French holdings no longer applied.[12] Charles Callan Tansill concludes that Pickering was more supportive of independence for Saint Domingue than was President Adams.[13]

In 1798, Toussaint showed the Adams administration that he preferred American trade to French privateers. He sent to Philadelphia his trusted assistant Joseph Bunel, a mulatto married to a black woman. Pickering greeted him and arranged for a dinner with Adams, "the first-ever breaking of bread between an American president and a man of color."[14] Needless to say, southerners were offended by this. Even a Pennsylvanian, Albert Gallatin, expressed outrage that the president had dined with a man "married to a black woman."[15] But Pickering pressed ahead. He sent out a consul general to Saint Domingue, Edward Stevens, who came from the West Indies and knew the islands well (P 10.600). Jefferson noted, ominously, that the appointment of a consul general for a country was tantamount to diplomatic recognition of that country.[16] Stevens did in fact bypass the French civil authority in Saint Domingue and go straight to the military commander, Toussaint, "as nothing could be done without his sanction."[17] Finding the general to be a man of "penetration and good sense," he became a partner with him in restoring America's heavy trade with his land.

Pickering was willing to share the Haitian trade with England, but not on the terms England was asking — that only one port be used, and that one under British supervision. England wanted to use this vantage point to keep Toussaint from establishing a free black republic. Rufus King, the United States minister to England, told the authorities at Whitehall that America, too, was intent on keeping Toussaint from a declaration of independence.[18] He did not realize that his superior in Philadelphia was already making the American frigates act as partners in the black revolution.

In order to forge his special relationship with Toussaint, Pickering had to fight on two fronts. He could not let Britain reduce America to a suitor at a British-controlled port. Stevens was to make an opening at two ports, with Toussaint in charge of them (P 10.606–7). When the British minister, Thomas Maitland, traveled to Philadelphia with a list of rules for America to follow in trading with Saint Domingue, Pickering was the sole negotiator with him (President Adams was at home in Quincy), and he presented the British agent with a fait accompli of trade agreements already in force. Maitland's instructions were to arrange for trade in ways that would not give Toussaint more power for declaring independence, but he found that Pickering was working on the assumption that independence would be gained.[19] Pickering took all the contested points in this dramatic negotiation. As Tansill notes,

> Secretary Pickering won a distinct victory. The British negotiators were forced to abandon the articles that the War Office and Foreign Office had strongly insisted upon, and they discovered that it was expedient to compromise on other items of less importance. After such a brilliant performance, it was only to be expected that President Adams would express his "fullest approbation" of the course followed by Secretary Pickering.[20]

Maitland left Philadelphia deeply humiliated and denouncing American perfidy.[21]

That was only part of Pickering's task. In order to bring off what

Stanley Elkins and Eric McKitrick call his "virtuoso maneuver," he had also to blunt the opposition of America's slave states to dealing with Toussaint.[22] Opposition to the rebellion in Saint Domingue had been expressed by men in Congress who were close to the vice president. Jefferson's son-in-law, John Wayles Eppes, said that a victory for the slaves on that island "will bring immediate and horrible destruction to the fairest portion of America" (by which he meant the South), and Albert Gallatin, Jefferson's Republican ally in the House, said that allowing free slaves to govern their own nation would "throw so many tigers on society."[23] Pickering knew that almost all southerners, and certainly the Virginians, would oppose any aid to Toussaint; but he thought he could make a wedge of the one slave state with a large merchant class, South Carolina. He arranged for Toussaint's mulatto spokesman, Bunel, to meet with South Carolina's senator Robert Goodloe Harper and the state's representatives in the House. Though South Carolina had initially sent aid to Saint Domingue's plantation owners, it was clear now that those owners had lost the island. Bunel assured Harper that Toussaint would not support slave insurrections elsewhere — in fact, he needed the good will of Americans to maintain his independence from the European powers.[24]

The logic of commerce prevailed, to Jefferson's great regret. He wrote to Madison that even South Carolina voted for what he called "the Toussaint clause" allowing trade with Saint Domingue, "the object of which, as is charged by the one party and *admitted* by the other, is to facilitate the separation of the island from France" (emphasis in original).[25]

> Even South Carolinians in the House of Representatives voted for it. We may expect therefore black crews and supercargoes and missionaries thence into the southern states; and when that leaven begins to work, I would gladly compound with a great part of our northern country, if they would honestly stand neuter. If this combustion can be introduced among us under any veil whatever, we have to fear it.[26]

Toussaint was now steering his course toward independence with the help of the United States Navy (a navy Pickering had helped develop as secretary of war). Secretary of the Navy Benjamin Stoddert ordered captains of ships in the Caribbean to "show every kind of civility" to Toussaint, since he had "a great desire to see some ships of war belonging to America."[27] Ships were marshaled to protect the trade with Saint Domingue, and to guarantee Toussaint's authority to receive it. The orders went out to Captain Fletcher of the *George Washington,* Captain Little of the *Boston,* Captain Barry of the *United States,* Captain Talbot of the *Constitution,* Captain Perry of the *General Greene.*

The ships intercepted aid being sent to Toussaint's rival for control of the country, the mulatto leader André Rigaud, who was a French loyalist. At the showdown engagement between Toussaint and Rigaud, the siege of five thousand of Rigaud's troops in the port city of Jacmel, the *General Greene* sailed to Toussaint's assistance. Captain Raymond Perry reported that he "engaged three of Rigaud's forts warmly for thirty or forty minutes, in which time we obliged the enemy to evacuate the town and two of the forts, and repair to their strongest hold; this fort however soon hauled down its colors."[28]

The first revolutionary regime in the New World was coming to the aid of the second one. Toussaint came out after the battle to thank Captain Perry on the *General Greene,* and the ship received him with a "federal salute." Toussaint wrote to Edward Stevens: "Nothing could equal his [Perry's] kindness, his activity, his watchfulness and his zeal in protecting me, in unhappy circumstances for this part of the colony. He has contributed not a little to the success by his cruise."[29] The navy continued to intercept French aid sent to support Rigaud's remaining forces. In fact, all ships were turned away that lacked a passport from Toussaint. At last, the armed American schooner *Experiment* captured *La Diana,* with Rigaud aboard, and sent him off to prison on St. Kitts. "The operations of these vessels probably contributed as decisively to Rigaud's final defeat as had the *General Greene* to his defeat at Jacmel."[30]

Jefferson and Saint Domingue, Again

America's relations with Saint Domingue were altered abruptly when, a year after the fall of Jacmel, Thomas Jefferson was sworn in

as president. Jefferson recalled Edward Stevens and, at the request of
the French minister Pichon, withdrew the title of consul general,
sending a replacement with the demeaning title of "general commercial agent," a post not even meriting government pay.[31] Levi
Lincoln, who was acting as secretary of state until Madison could
reach the capital, spoke on Jefferson's instruction when he assured
the French minister that United States collaboration with Toussaint
had violated neutral relations with France, and that future conduct
would "respect the rights and interests of your nation . . . to avoid
just causes of complaint."[32] To replace Stevens, Jefferson sent Tobias
Lear, former secretary to George Washington, a man rightly described by Paul Finkelman as "a cipher of limited abilities."[33] Lear
had mismanaged the papers of Washington given into his keeping
— offering Hamilton, for instance, a choice of suppressing some of
them. Nor was he likely to view freed slaves with favor.[34] Lear, all in
all, was totally unfit to deal with the shrewd Toussaint or with the
massive French invasion of Saint Domingue that was about to oc-
cur, and he complained that his official duties kept him from the
fortune-hunting he had counted on in the Caribbean.[35]

Toussaint realized, the moment Lear arrived, that he had lost
the good relations developed with Adams, Pickering, Stevens, and
the navy captains. He complained at the withdrawal of the consul
general title, the lack of a greeting from the new president, and the
informal nature of Lear's commission. He rightly attributed these
indignities to "my color."[36] Jefferson was losing no time making up
for what he had called American "disobligations" toward France.
Napoleon was now securely in power as First Consul, and was reversing the Directory's decree that abolished slavery. The success
of Toussaint was muddying Bonaparte's plan to expand French
power in the Caribbean, so he assembled at Brest his largest-ever
naval task force to defeat "the black Napoleon." Command of it was
given to his brother-in-law, General Charles Leclerc. Louis André
Pichon, the French minister in America, enquired for his government where America would stand while this massive invasion took
place. Jefferson assured the French minister that American sup-
plies would be available for French use: "Nothing would be easier

than to furnish your army and fleet with everything, and reduce Toussaint to starvation."[37]

Toussaint's rivals combined to make peace with Leclerc, who seized Toussaint at a parley and sent him off to prison in the French Alps, where he died in 1803. Jefferson backed off from his support for Leclerc's army when he became convinced that it meant to move on to Louisiana after conquering Saint Domingue. But the French army was wiped out by the combined action of yellow fever and the new black leader, Jean-Jacques Dessalines, who in 1804 proclaimed Saint Domingue an independent republic under its ancient name, Haiti.

From that moment, Jefferson and the Republicans showed nothing but hostility to the new nation. Already in 1802, Jefferson had expressed his continuing concern over black rebellion to Rufus King, lamenting that the "course of things in the neighboring islands of the West Indies appeared to have given a considerable impulse to the minds of the slaves" in the United States and "a great disposition to insurgency has manifested itself among them."[38] When he proposed an embargo of the island, over the objections of northern merchants who had a prosperous trade there, Republicans in Congress welcomed this as a great opportunity. In the congressional debates that led to passage of the embargo, Senator Eppes of Virginia (Jefferson's son-in-law) said that he would "venture the treasury of the United States that the Negro government should be destroyed" (PM 243). Senator Jackson of Georgia agreed that "the self-created emperor of Haiti must be subdued" (PM 244).

Jefferson refused to grant diplomatic recognition to the new nation of Haiti, though this went against the clear norms he had earlier established for granting such recognition. As secretary of state in 1792, he defended the recognition of the revolutionary French government:

> We certainly cannot deny to other nations that principle whereon our own government is founded, that every nation has a right to govern itself internally under what forms it please, and to change those forms at its own will; and externally to transact business with other nations through whatever organ it chooses, whether that be a

king, convention, assembly, committee, president, or whatever it be. The only essential thing is the will of the people. (J 24.800)

Timothy Pickering, now a senator from Massachusetts, protested the double standard Jefferson used for the French and the Haitian rebellions.[39] He wrote a heartfelt letter to the author of the Declaration of Independence:

> Dessalines is pronounced by some to be a ferocious tyrant; but, whatever atrocities may have been committed under his authority, have they surpassed, have they equaled in their nature (for in their extent they are comparatively nothing), those of the French Revolution, when "infuriated men were seeking," as you once said, "through blood and slaughter their long-lost liberty"? If there could ever be an apology for Frenchmen, will it not apply with tenfold priority and force to the rude blacks of Santo Domingo? If Frenchmen, who were more free than the subjects of any monarch in Europe, the English excepted, could find in you an apologist for cruel excesses of which the world had furnished no example, are the hapless, the wretched Haitians ("guilty" indeed of skin not colored like our own), emancipated by a great national act and declared *free* — are they, after enjoying freedom many years, having maintained it in arms, resolved to *live free or die;* are these men not merely to be abandoned to their own efforts but to be deprived of those necessary supplies which for a series of years, they have been accustomed to receive from the United States, and without which they cannot subsist? (P 14.147)

That letter is not mentioned by Gerard Clarfield in either of his two books on Pickering. In fact, his treatment of Pickering's dealings with Toussaint is skimpy to non-existent. It never comes up in the biography, and fewer than two pages are devoted to it in the book entirely devoted to Pickering's diplomacy, where Pickering's Toussaint policy is ludicrously described as a joint effort with England that "quarantined the island [of Saint Domingue]."[40] Though no one else goes quite that far in ignoring or dismissing Toussaint, Stephen Egerton notes that standard works on the Adams presidency — even fine studies like those of Stephen Kurtz, or Michael Dauer, or John Ferling — omit any treatment of Saint Domingue's revolution; and David McCullough "covers the affair in a single page and sets it in the non-existent colony of 'San Domingo.'"[41]

The oblivion over Saint Domingue is not confined to the Adams historiography. Historians of the Caribbean have long complained that United States historians have given too little attention to the full implications of the Haitian revolution, to its astonishing achievement and its effects throughout the region. It is almost as if the United States did not want to let another revolution in the New World rank with its own. Yet Haiti's was in many ways a more "impossible" and thorough overthrow of a European regime, and it had more immediate imitators in this hemisphere than did the "spirit of 1776."

> Haitians were the first, and remain the only, enslaved people in human history to have overthrown slavery and established an independent polity ruled by former slaves in place of the one controlled by their masters. Not surprisingly, the Haitian Revolution shook the confidence of white slaveholders in other parts of the Americas and influenced the direction of antislavery movements in France, Great Britain, and the Americas.[42]

The United States ousted a colonial power in its revolution, but it did not overthrow the entire social order on its shores. Saint Domingue did that:

> The Haitian Revolution represents the most thorough case study of revolutionary change anywhere in the history of the modern world . . . It was a unique case in the history of the Americas: a thorough revolution that resulted in a complete metamorphosis in the social, political, intellectual and economic life of the colony . . . The Haitian model of state formation drove xenophobic fear into the hearts of all whites from Boston to Buenos Aires, and shattered their complacency about the unquestioned superiority of their own political models.[43]

It is no wonder that some Americans did not want to remember this "terrified consciousness of the Caribbean" (as Anthony Maingot calls it).[44] But there is no reason we should continue hiding its importance in our account of the past. And as our understanding of the role of slavery in our past grows, it will become clearer just how much it affected all aspects of the nation's life, including its diplomacy. Seen from that vantage point, Pickering's support of Toussaint's revolution will be recognized as one of the bright spots in our diplomatic past, while Jefferson's betrayal of the same revolution will register as one of its least admirable (but more lasting) tendencies. The United States would not recognize Haiti as an independent nation until 1862, when Lincoln no longer had to cater to southern sensibilities.

[11]

"Second Revolution"

I t became clear in retrospect that the election of 1800 was a great tip-
ping point in American history, signaling the demise of Federalist
domination of the government and the advent of Republican rule. But the
election was more ambiguous than that for those living through it and
contesting its outcome. Reports of the voting in each state were slow to
come. It seemed that the election could go either way. Despite the sabotag-
ing of John Adams by members of his own party (principally Alexander
Hamilton), he made a surprisingly strong showing. If Jefferson had not
had the slave count, he would not have won, given static results elsewhere.
If Pennsylvania's electoral vote had been blocked by the state legislature (as
it almost was), he would have lost even with the slave count. On the other
hand, if Republicans had succeeded in making Pennsylvania vote as a bloc
in the Electoral College, he could have won even without the slave count —
but only provided Burr succeeded in sneaking a Republican legislature
into Albany, to give Jefferson the New York electors. There were many vari-
ables. But the steadiest, least fluctuating element in all these shiftings of
the equation is the twelve to fourteen votes given to the southern candidate, no matter what. An understanding of the 1800 election does not end
with that matter; but it should begin with it.

3

1800: Why Were Slaves Counted?

How could the Constitution so "disproportion the appor-tionment" of delegates to the national legislature as to al-low a man to gain three hundred extra votes in Congress by owning five hundred human beings? This offered not only a reward for injustice, but the means for protecting and perpetuating the in-justice. As Gouverneur Morris put it during the debates that framed the Constitution:

> The admission of slaves into the representation, when fairly ex-plained, comes to this: that the inhabitant of Georgia and South Carolina who goes to the coast of Africa and, in defiance of the most sacred laws of humanity, tears away his fellow creatures from their dearest connections and damns them to the most cruel bondage, shall have more votes in a government instituted for protection of the rights of mankind than the citizen of Pennsylvania or New Jersey who views with a laudable horror so nefarious a practice. (F 2.22)

And if slaves were to be "represented" at all, how did the figure three-fifths become the measure of such misrepresentation? The only way to understand that number, or to see how the very idea of counting slaves in Congress arose, is to look at the way the three-fifths count was first proposed, in an entirely different context, as a measure of *taxation* under the Articles of Confederation, where *representation* was not at issue.

It has already been noticed that each state was given, in the Articles, only one vote in Congress, no matter how many delegates from each state attended the sessions. There was to be no proportionate representation. In fact, despite the revolutionary slogan linking the two, taxation could not follow the rule of representation in this case. If the states were requisitioned for equal amounts of money, to correspond with their equal votes, then a little state like Rhode Island would pay as much as New York or Virginia to the defraying of national expenses.

How, then, were financial quotas to be set for the states? The first draft of the Articles, drawn up by a committee of the revolutionary Congress, but submitted in the handwriting of John Dickinson, said in Article XI that funds for war and other expenses "shall be supplied by the several colonies in proportion to the number of inhabitants of every age, sex, and quality, except Indians not paying taxes." How was the number of inhabitants to be ascertained? The document proposed that they "shall be triennially taken and transmitted to the assembly of the United States."[1] This offered little help in the immediate circumstances, when taking a census was impossible because of the war, with armies shifting the population about and the enemy occupying places to be surveyed. Besides, by including those of "every quality" but one (Indians), the draft proposed counting slaves, both indentured and chattel, both white and black. The southern states, which would be urgent for counting slaves later on (when it would boost their representation), were opposed to counting them at all when it boosted taxes. This was, they claimed, taxation without representation.

The South therefore mobilized against the draft's Article XI. Samuel Chase of Maryland said that only free whites should be counted (H 5.548). The slaves were property, comparable to such property, held in the North, as "cattle, horses, etc." If the southern states paid according to the slave population, they would be taxed, according to Jefferson's notes on these debates, "according to their numbers and their wealth conjunctly, while the northern would be taxed on numbers only" (J 1.320). John Adams answered that laborers, free or slave, would be taxed under the system proposed, and "the condition of the laboring poor in most countries, that of the fishermen particularly of the northern states, is as abject as that of slaves" (J 1.321) — an argument that would come back in a far different context, years later, when John Calhoun equated southern slaves and northern laborers.

It was at this point that Benjamin Harrison of Virginia made the first proposal for a *partial* representation of slaves, counting each as one-half of an inhabitant, since they did not work at the same rate as freemen in the North. James Wilson of Pennsylvania objected that this made a positive advantage of owning slaves, not only cutting the amount of taxes their owner would pay but reducing the number of men they would have to supply for the common defense. "It is our duty to lay every discouragement on the importation of slaves, but this amendment would give the *jus trium liberorum* [tax break for large families] to him who would import slaves" (J 1.322). Witherspoon of New Jersey said that quotas should be set by "lands and houses," and the South threw its weight behind this proposal. After debates running into October of 1777, during which all the New England states opposed the Witherspoon concept, a five-to-four vote altered the draft to say that funds "shall be supplied by the several states in proportion to the value of all land within each state, granted to or surveyed for any person, as such land and the buildings and improvement thereon shall be estimated according to such mode as the United States in Congress assembled shall from time to time direct and appoint" (H 9.785). This is what was ratified in the Articles.

Hard experience of trying to finance the war proved this article unworkable. States were accused or suspected of underreporting their land values to reduce taxation (M 6.23–24, 37, 173–74, 215–16, 489). Even honest estimates were hard to come by in wartime, when land values fluctuated because of occupation or devastation, and some state claims on territory were disputed or unsurveyed (M 6.188, 195–96, 247). Besides, the Congress had not been able to establish norms for determining the value of different kinds of lands (arable, pastured, wooded, watered, or whatever) or of improvements (mills, houses, workshops, etc.), as Madison recorded in his notes (M 6.36, 150, 213). In 1783, therefore, Congress tried to go back to the original idea of a tax keyed to population.

This raised the same old problem, of course — how to count (if at all) the slaves? The first proposal was that advanced earlier by Harrison, that slaves be counted as one-half of other inhabitants. Attempts at numerical calculations of slave productivity were then indulged. Northerners (Oliver Wolcott from Connecticut, Stephen Higginson and Samuel Holton and Samuel Osgood from Massachusetts) claimed that slaves did three-quarters the work of freemen. Southerners countered that it was more like one-fourth (Daniel Carroll from Maryland) or one-third (John Rutledge from South Carolina), producing a deadlock (M 6.407). A vote was taken on counting slaves at a two-thirds rate — probably at the suggestion of Madison, according to the editors of his papers — but it lost. Madison then, "to give a proof of the sincerity of his professions of liberality," proposed the three-fifths rate for taxation. This was a compromise between the one-half count favored by the South and the three-fourths favored by the North. It would count a slave's productivity at 60 percent of a free person's, as opposed to the 50 percent favored by the South or the 75 percent desired by the North. (Madison split the difference with a tilt in the South's favor.) The compromise prevailed by a vote of five to three, with the southern states voting for it (M 6.408). A later vote reached eleven to two in favor of the motion (M 6.471), but since this was an amendment to the Articles, it required unanimous agreement in order to be passed.

It is often said that the three-fifths ratio was adopted under the Articles of Confederation. Clinton Rossiter even claimed that the ratio was "a legacy from the Congress of 1783."[2] That is not true. It was an amendment that never passed. But the ratio had been voted on by a congressional majority, so the number came into the Constitutional Convention with an air (however spurious) of precedent — though it was about to be put to an entirely different use, for fixing representation, not taxation. The original (Virginia) plan for the Constitution, submitted to the convention on May 29, did not use the three-fifths formula for representation. It said that "the national legislature ought to be proportioned to the quotas of contribution, or to the number of free inhabitants, as the one or the other rule may seem best in different cases" (M 10.15). Madison, however, moved the very next day to remove the term "free inhabitants." Hamilton moved to retain it, and Delaware said that it was not authorized to change the rule of representation. The convention tabled the matter as a hot potato (F 1.35–38). On June 11, Roger Sherman of Connecticut tried to return to the representation of "free inhabitants" alone, but two of the men from South Carolina (Pierce Butler and John Rutledge) objected. At this point, seeking compromise, James Wilson introduced the three-fifths count, a concept Charles Pinckney had been lobbying for (F 1.196, 201). Predictably, some northern delegates opposed counting the slaves at all, while some southerners wanted to count them fully.[3] But the South deftly switched its emphasis from taxation and productivity arguments, those used in the Articles debate, to a new concern — a balance of representation between the North and the South.

Under the Articles, the North outnumbered the South by eight states to five.[4] But a majority of nine was required for most important matters (Articles IX, X, XI) and unanimity for any amendment (Article XIII); so the South had a veto on matters that challenged its vital interests. Under the Constitution taking shape, however, that would no longer be the case. The South had to fear an edge given to the North, both in terms of the unit vote in the Senate and the popular vote in the House, since 60 percent of the white population was in the North. Counting slaves fully would have made the two regions roughly equal. Counting them at three-fifths would give the South, which had only 41 percent of the white population, 47 percent of the delegates in the House of Representatives.[5]

Madison made regional balance the central concern of representation, subordinating other concerns that are usually given more attention (e.g., the division between large states and small ones).

> The great danger to our general government *is the great northern and southern interests of the continent being opposed to each other. Look to the votes in Congress and most of them stand divided by the geography of the country, not according to the size of the states.* [M 10.88, emphasis in original]

The states were divided into different interests not by their difference of size, but by other circumstances: the most material of which resulted partly from climate, but principally from the effects of their having or not having slaves. These two causes concurred in forming the great division of interests in the United States. It did not lie between the large and small states: it lay between the northern and southern. And if any defensive power were necessary, it ought to be mutually given to these two interests. (M 10.90)

Mr. Madison said that having always conceived that the difference of interest in the United States lay not between the large and small but the northern and southern states . . . (F 1.601)

Even an equal vote of the states in the Senate should be rejected, he argued, because of "the perpetuity it would give to the preponderance of the northern against the southern [states]. Scale was a serious consideration. It seemed now to be pretty well understood that the real difference of interests lay, not between the large and small but between the northern and southern states" (M 10.102).

As a bargaining chip to secure both his concerns — proportional representation in the Senate as well as the House, and representation of the slaves — Madison offered a suggestion that only free whites should be counted in one chamber and slaves should be fully counted in the other. He said he would not push this, because it looked divisive, and whichever count was used in the House would have greater weight than in the smaller (but still proportional) numbers in the Senate (F 1.486–87). But he brought the proposal up again ten days later as the "proper ground for compromise" (F 1.562). He was hoping that a compromise of this compromise would lead to proportional representation in the Senate and at least partial counting of slaves in the House. Madison's stress on regional conflict was voiced by Charles Pinckney, too: "There is a real distinction [between] northern and southern interests. North Carolina, South Carolina, and Georgia in their rice and indigo had a peculiar interest which might be sacrificed" (F 1.510).

The three-fifths provision was defeated (six to four) on July 11, but prevailed on July 12 (six to two, with two states divided). The deciding factor, as Gouverneur Morris admitted, was the threat of the South not to ratify unless this concession were made. He was against granting the concession:

> Mr. Gouverneur Morris was compelled to declare himself reduced to the dilemma of doing injustice to the southern states or to human nature, and he must therefore do it to the former. For he could never agree to give such encouragement to the slave trade as would be given by allowing them a representation for their Negroes, and he did not believe those States would ever confederate on terms that would deprive them of that trade. (F 1.588)

William Davie, a delegate from North Carolina, put the South's ultimatum this way:

> Mr. Davie said it was high time now to speak out. He saw that it was meant by some gentlemen to deprive the southern states of any share of representation for their blacks. He was sure that North Carolina would never confederate on any terms that did not rate them at least as three fifths. If the eastern states meant therefore to exclude them altogether, the business was at an end. (F 1.593)

Morris answered Davie by saying that a union of North and South was therefore impossible:

> It is in vain for the eastern states to insist on what the southern states will never agree to. It is equally vain for the latter to require what the other states can never admit; and he verily believed that the people of Pennsylvania will never agree to a representation of Negroes. (F 1.593)

The three-fifths rule was adopted not because of any estimate of the blacks' productivity, or even of a tradeoff between representation and taxation.[6] It was because the South felt it needed a greater share in the representation. As Davie explained the matter to his fellow North Carolinians:

> The eastern states had great jealousies on this subject. They insisted that their cows and horses were equally entitled to representation; that the one was property as well as the other. It became our duty, on the other hand, to acquire as much weight as possible in the legis-

lation of the union; and as the northern states were more populous in whites, this only could be done by insisting that a certain proportion of our slaves should make a part of the computed population. (F 3.342)

Pinckney made the same point to South Carolinians:

We determined that representatives should be apportioned among the several states by adding to the whole number of free persons three fifths of the slaves. We thus obtained a representation for our property; and I confess I did not expect that we had conceded too much to the eastern states when they allowed us a representation of a species of property which they have not among them. (F 3.253)

Alexander Hamilton admitted that the three-fifths proviso was the sine qua non of ratification: "Without this indulgence, no union could possibly have been formed" (F 3.333). Morris agreed:

The states in which slavery is prohibited ultimately, though with reluctance, acquiesced in the disproportionate number of representatives and electors that was secured to the slave-holding states. The concession was, at the time, believed to be a great one, and has proved to have been the greatest which was made to secure the adoption of the Constitution. (F 3.430)[7]

Even with the three-fifths provision in place, the South was outnumbered in the first Congress — which, before a census could be taken, was based on an agreed-upon estimate. The North would have a 53-to-47 edge. But the South felt that it would soon, with the help of the federal ratio, catch up with and go beyond the North's numbers, especially as new states were added to the Union. These would come first of all in the Southwest, where population was flowing toward what would become Kentucky, Tennessee, Alabama, Arkansas, and Louisiana — slave states all (F 3.578–79, 604). As Madison pointed out, "The extent and fertility of the western soil would for a long time give to agriculture a preference over manufacture" (F 3.585). This would be plantation territory, with slave labor. Madison said that representation in Congress could not be frozen at the original numbers, but must reflect changes in the census — otherwise, "as soon as the southern and western population should predominate, *which must happen in a few years,* the power would be in the hands of the minority" (F 3.586, emphasis added).

In other words, the South was not demanding slave representation to achieve a near-parity at the moment, but as a way of achieving majority control in the immediately foreseeable future. Even before he arrived at the Philadelphia Convention, Madison had told Jefferson why he thought that representation by population would supplant the unit vote of the Articles: "It is recommended to the eastern states by the actual superiority of their populations, and to the southern by *their expected superiority*" (M 1.318–19, emphasis added). Madison wrote the same thing to Patrick Henry and George Washington (M 9.371, 385). This promise of future preponderance was used, after the convention, as an argument for the South to ratify the Constitution. As George Nicholas told the Virginia ratifying convention:

> The influence of New England and the other northern states is dreaded . . . [but] it must be supposed that our population will, in a short period, exceed theirs, as their country is well settled and we have very extensive uncultivated tracts. We shall soon outnumber them in as great a degree as they do us at this time. Therefore this government, which I trust will last to the remotest age, will be very shortly in our favor.[8]

Morris had agreed with this view in Philadelphia:

> It has been said that North Carolina, South Carolina, and Georgia only will in a little time have a majority of the people in America. They must in that case include the great interior country, and everything was to be apprehended from their getting the power into their hands. (F 1.604–05)

Given this prospect of large gains in the Southwest, it must be asked why the North gave in to the demand for a three-fifths representation of the slaves. The imminent surge of population was hardly a great secret guarded by the South. Lance Banning describes what must have been obvious to everyone:

As of 1786, the West was everywhere perceived as an extension of the South. Western settlement was still almost exclusively on lands southwest of the Ohio. Settlers in Kentucky or in Tennessee were often literally the kin or former neighbors of important southern families, and a great deal more than family ties and family fortunes seemed at stake in their continued membership in the American union. For years, Virginians had identified the economic future of their commonwealth with improvements that would make the Chesapeake the entrepot for European imports to the West. More recently, as population had moved increasingly into the old Southwest, it had become increasingly apparent that admission to the Union of new southwestern states could fundamentally affect the federal balance, guaranteeing southern dominance within the federation or assuring the emergence of a national majority whose agricultural character and interest would accord with Virginia's republican ideals.[9]

The North knew enough of these developments not to have gone blindly into the three-fifths bargain. Why did they strike the bargain, then? They had little choice. The Deep South had made it clear that without this edge it would not ratify (it was a close call even with it). It was part of a determination of the South to buttress slavery against all assaults on it. When prolonging the slave trade was attacked as "dishonorable to the American character to have such a feature in the Constitution," Charles Pinckney answered simply: "South Carolina can never receive the plan if it prohibits the slave trade" (F 2.364).[10] John Rutledge chimed in: "If the convention thinks that North Carolina, South Carolina, and Georgia will ever agree to the plan unless their right to import slaves be untouched, the expectation is vain. The people of those states will never be such fools to give up so important an interest" (F 2.373).

Here, as with the slave representation (where the "compromise" awarded a three-fifths rather than a full count), the most the North could wheedle from the South was a proviso that the slave trade would be *guaranteed* only for the next twenty years (leaving open the possibility of renewing it then). As Madison put it, "South Carolina and Georgia were inflexible on the point of slaves"

(M 10.214). On all matters affecting slaves, concession to the South was the price to be paid if there was to be any union at all. Northerners might hope for amendment once the government was functioning. The main task was first to get it functioning.

This did not mean that the North was happy with the concession. Morris, as we have seen, considered it immoral: "He never would concur in upholding domestic slavery. It was a nefarious institution — it was the curse of heaven on the states where it prevailed" (F. 1.221). But he gave in, to his later regret, and wrote the final draft that deployed euphemisms to avoid mentioning slavery. Others were opposed to the slave count, but said they would accept it if it were the sine qua non of union. Rufus King of Massachusetts expressed the frustration of those encountering the South's inflexibility on the slave issue:

> The admission of slaves [into the rule of representation] was a most grating circumstance to his mind, and he believed would be so to a great part of the people of America. He had not made a strenuous opposition to it heretofore because he had hoped that this concession would have produced a readiness, which had not been manifest, to strengthen the general government and to mark a full confidence in it. (F 1.220)

Some ratifying conventions swallowed with difficulty the three-fifths provision. Luther Martin urged his fellow Marylanders to reject the Constitution because of it:

> To have a provision not only putting it out of its power to restrain and prevent the slave trade, but even encouraging that most infamous traffic, by giving the states power and influence in the union in proportion as they cruelly and wantonly sport with the rights of their fellow creatures, ought to be considered as a solemn mockery of and insult to the God whose protection we had then implored. (F 3.211)

There was further grumbling when the first census showed that the South would have twelve extra votes in the next Congress because of the slaves, "above the proportion of other states, whose property (though of superior value) was not entitled by the Constitution to any representation at all."[11] Fisher Ames complained in the same forum of the disproportionate representation.

In the long run the South did not outnumber the North as expected; but it experienced a great surge in the early years, making other regions feel a certain panic. The first three states added to the South, large and growing states, added fifteen members to the South's delegation in Congress, while the first two states added to the North in that same period produced only two more members. Each of the early censuses told the same tale. Timothy Pickering noted, ominously, "On the census of 1790, Kentucky was entitled to two representatives; under that of 1800, she has six." This is what would make the prospect of adding Louisiana and the Floridas — and, after that, Mexico and California — so threatening to northerners. It was mentioned earlier that Oliver Wolcott and others feared the slave vote would tip the margin in the 1796 election. When it did just that in 1800, some were prepared to break the bargain that had been struck in Philadelphia.

4

1800: The Negro-Burr Election

IN 1800, OTHER THINGS being equal, the outcome was determined by two factors — the twelve votes given Jefferson by the
slave count, and Aaron Burr's brilliant campaign effort in New
York, which added twelve more votes. Without either one, the Republicans would have lost. The Negro factor and the Burr factor
would be fused in the mind of Timothy Pickering, who briefly
hoped that Burr, because of his experience in 1800, would lead a
northern secession from the slave power. Burr's contribution to the
Republican cause in 1800 is often overlooked, since people concentrate rather on his actions during the election in the House, made
necessary because of the electoral-vote tie between Jefferson and
him. But the Republicans would never have reached that stage in the
election but for what Burr did in New York.

Jefferson, like some of his allies, was not comfortable with Burr as
a Republican running mate (for a second time) in 1800. Burr was
what Jefferson despised — a mobile and urban operator, despite his
old family ties with New England's theocracy. He was a professional
politician before that had become a profession. As the grandson of
the nation's great theologian-orator, Jonathan Edwards, and the son
of the theologian-president of the College of New Jersey (Princeton), Burr should have been a religious conservative distrustful of
worldly scheming. He belonged with his cousin Timothy Dwight,

who became the president of Yale, or his tutor (and brother-in-law) Tapping Reeve, the most famous law professor of his time. But Burr rarely stayed where he belonged. After attending Princeton, the family domain, he became an officer during the Revolutionary War, brave and headlong, restive under Washington's authority, but able himself to discipline those who (like him) disliked discipline. In all these aspects, he resembled another prickly young officer who maneuvered out from under General Washington's strict gaze — Alexander Hamilton.

These two men, with outsize ambitions belying their slight stature, became each the other's evil twin. Both romantics, both adventurers, they frightened outsiders and each other with the sweep of their ambition. Each was a leader — Hamilton narrow-eyed, aimed, bowling over opposition (or trying to), the first over the ramparts at the capture of Yorktown; Burr, with liquid accepting eyes, drawing people in rather than shoving them aside, the rescuer of stranded troops (including Hamilton's) at Brooklyn Heights. Hamilton was all edge, Burr a thing of curves and sidles. Jefferson would seek in Burr an anti-Hamilton, hoping he was the more detested man's antidote — only to find the cure as bad as the disease.

In 1791, Jefferson and Madison made an unprecedented tour northward off their native turf, purportedly to "botanize" among odd flora, but in fact to sound out men who could make their nascent Republican party more than a regional force. New York seemed the only place north of Pennsylvania that was open to their inroads. George Clinton had organized a proto-Republican machine to oppose aristocratic families descended from colonial New York's Dutch patroons. Those aloof Dutch types still had their representatives in families like the Van Rensselaers and Schuylers, and Alexander Hamilton had married into the latter family. Clinton was using Aaron Burr, Hamilton's rival as a Revolutionary War hero and rising young lawyer, to counter the ambitions of Hamilton.

Since Clinton was the local Republican power, Jefferson and Madison, those botanists from Virginia, paid special attention to what Robert Troup called the specimen *clintonia borealis*.[1] But Clinton would be a difficult man to manage from out of state. He was a proud guardian of his domain — which is why he had fought so hard against ratification of the Constitution. The Virginians there-fore needed a backup candidate to carry the party's effort in New York if Clinton proved unmanageable. They looked for this to Burr, Clinton's protégé but a restive one. Burr might be used as a prod to Clinton, or even a substitute for him, and he could be counted on, in any event, to bedevil Hamilton.

Clinton had actually been the first to try the Jeffersonian tactic of using Burr against Hamilton. The Clinton machine jumped Burr up to the office of New York attorney general in 1789. When, two years later, Hamilton went to Philadelphia to be the nation's first secretary of the treasury, Clinton's tame legislature sent Burr right after him to be New York's senator — rejecting the incumbent, who happened to be Hamilton's father-in-law, Philip Schuyler. This was particu-larly galling to Schuyler since, as a member of the first Senate, he was part of the third of that body that could serve only two years, in order to set up the rotating scheme that would later give everyone a staggered six-year term. Schuyler had just settled in to enjoy a work-ing relationship with his son-in-law at Treasury, an advantage giv-ing him an edge (he thought) to win re-election to a full term. In-stead, the Clinton-dominated legislature yanked him back home, to be supplanted by his son-in-law's smooth alter ego. The insult was never forgotten by Hamilton's allies in New York.

As senator, Burr tried to establish claims on southern Republi-cans that would make them favor him over Clinton as the man to work with in New York. Burr supported the Virginians on all the issues that mattered most to them in the 1790s. He opposed (in-evitably) Hamilton's bank, and attacked the Jay Treaty (Jay was a member of the Schuyler faction in New York). He defended the Democratic-Republican Societies criticized by Washington, and supported Albert Gallatin's claim to a contested Senate seat from Pennsylvania. Even after Burr left the Senate, he championed the South's cause by trying to scotch the New York legislature's con-demnation of the Kentucky and Virginia Resolutions (B 1.393–95).

But while Burr labored at being a party regular, he was also creat-ing a network of personal followers for himself. His service in all the sectors of the Revolution had created friends and acquaintances among the officers and veterans in many states, and he distinguished himself in the Senate by extending and confirming provisions for disabled veterans and for the widows and orphans of those who died in service (B 1.93–95). He was a man in a hurry. Put in the Senate by George Clinton's tame legislature in 1791, he tried to run against Clinton for governor the very next year. He was betting that Federalists wanted so desperately to dethrone Clinton, who was running for his sixth successive term, that they would vote for a dissident Republican — all prior *Federalist* candidates had failed. Nonetheless, Federalists tried to put up again a former candidate, Judge Robert Yates, only to find that Yates was promoting, across party lines, his friend Burr. In some panic at this point, the Federalists pleaded with John Jay to resign from the Supreme Court, where he was Chief Justice, and come back to New York for their rescue. When Jay accepted this offer, Burr had to give up his bid (B 1.103–6).

Jay almost certainly won more votes than Clinton in the ensuing election, but there were irregularities in reporting returns from three western counties. The committee empowered to adjudicate the dispute over these votes split along party lines, and asked for the opinion of the two New York senators. Burr did not want to commit himself, but his Senate colleague, Rufus King, was determined to give the disputed votes to Jay — which forced Burr to stick to legalities and discount the votes, as the commission too decided, giving another term to Clinton (B 1.106–22).

The 1792 Race for President

But the electoral battles of 1792 were not over. That was also the year of the second election for president, the first competitive one after the early acclamation of Washington and Adams. Washington, of course, was certain to win if he decided to serve a second term. But if Washington was undefeatable, his vice president was not. Clinton had exerted all his electoral pressures to win as governor in New York, hoping that would put him in a strong position for replacing Adams as vice president. He had been approached by Madison and Monroe to mount a challenge to the all-Federalist ticket of Washington and Adams. But the narrow and nasty character of Clinton's victory against Jay made some Republicans at the national capital in Philadelphia think Clinton was tainted, and that Burr, the man who had wanted to displace him as governor, should step ahead of him to the vice presidency (M 14.376–77, 379–81). This possibility disturbed Hamilton so much that he launched a letter-writing campaign against it (B 1.140). Madison and Monroe conferred, and decided to stick with Clinton, for fear of offending the nascent Republican party in New York (M 14.378–39, 382). Burr graciously retired from the challenge his friends were urging upon him — but this bid (however curtailed) meant that, by the time Burr won as vice president in 1800, it was his third try for the spot. He had been a candidate in three of the nation's first four national elections — and had thus been running for top executive honors even longer than Jefferson.

The 1796 Race for President

In the next presidential race, Burr would run *with* Jefferson. Members of the Republican caucus in Philadelphia, men who had worked with Burr while he was there in the Senate, decided that Clinton was too much a man of the past; the northerner to go with was Burr. Some of these men had succumbed to his great personal charm — a friend of Hamilton once lamented that Burr "has an address not resistible by common clay. Hamilton himself said that Burr had the glow of his great ancestors about him. Prominent Philadelphians were his promoters in 1796 — the scientist Benjamin Rittenhouse, the revolutionary governor Thomas McKean, but especially Albert Gallatin (B 1.267–68). In 1794, when Gallatin was refused a Senate seat because of his foreign birth, Burr had not only given a lawyerly speech in his favor, but supplied him with legal documents and arguments about the date of his naturalization (B 1.160–63).

Once Burr was chosen as Jefferson's running mate, he went down to Monticello to confer with his colleague. There is no record of what they talked about, but common sense suggests they were deciding on a campaign strategy. Burr, presumably, was to organize the party in the North. But when Burr threw himself energetically into a six-week blitz of the northern states, some Republicans were disturbed by his forthright self-promotion. It was still unusual to campaign for oneself — even four years later, Monroe would have to remind Jefferson that he should not attend a rally for himself in Richmond. Jefferson, losing his normal reluctance to appear openly, had written, "Sometimes it is useful to furnish occasions for the flame of public opinion to break out."[2] Jefferson did not repeat this uncharacteristic lapse.

John James Beckley, the Pennsylvania organizer who had concerted strategy with Madison and Monroe in 1792, now expressed concern that Burr's efforts "are more directed to himself than anybody else" (B 1.269). He feared that if all the Republican votes went equally for Jefferson and Burr, and if Burr picked up some Federalist votes as well, Burr not only could tie with Jefferson but might even sneak past both Adams and Jefferson in the electoral count: "Would it not be prudent to vote one half of Virginia for Clinton?" In the event, Burr did not get even half of Virginia's 1796 vote. Of the state's twenty-two votes, he received exactly one, while Samuel Adams (an anyone-but-Burr substitute) received fifteen.[3] Ironically, this attempt to "keep him in his place" is what set up Burr's tie vote with Jefferson four years later. Burr, angered that he had been betrayed by his own party, refused to join the Republican ticket again, in 1800, unless he was assured that there would be no repetition of the humiliating snub he had received the first time. Virginians toed the line the second time around — with exactly the results they had tried to avoid in 1796.

The 1800 Race for President

Burr did not show his anger publicly in 1796 — even years later, in his memoirs, he was silent about the 1796 election — but it had to gall him that he received only half the votes given to Adams's running mate, Thomas Pinckney. Yet he continued to run New York's Republican opposition to Hamilton, and in the run-up to the 1800 election he completely flummoxed his old foe. The key to New York's presidential vote was the race for the New York Assembly, since it would choose the presidential electors. Once again, Burr conferred on strategy with Jefferson (this time meeting him in Philadelphia). He told the vice president that everything would depend, in New York, on the twelve New York City delegates to the assembly, and he thought he could win those crucial seats for the party. This news comforted Jefferson, since it looked as if Pennsylvania, which had given Jefferson fourteen of its fifteen votes in the last election, would not be casting any votes in 1800. New York, in that case, would be the only middle state going Republican, *if* it did. Without New York, Jefferson said, "it would then require a Republican vote both from New Jersey and Pennsylvania to preponderate against New York, on which we could not count with any confidence."[4]

The deadlock in Pennsylvania, which promised to keep the state out of the election, reflected a general struggle between states that chose electors statewide (which gave an advantage to the majority within the state) and those that chose by district (which gave votes to minority enclaves). Republicans saw that they had lost the 1796 election by a mere three electoral votes, and blamed this on the district system that had let Federalists reap one extra vote from three generally Republican states (Virginia, Pennsylvania, and North Carolina).[5] In all three states they tried to remedy this situation. Jefferson said that registering minorities was more democratic, but that Virginia could not continue the practice without putting itself at a disadvantage vis-à-vis states with a winner-take-all procedure.

> All agree that an election by districts would be best, if it could be general; but while ten states choose either by their legislatures or by a general ticket, it is folly and worse than folly for the other six not to do it. In these ten states the minority is entirely unrepresented, and their majorities not only have the weight of their whole state in their scale, but have the benefit of so much of our minorities as can succeed at a district election.[6]

Federalists had carried five Virginia districts in the 1799 congressional elections. To prevent that vote from being repeated a year later, in the presidential contest, Madison proposed and drafted a change in the law that called for statewide election, making possible a Republican sweep (M 17.337, 359–61). Federalists claimed that this would prevent a third of Virginians from having any say in the election.[7] Though the change did favor the majority party, its work was not finished. Voters, instead of naming a known person from each district, had to vote for statewide candidates singled out by the central party. The information on these candidates had to be spread, along with their connections to the Jeffersonian establishment. One means for coping with this problem was to make sure that most electors were well known outside their districts. Madison himself was put up as one of the electors, along with famous men like Edmund Pendleton and George Wythe.[8] Jefferson himself arranged for ample printed material to be distributed to each district, while warning his agents to keep his role in the effort secret. It was a practice he had instituted in 1799 and maintained through the election year: "Do not let my name be connected with the business," he told the party's state chairman. "I trust yourself only with the secret that these pamphlets go from me."[9]

Pennsylvania Republicans wanted to adopt a general-ticket system, but Federalists, who controlled the upper house and wanted to retain the district vote, refused to pass the legislation required to set procedures at each election. This deadlock promised to leave the state without votes, as had happened to New York in 1789, the first election for president. The deadlock was not broken until the last minute (in December), by a compromise that denied the Republicans their former statewide ticket. Each house was allowed to put up eight candidates, from which a vote of both chambers picked the required fifteen (H 24.449–50). This gave Republicans only a slight edge, eight out of fifteen, instead of the fourteen-to-one vote in 1796. So Jefferson knew how much depended on Burr's success in New York. As he wrote to Madison, "If Pennsylvania does not vote [or does not vote solidly Republican], then New York determines the election."[10]

Burr's task was a difficult one. Federalists, under Hamilton's guidance, had won all the previous year's elections in New York City.[11] This time, Burr would have to take them all if he meant to shift decisively the balance in the legislature. Hamilton did not realize that Burr had identified a crucial factor in the coming race. The state assembly had recently been moved from New York City to Albany, and many of the Federalists' Manhattan lawyers and merchants were unwilling to give up their interests for three months of rustication up-state. This made it difficult for Hamilton to fill his party's slate with eminent men. He assumed that Burr would have the same problem, and he settled for candidates that Burr's friend, Matthew Davis, mocked as "two grocers, a ship chandler, a baker, a potter, a book-seller, a mason, and a shoemaker" (B 1.423). Burr capitalized on this situation with a threefold strategy.

First: He removed his own candidacy from the city, running in-stead from Orange County. He did not want his presence on the ticket to be a distraction or a deterrent, since he meant to woo his old patron-rival, Governor Clinton, out of retirement to head the city ticket. He wanted no disputed leadership in the city delega-tion.[12]

Second: Burr calculated that if he got Clinton to run, other prom-inent men would join him, despite their initial refusals. These in-cluded Horatio Gates ("the hero of Saratoga") and Robert Living-ston (signer of the Declaration of Independence). They headed a distinguished ticket.

Third: Burr kept his own slate a secret until, belatedly, Hamilton published the only names he had been able to come up with. Once that occurred, on April 15, Burr called a public meeting for April 17 to unveil his candidates — too late for Hamilton to replace his non-entities with worthier choices.

Frustrated as Hamilton was by these maneuvers, he did not give up. During the three days of voting in the city, he took to the streets, haranguing voters at the polling place, while Burr did the same thing — and Hamilton could not equal the efficiency of Burr's oper-ation. The Burr home had been turned into a communication head-quarters, from which young volunteers went out to campaign door to door (German-speaking emissaries to the German neighbor-hoods). They brought back dispatches, catching sleep on mattresses spread over the floor, bolting food kept ready on tables.[13] On the last day, Burr himself spent ten hours at a polling place where Federalist cheating was anticipated (B 1.425). The result was a clean sweep for Burr's men — all twelve would travel to Albany, where they could provide the margin for a majority vote in the legislature, one giving all New York's vote to the Republicans.

Hamilton was so infuriated at what Burr had done to him in the city election that he attempted an electoral coup, asking the governor, John Jay, to summon back into session the lame-duck assembly just voted out and make *it* choose the presidential electors. He wrote: "In times like this in which we live it will not do to be overscrupulous. It is easy to sacrifice the substantial interests of society by a strict adherence to ordinary rules" (H 24.464–67). This is exactly what Jefferson would say in 1807, brushing aside the laws in order to send Burr to the gallows. Something about Burr caused his enemies to come unhinged. Hamilton's erratic course would take him, in 1800, from urging Jay to do anything to prevent Jefferson from becoming president ("an atheist in religion and a fanatic in politics") to urging Federalists in Congress to break the electoral tie by making Jefferson president. The only common element in these two recommendations was their expression of a hatred for Burr.

Yet despite what Burr had done against Hamilton and for the party, Republicans hesitated to put him on the ticket again. They decided to sound out Clinton instead, and he toyed with the idea while setting a whole series of conditions. Meanwhile, Burr's friend Gallatin was deputed to sound him out, just in case. Gallatin's wife and father-in-law both spoke with Burr, and the latter reported that Burr "seemed to think that no arrangement could be made which would be observed to the southward, alluding as I understood to the last election, in which he was certainly ill used by Virginia and North Carolina. [But] I believe he may be induced to stand if assurance can be given that the southern states will act fairly" (B 1.433). If Burr ran with them this time, the Virginians would have to pledge him all their votes. Gallatin assured him that they would — and the pledge was honored.

Perhaps it was more than honor that made the southerners keep their word. Hamilton, continuing his aberrant behavior in this year of hatred for Burr, publicly urged Federalists to vote in lockstep for Charles Cotesworth Pinckney of South Carolina, who was running with Adams. He was hoping that some South Carolinians might vote for Jefferson as their presidential choice, but for their favorite son in the second place — that, after all, is what they had done in 1796, all eight electors giving one of their votes to Jefferson and the other one to the Federalists' "second man," Pinckney's cousin Thomas. In this way, the second choice might edge out both men intended for first place.[14]

Virginians, aware of this scheme, felt they could not afford to throw away any of their votes this time. There would be no more grandstanding with Samuel Adams. Hamilton's scheme to elect Pinckney failed. Throughout the 1800 campaign, as Hamilton's admiring biographer puts it, "Two extremely shrewd politicians had locked horns, and Burr had won."[15] But with the Republicans' tie, the election still had to be decided in the House of Representatives, and that would pit two other shrewd politicians against each other — Jefferson and Burr.

5

1801: Jefferson or Burr?

NOT ONLY WAS the 1800 election more ambiguous than it has seemed. The second election, that of 1801 in the House of Representatives, was not as simple a matter as Jefferson would later make of it. Congress had to resolve the tie between Jefferson and Burr. It was not given much time for this, since the reporting of the votes took so long. Jefferson, in his capacity as vice president, opened the electoral votes before a joint session of the Congress on February 11, little under a month from the date when one of the two who were tied must be inaugurated. The House determined to stay in continual session until a president was decided on; but it took six days and thirty-six ballots to reach a decision. What happened during those days is murky in itself, but conventional wisdom clears away the murk, producing a neat and celebratory version of the outcome. This canonical view makes seven interlocking points:

1. That the House's choice of Jefferson represented a triumph of the majority will.
2. That Aaron Burr tried to defeat this popular will.[1]
3. That a public-spirited Hamilton urged Federalists to do the right thing and vote for Jefferson.

4. That, nonetheless, some Federalists were on the verge of usurping the presidency.

5. But that a noble Federalist, James Bayard of Delaware, "deferred to the will of the people" and became "the savior of the Constitution."[2]

6. And that, as a result, the sore loser Adams stormed out of town without even waiting to see the transfer of power.[3]

7. That, in short, America was blessed with a Second Revolution, rescuing the endangered principles of the first one.

What is wrong with this case? It is important to remember what the Constitution called for. Technically, Burr had received seventy-three votes *for president* — the same number as Jefferson — and could have received no vote at all *except* for that post. Looking back at the election through the lenses of later party procedure, we can say that the Republicans voting for Jefferson and Burr had *intended* what they could not yet *say*, constitutionally — that they wanted Burr only for the second spot, though the Constitution allowed no explicit vote for that. And, looking through those same lenses, it is possible to maintain that only those voting for the Republican ticket should have the right to sort out their own preferences — therefore, that Federalists who capitalized on the constitutional technicalities by asserting their preference between the two Republicans were acting in bad faith. But the historical situation should not be read anachronistically.

The Historical Situation

1. Voting by party slate was a new thing only partly recognized in 1800. As recently as the previous election, voters' preference had been for the top two men from different proto-parties, matching Jefferson as vice president with Adams as president. In fact, half the states voting that time had failed or refused to vote the suggested slate of the two parties' congressional caucuses.[4]

2. The only obligation resting on the House of Representatives was to choose the person its members considered most fit to rule the country. They were as free to make a decision by their own lights

as were the presidential electors themselves. The latitude of decision envisaged by the Constitution can be seen from the fact that, where no electoral vote produced a majority for one candidate, the House was given its choice among the top *five* candidates. They were to exercise their own judgment, not to seek "the popular will." The very rules under which they operated — only one vote per state — were at odds with any representation of the people in terms of number or a presumed "popular will."

3. In fact, the popular will was not manifest to many of those required to determine the outcome, for reasons already touched on. The Republican number included the totally non-representative slave bonus of twelve votes. And even restricting the election to free white voters led to ambiguities. Electors were mainly chosen by state legislatures, not by direct vote — which allowed Burr by his spring coup in the New York Assembly race to make that legislature rule out any Federalist electors. In cases where a direct vote was used, minority votes were not counted in states like Virginia and South Carolina, which had enacted statewide legislation to exclude Federalist district votes. This very election hinged on the last-minute compromise in Pennsylvania that almost prevented its participation in the election. The situation was far more confused than Jefferson maintained when he attributed his recent installation in the White House to "the mighty wave of public opinion which has rolled over it [the nation]."[5]

4. There was a case to be made for choosing a Republican acceptable to Federalists, rather than confining the issue to Republicans' own preferences. The outcome should reflect a broad agreement. Jefferson would famously (some say fatuously) claim to be representing the other side as well as his own in his inaugural address: "We are all Republicans, we are all Federalists." Burr could more convincingly have voiced that claim. The logic of a coalition choice was expressed by Jefferson himself when he said that he would gladly take the second spot to Adams in 1796, since by working with a moderate Federalist he could undermine the radical Federalists (that is, the "monocrats" around Hamilton).[6] He wrote to Madison about Adams: "it is to be considered whether it would not be on the whole for the public good to come to a good understanding with

him."[7] If Jefferson could envisage a collaboration with a moderate Federalist, what was there to prevent Federalists from arranging for collaboration with the moderate Republican, Burr? Yet they have been scorned as schemers trying to "undo" the election by choosing Burr. Some of them were clearly thinking in terms of a coalition as checking the extremes of both parties. The Speaker of the House, Theodore Sedgwick, said that Burr, as less firmly lodged in the Republican fold, "will not be able to administer the government without the aid of the Federalists," making his administration more centrist (B 1.482). Pickering, though he was not in Washington at this time, expressed the same views on Burr as a compromise. Even Burr's faults made him useful:

> He holds to no pernicious theories, but is a mere matter-of-facts man. His very selfishness prevents his entertaining any mischievous predilections for foreign nations . . . So that although Burr's promises were but as cobwebs to bind a giant, both the great parties in the nation would have concurred in imposing the necessary restraints . . . [He] would not, because he could not, have projected and procured the adoption of measures productive of so much mischief . . . no possible mischief was to be apprehended from him as the executive chief of the union. (P 47.242)

In 1807, Pickering would make a similar case for a coalition of Federalists and Republicans to elect Burr the governor of New York.

5. Burr did have national, not merely regional, claims. He was the most successful Republican outside the South. He had added the essential twelve votes from New York that were the major non-southern component in the election. Yet he also had support in the South. The popular Charles Cotesworth Pinckney of South Carolina considered Burr more honorable than Jefferson, and thought it "politic and judicious" to have Federalists vote for Burr in the House — which is what his brother did there.[8] James Bayard of Delaware, the man making the closest daily canvass of the House's intentions, said that some southern delegates were suppressing their preference for Burr "out of complaisance to the known intentions of the party," but might feel free later in the balloting process to "give their votes for Mr. Burr, the man they really preferred" (B 1.482). For Federalists

of Pickering's stripe, who resented having a "Negro president," Burr was far preferable to Jefferson, even though as a Republican he too had profited by the slave bonus. He was not a slave owner, not a supporter of slavery; in fact, he was a lifelong opponent of slavery. If the Republicans were sincere in claiming that their coalition rested on something more than solidarity of the slave-owning South, a man who represented the party outside that context had much to recommend him.

6. But most people would now say that the preceding considerations lack any real force, since no one in good faith could have felt that Burr was "the best man" to be president. This judgment is based largely, though not entirely, on Burr's later reputation (whether earned or not) as a fomenter of treason in the West. But even in 1800 many people called Burr a sinister force. Similar charges, of course, can be unearthed against most leaders of the time. But, just as for them, there was a considerable body of people who thought well and spoke well of Burr. George Clinton thought Jefferson was the trimmer and told Burr he would have preferred him.[9] The British minister in Washington, reporting on the election, wrote to Whitehall:

> The Federal party in the House of Representatives seem determined to support the choice of Mr. Burr to be the president of the United States — provided he is willing to agree to certain conditions . . . He is regarded by some of them as a man possessing talents at least equal to those of Mr. Jefferson, with greater energy and consistency of character.[10]

People would later treat a preference for Burr as almost unthinkable. But that is not how it looked to those actually facing the choice. House Speaker Sedgwick wrote in his diary for January 30 that the "disposition to prefer Mr. Burr to Mr. Jefferson has been increasing until it has become nearly unanimous" (B 1.485).

Gouverneur Morris wrote, "It seems to be the general opinion that Colonel Burr will be chosen president by the House of Representatives."[11] Bayard, who would be credited with ending the stalemate, had all along wanted to vote for Burr, since "I considered Mr. Burr personally better qualified to fill the office of president than

Mr. Jefferson."[12] Even half a year after Jefferson had won the election, Gallatin thought Burr a real threat to Jefferson's re-election. If New York Republicans had to resort to him as their leading candidate, Federalists in that state might combine with them.[13] This was before Burr dashed his own hopes by killing Hamilton; but Gallatin in 1881 still saw Burr's strength in his ability to draw both Republican and Federalist votes. He *was* a coalition candidate, at a time when open partisanship was still somewhat shamefacedly avowed by many Americans.

All the above considerations have to be kept in mind if we are to judge properly what went on, in the House, during the tense days of non-stop balloting in February of 1801. Jefferson had won exactly half of the states (eight of sixteen), and needed just one more to reach a majority; but he was faced with an apparently unbudgeable bloc of six states firmly Federalist, along with two disqualified from casting their one vote because their delegation was divided into equal numbers. Delaware had only one congressman, so the whole state's vote depended on that man, James Bayard. The Federalists in the divided states of Maryland and Vermont commissioned him to sound out the candidates, to see if one of the two could be pledged not to conduct a purge of Federalist men and measures. Then the three states would decide whether to break the logjam. Burr seemed the more likely man to make such an assurance, but he refused to negotiate with any Federalists. "Mr. Burr would not cooperate with us."[14] He had given his word that he would not do so, and he kept it.[15] During the height of the struggle for House votes, he made himself incommunicado, attending his daughter's wedding in Albany.

Burr's non-bargaining attitude toward Bayard was not enough for some Republicans. They expected him to withdraw his claim at once, or to announce that he would not accept the presidency, even if offered it. Jefferson tried, in a typically indirect way, to get a previous assurance on this point. On December 15, when the possibility of a tie vote was manifest, he wrote to Burr making it clear who would be first in case that occurred. He congratulated Burr on the prospect of becoming *vice* president in *his* administration, and expressed sorrow that this would preclude him from his desire to put Burr in the more active role of a cabinet member:

> I had endeavored to compose an administration whose talents, integrity, names and dispositions should at once inspire unbounded confidence in the public mind and ensure a perfect harmony in the conduct of the public business. I lose you from that list. (B 1.469)

Burr responded with the assurance Jefferson was angling for, saying that he and his friends "can never think of diverting a single vote from you" (B 1.474). But he could not resist a mischievous dig that let Jefferson know he was on to his little game of regretting the loss to his cabinet. "I will cheerfully abandon the office of vice president if it shall be thought that I can be more useful in any active state" (B 1.474).

Jefferson was not completely comfortable with Burr's words. Burr said he and his friends would not divert a vote; but Jefferson wanted more than that. Would Burr positively refuse the presidency if he were offered it? Jefferson's agent in this matter, Samuel Smith of Maryland, kept pestering Burr with ever more insistent demands that he renounce any possibility of being president. Smith wrote Burr on December 10 for a declaration of intent. Burr answered (December 16) that in case of a tie "I should utterly disclaim all competition" (B 1.471). Smith followed up with another letter on December 12, to which Burr gave the reassuring news, on December 17, that he did not even plan to attend the inauguration of the new president (B 1.472). This was not enough for Smith. He wanted a more definite commitment. Burr replied on December 24 that "I have not now time to quarrel with phantoms" (B 1.475). Nonetheless, Smith pressed him for a fourth time — would he positively refuse the presidency if it were offered him? On December 29, Burr called this an "impertinent" question to which he had made no answer when others asked it. But "if I had made any, I should have told that as at present advised I should not [refuse]" (B 1.479). This was a thunderclap to Smith. He then confronted Burr in person. When Burr said that "at all events the House could and ought to make a choice, meaning if they could not get Mr. Jefferson they could take him," Smith said that if Burr tried to accept the office, "Republicans would not give up on any terms" (B 1.484). From this moment on, reports of Smith's conversation, quickly sent around Republican circles, made Burr a "usurper" in the eyes of Jefferson's supporters.

The Constitution

Yet why should Burr turn down an office if it came to him by the proper constitutional procedure and without any scheming on his part? Technically, every vote cast for him was cast for the president. If the House decided he was the best man to unite the country, it was within its rights, and even its duties. For that matter, who was he to take away from the House its role in making that decision? This was a constitutional point Gallatin made to Jefferson. He questioned "the two candidates having a right to make the selection of the two offices if the House shall not do it, [so that] they may themselves decide which of the two shall be president and which vice president." This would be "predicated on an assumption of executive power on our part . . . an assumption of power not strictly warranted by the forms and substance of our constitutions [federal and state]."[16] Gallatin would no doubt have had the same objection to Madison's plan for an executive means of breaking the legislative deadlock.

Madison suggested that if the tied vote should persist in the House beyond the target date for inauguration (March 4), Burr and Jefferson should act as joint chief executives and assemble the new Congress (expected to be Republican) early, to give a different House of Representatives the chance to vote on which of the two men summoning it actually had the power to do so. He offered, as "what my present judgment favors," a plan "for Congress to be summoned by a joint proclamation or recommendation of the two characters having a majority of votes for president."

The prerogative of convening the legislature must reside in one or other of them and, if both concur, must substantially include the requisite will. The intentions of the people would undoubtedly be pursued. And if, in reference to the Constitution, the proceeding be not strictly regular, the irregularity will be less in form than any other adequate to the emergency. (M 17.454)

Saying that two potential presidents must "include" the powers of an actual one is like saying that two bridges stretching halfway across a river are as good as one that goes all the way across.

With no easy way to break the deadlock, minds raced to the consideration of actions to be taken if it continued to be jammed. The Constitution made no provision for this eventuality. Who would have the authority to deal with the impasse? Not the president, clearly — he cannot name his successor. Not the House, since its deadlock was precisely the problem. Not the Supreme Court, since no law was at hand for it to enforce — the Constitution, after all, was what had backed people into this corner. Not individual states, since this was manifestly a federal matter. That left only one body at the federal level — the Senate. There was a constitutional logic for turning to the Senate. Article II had prescribed that, in case of a tie for the *second* highest vote, the Senate should resolve it. This is what Jefferson considered the gravest danger, since Federalists had a majority in the Senate.

There was a more direct way to involve the Senate. The Constitution had said that Congress should have the power to choose a successor to the presidency in case both the president and the vice president were unable to function. According to Article II, Section 1,

> Congress may by law provide for the case of removal, death, resignation, or inability both of the president and vice president, declaring what officer shall then act as president, and such officer shall act accordingly until the disability be removed or a president shall be elected.

Acting on that provision, Congress passed the first Succession Act in 1792, designating the president pro tem of the Senate as the proper successor. By taking "inability" to cover the lack of a functioning president, Congress might give the office to any senator they chose by making him president pro tem. To prevent this, Jefferson was careful to preside continually over the Senate, where he could block voting for a president pro tem (B 1.488).

Not only that, he personally asked John Adams, just as voting was about to begin in the House, to prevent a usurpation by a Senate president pro tem by vetoing any bill calling for his succession. The two met while walking on Pennsylvania Avenue, and Jefferson made his plea. But Adams saw no usurpation in such a process, following on a law passed by the Congress and not vetoed in 1792. For that matter, declaring the presidency and vice presidency vacant after March 4 need not require a new bill to be approved or vetoed. The succession would be automatic according to the Succession Act. But Adams's refusal to make a pledge of future conduct just proved, for Jefferson, that the president would go along with the plot to deprive him of a prize that belonged to him: "Finding his mind made up as to the usurpation of the government by the president of the Senate, I urged no further."[17]

Even if one did not consider following the Succession Act a usurpation, there were problems with applying it to 1801. There was a president in power until March 4. After that, if the tie continued, there was technically no president to be "disabled" since one had not been previously "abled." And the appointment extended only "until the disability be removed or a president shall be elected." This presumes that there had been an election before the disablement. In this case, there would have been none. One would be *beginning a term* with a non-elected president. Was he to serve a whole four years? If not, what does it mean to say "until . . . a president shall be elected"? One way of addressing this would be for Congress to call for a new election. The Republicans were adamant against this. With entirely new options, Federalists might adopt Burr as their candidate, hoping to pick up some Republicans. They had been only eight votes short of a majority the last time.

Well, if the Senate president pro tem was not a solution to the problem, what might be? Congress, it was suggested, might appoint an ad hoc commission to adjudicate the problem. Looking ahead into history, not for a precedent but for a kind of post-cedent, we find that Congress appointed an electoral commission of fifteen members to decide on the disputed votes that were preventing a House count in the Hayes-Tilden election. There was a kind of precedent for that, too. In 1800 itself, when the upper and lower houses in Pennsylvania were not reaching an agreement on how to choose the state's electors, Governor Thomas McKean, fearing that Republicans might be denied the sweeping Pennsylvania returns of the previous election, had threatened to impose a new voting procedure there by executive order. The Federalist senator from Pennsylvania, James Ross, introduced a bill to choose an electoral commission to deny the validity of such a procedure. Though the bill passed the Senate only to die in the House, it might have been resuscitated if McKean had carried through on his proposal.

The Republicans declared, ahead of time, that any of these procedures would be a "usurpation," a violation of the Constitution — any, that is, but Madison's, which was arguably the only unconstitutional one. All the courses suggested were certainly (inevitably) *non*constitutional, in the sense that they did something not expressly provided for in the Constitution. But does that make them *un*constitutional? Going beyond the Constitution is not, necessarily, going against the Constitution. These efforts were made in accord with constitutional principles — that the people must act through their representatives in Congress, both houses of which had been given roles in the conduct of elections (both houses setting their time, the Senate president opening the votes, the joint houses counting them, the House breaking presidential ties, the Senate breaking vice presidential ties). If legislation were passed for emergency measures, it would have to be by the normal procedures for passing a law. Republicans themselves admitted that the process would have been normal when Jefferson asked Adams to veto such legislation. Their real objection was not that Congress had no authority, but that both houses had, at the moment, a Federalist majority, which might use admittedly constitutional procedures to deny Jefferson the election. Federalists, of course, said that objections to special procedures should be solved by a constitutional House vote for Burr, making more drastic measures unnecessary. But this, too, the Republicans were calling a usurpation.

Anticipated Resistance

The fear of impending "usurpation" led to threats of armed resistance. Governors McKean of Pennsylvania and Monroe of Virginia were preparing their legislatures for this.[18] These threats were later minimized, when not denied, but documents were destroyed that might have verified them.[19] McKean admitted that he had drawn up a proclamation that Jefferson was president and all military officers must obey him as such. The proclamation was approved by the legislature, which voted to equip twenty thousand militia for opposing any "usurper."[20] Republicans were becoming hysterical. As James Lewis says, "Republican fears clearly exceeded Federalist plans."[21] One fervid Pennsylvanian said in the newspaper:

> Dare to designate any officer whatever, even temporarily, to administer the government in the event of a non-agreement on the part of the House of Representatives, and we will march and dethrone him as an usurper.[22]

The calmest voice among Republican leaders was that of Albert Gallatin. He pointed out that any of the measures being bruited — an interim presidency, a new election, an ad hoc commission — could be undone when the next Congress assembled, since it would certainly be Republican. Elections in Tennessee and Kentucky should be moved up by those states to insure the new majority. In the meantime, force was to be avoided at all costs, "preventing every partial insurrection, or even individual act of resistance." States with Republican majorities should not disturb those without them. Laws should all be obeyed, but ones coming solely from a "usurping" authority could be quietly ignored in Republican states. Attempts to impose a Republican choice (e.g., Madison's suggestion that Burr and Jefferson issue a joint executive order before either had validated executive authority) should be avoided as setting a terrible precedent.[23] This approach was opposed by Samuel Tyler, who wrote Monroe that the Republican states, centered on Virginia, Pennsylvania, and New York, should secede from the Union if the usurpation occurred.[24] But A. J. Dallas, soon to be appointed a district attorney in Pennsylvania by Jefferson, agreed with Gallatin: "By all means preserve the city [Philadelphia] quiet. Anything which could be construed into a commotion would be fatal to us."[25]

This was sound advice, which Jefferson ignored. He fanned the talk of armed resistance. In his Pennsylvania Avenue conversation with John Adams, he told the president that any act to block his election "would probably produce resistance by force and incalculable consequences."[26] Considering this threat of violence, perhaps we should not be surprised that Adams did not stay in Washington for Jefferson's inauguration. Perhaps that threat was still ringing in his ears. Nor was this an isolated remark of Jefferson's. He gave de facto encouragement to the two governors considering resistance by telling each the other was in motion. He wrote Monroe that, in case of a usurpation, "the middle states would arm, and that no such usurpation, even for a single day, should be submitted to." He wrote McKean that things were "bristling up" in the South. To Madison Jefferson expressed without disapproval "the certainty that a legislative usurpation would be resisted by arms." Interesting term, that — legislative usurpation. Taking the matter *out* of the hands of the legislature would be the only real usurpation. Jefferson contemplated without express disagreement a solution in the form of marching militias. Jefferson would later claim to Joseph Priestly that violence was never contemplated, but he wrote to Madison that only a threat of it thwarted Federalist plans for usurpation.[27]

Was Jefferson serious about taking the presidency, if necessary, by force? To answer that we have to gauge how seriously he believed his own rhetoric that the Federalists were on the verge of restoring the monarchy. He was ready to defy constitutionally passed legislation with the Kentucky Resolution in 1798, when Congress itself had succumbed to "the time of the witches." He had been telling his friends and himself, for the last two years, that the time for rescuing the country was running out. There is much debate about whether his election was a real "revolution." This misses the point. For him, any way that the Federalists could be ousted was a revolution, since it prevented the imminent triumph of the monocrats. That ouster was the first priority for national salvation. To accomplish it was a proleptic revolution: the king was uncrowned before he reached his throne. And then, at the last minute, Jefferson saw this revolution slipping away. If the Federalists could rob him of the presidency, there was no end to what they might attempt in the suppression of freedom. The man who thought Shays's army watered the tree of liberty with blood was not one to hesitate at using force against "usurpation." Jefferson was getting desperate — which explains his final act in this drama, his dealing through an intermediary with James Bayard.

The Showdown

Bayard, we have already seen, was commissioned by Federalists in the tied states to sound out the candidates, to see who would work better with Federalists once he was in office. He tried to get assurances from Burr through another New Yorker, Edward Livingston, but got nowhere with him (he did not know that Jefferson had already promised to make Livingston's brother the secretary of the navy, with the prospect of a federal post for Edward himself).[28] Despite Burr's unresponsiveness to their solicitings, Federalists got Bayard to delay making a final commitment with the hope that letters would come at the last minute with assurances from Burr. It was not till the eve of the final ballot that a missive confirmed that Burr had "explicitly resigned his pretensions [claims]." The Speaker of the House, Theodore Sedgwick, was crushed: "The gig is therefore up" (B 1.486). From this time on, Bayard considered Burr a fool: "The means existed of electing Burr, but they required his cooperation" (B 1.487).

Bayard's approaches to Jefferson had a different outcome. He wanted to get from Jefferson the same pledge that others had failed to elicit — that he would not dismantle Federalist programs like the navy. That is what Adams had asked from Jefferson on Pennsylvania Avenue, and Gouverneur Morris in a private conference.[29] Bayard tried to approach Jefferson through his friend, John Nicholas, who told him that he was sure Jefferson did not intend to dismantle the government in place. That was not good enough for Bayard. He wanted Jefferson's own commitment. The next emissary he chose, Samuel Smith of Maryland, who lived in the same boarding house as Jefferson (Conrad's), said that he would get those assurances from him that very night. Later testifying under oath, Smith said that Jefferson told him he could make no promises, but he would be glad to converse with Smith about his views — in a way that just happened to address all Bayard's concerns. Jefferson, at this late stage, was desperate over the prospect of Federalist "usurpation." If "Paris is worth a Mass," the presidency had become worth some casuistry over the difference between promises and a conversation. Here is what he told Smith:

> As to the public debt, he had been adverse to the manner of funding it [Hamilton's credit scheme], but that he did not believe there was any man who respected his own character who would or could think of injuring its credit at this time; that, on commerce [New England merchant interests], he thought that a correct idea of his opinion on that subject might be derived from his writings, and particularly from his conduct while he was minister at Paris, where he thought he had evidenced his attention to the commercial interest of his country; that he had not changed opinion, and still did consider the prosperity of our commerce as essential to the true interest of the nation; that on the navy he had fully expressed his opinions in his *Notes on Virginia;* that he adhered still to his ideas then given; that he believed our growing commerce would call for protection; that he had been averse to a too rapid increase of our navy; that he believed a navy must naturally grow out of our commerce, but thought prudence would advise its increase to progress with the increase of the nation, and that in this way he was friendly to the establishment.[30]

That was good enough for Bayard. When the conversation was repeated for him in the morning, he took this to mean (as it was clearly meant to) that Smith "was authorized by him to say that they [Bayard's concerns] corresponded with his own views and intentions, and that we might confide in him accordingly."[31] Bayard then set in motion a coordinated set of Federalist withdrawals from the balloting. He did not vote for Delaware. The 50-percent Federalist votes in Vermont and Maryland were withdrawn, letting them become Jefferson's ninth and tenth states (with two states not participating and four still voting for Burr). Jefferson won without a single Federalist vote switching or being cast for him. The most that Bayard and others would do for him was abstain.

Jefferson much later said he could not recall the conversation with Samuel Smith. If it occurred, he said, it had nothing to do with deliberations in the House. But Bayard was not one to be lightly assured — Livingston's and Nicholas's second-hand reports had not satisfied him. Clearly he thought he had a commitment. Samuel Smith, testifying under oath, gave the same account of it as Bayard. Joanne Freeman rightly concludes that "the manner in which Jefferson communicated his thought to Smith was what ultimately determined the election, and therefore Burr's *Memoir* is essentially correct. From Burr's point of view Jefferson did intrigue for the presidency."[32] Burr no doubt considered this just the last in a string of betrayals by the Virginians. They had left him stranded in 1796. They had tried to deprive him of the reward of winning New York for them in 1800. During the House debates, Madison's correspondence became known, calling him "the creature of a counterfeit faction" (M 17.452). The animus felt toward him then is felt by some Jeffersonians to this day.

Reflecting on these flaws in the accepted version of the 1801 election does not mean that I wish Burr had won, any more than I wish Adams had won in the preceding year. But it does change the way one evaluates Jefferson's claim that his "Second Revolution" followed on and was justified by the "will of the majority." His swift action against Federalist office holders and the judiciary was evidence of a subservience not to popular wishes but to a fear that the "usurpation" might still take place, launched from those posts. It was not confidence in the system, but insecurity about it, that led to the immediate aftermath of the 1801 election.

What is astonishing is that Burr is presented as the villain in the whole matter, the one who tried to tamper with the system or thwart justice. Actually, his stand-off air, compared with the busy scurrying of the Jeffersonians, of governors preparing to resort to the militia, looks more like Albert Gore's passivity in the 2000 election when faced with the Bush team's legal blitzkrieg. The 1801 election may throw its own light on the way Jefferson pursued Burr so relentlessly in 1804, when — as Stanley Elkins and Eric McKitrick said — Jefferson showed a "thirst for the man's very life on the flimsiest of grounds."[33] Some resent nothing more than a person they have wronged.

Whatever we think of the clash between Jefferson and Burr, James Oakes, the historian of slavery in the South, makes a valid point when he says that the man with the strongest claim against "usurpation" was John Adams. He was ejected from Washington only because his opponents owned slaves.

6

1801 Aftermath: Turning Out the Federalists

B Y JEFFERSON'S LATER ACCOUNT of it, the Second Revolution occurred when the majority of the American people voiced its will in 1800. But a train of subsequent acts is what really accomplished the overturn — an unprecedented series of appointments, dismissals, repeals, and impeachments. This was the first partisan victory at a presidential level — the first opportunity, therefore, for a wholesale takeover of executive offices. This, of course, is what House Federalists feared while they were making up their minds between Burr and Jefferson. They tried, accordingly, to get assurances that there would not be a mass turning out of Federalists. They failed to get any commitment from Burr, but thought they had one from Jefferson.

They would have been justified in thinking a pledge was being honored when Jefferson delivered his inaugural address: "We are all Republicans, we are all Federalists." How could Jefferson discriminate between parties when there were no longer any differences? He declared to his cabinet members that he would remove Federalists from office only for incompetence or malfeasance, not for their views. Albert Gallatin, the secretary of the treasury, drew up guidelines for his department based on that principle. Levi Lincoln, the attorney general, was told by his president that he (the latter) would not assume "the office of an executioner, lopping off."[1] Timothy

Pickering later said that all these words were disingenuous, that Jefferson's actions belied his words. The words were part of a stealth campaign, to effect a kind of silent coup.

In a sense, Jefferson could only get away with mass displacements by pretending no such thing could happen. He and most other Whig proponents of the "country ideology" condemned executive appointments when they were used as instruments of political purpose. It was the power of creating "places" that had corrupted the British constitution. The king, by dispensing ministries and pensions, divided the loyalties of men in Parliament, giving them two masters, the king on one side, their constituents on the other, with the king proving the stronger and more persistent partner, since parliaments met discontinuously.[2] Jefferson believed that David Hume was brazenly promoting corruption when he called placemen a necessary balance to excessive power in the Parliament:

> The crown has so many offices at its disposal that, when assisted by the honest and disinterested part of the House [of Commons], it will always command the resolutions of the whole, so far at least as to preserve the ancient constitution from danger. We may, therefore, give to this influence what name we please — we may call it by the invidious appellations of "corruption" and "dependence" — but some degree and some kind of it are inseparable from the very nature of the constitution and necessary to the preservation of our mixed government.[3]

Byron played on this old conflict of patriot "country" and corrupt "court" in *Don Juan*'s satirical picture of a placeman, one who claims to combine place and patriotism, not for pay but for the service of the nation.[4] He concludes, like a slyer Hume:

> Sooner, "Come place into the civil list,
>   And champion him to the utmost!" He would keep it
> Till duly disappointed or dismissed.
>   Profit he cared not for, let others reap it.
> But should the day come when place ceased to exist,
>   The country would have far more cause to weep it,
> For how could it go on? Explain who can!
> He gloried in the name of Englishman.[5]

Gordon Wood shows how the "countryman" ideology was applied in America. Royal governors were able to recruit the loyalty of colonial Americans in and out of their representative assemblies by giving them royal commissions, "whether supported by place or pension."[6] This attitude perdured in the independent government of the United States: presidents should not be like kings, creating placemen, men appointed, not elected. George Washington tried to avoid appointing too many southerners with a separate "interest." John Adams had not replaced officials when he became president — not even Timothy Pickering, who was not beholden to him. How was Jefferson to justify a more sweeping ouster of "places"? He would ease the nation into a different set of standards, beginning with his firm determination to get rid of Adams's "midnight appointments," the sixteen new judges he created before leaving office, by repeal of the congressionally passed Judiciary Act of 1801. Jefferson meant to get rid of other judges as well, but he could do that only by impeachments, and they would have to wait. First, repeal — and, only later, impeachment.

Repeal of the Judiciary Act

The Judiciary Act of 1801 set up federal circuit courts to replace the periodic tours of Supreme Court justices riding circuit in the areas of their appointment. To do this in the "lame duck" time before a new administration took office was anti-democratic, according to Jefferson and his supporters. Creating a largely Federalist judiciary went against the will of the people expressed in the Second Revolution, which gave the executive and legislative branches to Republican control. It might be argued, of course, that some balance between the parties should be reflected in the structure of the government, and that a new Republican dominance of the executive and legislative branches was appropriately balanced by Federalist control of the third. But the euphoria of the Second Revolution made Republicans anxious to seize all three elements of government. Two had come to them by election. The third could come only by using these two against the third (though the Constitution had been contrived to resist just such pressure).

There was a constitutional obstacle to this campaign. According to the Constitution, judges have tenure during good behavior, and their salaries cannot be decreased during their term. The Republicans meant to remove judges for their views — the very thing the constitutional tenure was enacted to prevent. The sixteen new judges had not had time to do anything showing bad behavior, and their salaries were going to be not merely decreased but abolished. In order to deny that the judges were being removed for their views, the Republicans had to pretend that the courts were being dissolved solely because they were unnecessary — that the old arrangement was satisfactory, the Supreme Court justices had done very well when on circuit. Actually, they thought the Supreme Court justices had done very ill, especially Justice Chase, enforcing the Sedition Act while on circuit. But consistency was not the desideratum here — finding a fig leaf for the new judges' removal was what mattered.

The fig leaf was a transparent one. The new courts *were* needed. Even a defender of Jefferson's policy on the judiciary had to admit that Jefferson gave a false picture of the case loads at the circuit level:

> To assist the Congress in its determination of the necessity of the recent expansion, Jefferson laid before it a highly inaccurate and hastily prepared statement of the number of cases decided by the courts since their first establishment and the number of cases pending when the Judiciary Act of 1801 was passed.[7]

Memorials of protest were sent from districts where the need for the new courts was felt to be acute — from New York, New Jersey, and Pennsylvania.[8] The one from Pennsylvania was especially telling, since it was drafted by Alexander Dallas, a Republican Jefferson had just appointed to be district attorney for the eastern part of the state. Dallas wrote:

> The mere repeal [of the Judiciary Act of 1801] will reinstate a system which every man of common sense and candor must deprecate. It will entirely destroy institutions [the new courts] susceptible of being modeled into a form economical as well as useful. It will deprive some states of tribunals which have been found highly advantageous to the dispatch of business. I allude particularly to Pennsylvania. In

this state justice, as far as respects our state courts, is in a state of dissolution from the excess of business and the parsimony of the legislature. (B 666)

The rush to get rid of the circuit courts would come back to haunt Jefferson when Aaron Burr was brought to trial for treason in the state of Virginia (where, it was alleged, his crime had occurred). After the repeal of the Judiciary Act, there was no sitting federal judge in that circuit, so the Supreme Court justice assigned to the area had to take charge — John Marshall, a man Jefferson considered as much his enemy as Burr himself. The lack of circuits would also complicate the Republicans' effort to impeach Judge John Pickering (no relation to Timothy), who was drunk and incompetent, but was guilty of no "bad behavior" as that had been legally defined. Under the Judiciary Act of 1801, neighboring circuit judges could take on a disabled judge's case load, something impossible for a periodically appearing Supreme Court justice.

In the Senate debate over repeal of the Judiciary Act, which occurred in January of 1802, all eyes turned to Aaron Burr, presiding over the Senate for the first time when serious business was being transacted and he might have a tie-breaking vote to cast. The Republicans came out of the election of 1800 distrusting and disliking Burr for "refusing to refuse" election by the Congress. There was great and successful pressure on Jefferson not to give Burr a normal say in appointments. This public insult was noticed. Burr's enemies gloated that he was "completely an insulated man in Washington, wholly without personal influence," and that "little or no consequence is attached to him in the general estimation."[9] How would he respond to these snubs in the chair of the Senate? Some scholars say that he revealed himself as "a schemer prepared to court Federalist votes for his own purposes."[10] They think the repeal was self-evidently justified. Burr was not so sure. He asked for advice from Republican sources — the passage quoted above from Alexander Dallas was written in reply to Burr's request, and it shows that a "non-scheming" Republican could have misgivings about the repeal. Burr asked his correspondents whether the repeal bill was a) constitutional, b) prudent, and c) expedient (B 659). Dallas said that it was constitutional but both imprudent (as challenging judicial independence) and inexpedient (as upsetting needed court action). Marinus Willett thought the bill unconstitutional but necessary, on grounds both of prudence and expedience (B 670). Barnabas Bidwell, on the other hand, thought the bill passed muster on all three counts (B 675–76). There was certainly a spread of opinion, even among Republicans.

Burr would not need to take a position if a purely party vote were mustered in the Senate, since the Republicans held an 18-to-14 majority. But one Republican was absent, and one Republican defected, when the vote was taken to bring the bill forward for a third and final reading. The result was a 15-to-15 tie. Burr voted to send the bill on to its final reading, angering Federalists. Gouverneur Morris wrote: "There was a moment when the vice president might have arrested the measure by his vote, and that vote would, I believe, have made him president at the next election."[11]

But on the next day Senator Jonathan Dayton voted to recommit the bill to committee for further study. Again there was a tie vote, but this time Burr voted for recommitting. His explanation was reported:

> I am for the affirmative, because I never can resist the reference of a measure where the Senate is so nicely balanced, when the object is to effect amendment that may accommodate it to the opinions of a larger majority, and particularly when I can believe that gentlemen are sincere in wishing a reference for this purpose. Should it, however, at any time appear that delay only is intended, my conduct will be different. (B 656)

Whether that was sincere or not, it made sense. When there is a dead tie of all the actual senators voting, an attempt to work out a bill that will produce a real majority is always desirable. Even some Republicans who favored repeal were quick to praise Burr for his measured approach (B 673). That the matter was a close one was confirmed by the final vote, in which some Republicans broke ranks despite a great deal of pressure on this party-line matter. One Republican in the Senate and two in the House voted against repeal, and others withheld their votes. The sixteen judges were ejected from office by the slimmest of margins in the Senate, 16 to 15 — and even this margin could not have been achieved without unparalleled (to that point) executive influence.

Jefferson came into office saying that the executive branch had become too powerful under the Federalists, and that the legislative branch should operate with autonomy. But the repeal of the Judiciary Act made him for the first (but not the last) time use all his resources to bring Congress to a specific action.

> Jefferson's commitment to repeal of the Judiciary Act of 1801 was now total. He occupied himself with the duties and difficulties of uniting his party's majority in Congress, and the movement for repeal became known as "the President's measure." It was not long before many Federalists and even some Republicans began to complain of executive influence in the legislative branch.[12]

This whipping of a party line was something so new in the Congress that charges of compulsion were raised. Richard Ellis, a defender of Jefferson, writes that this was the beginning of a "bullying" approach on Jefferson's part.[13]   One Republican congressman is reported to have said: "If the question on the repeal were taken by ballot, they would certainly lose it, but by calling for the yeas and nays they could hold every man to the point."[14] Some Republicans continued to doubt the constitutionality of the repeal, though Jefferson had privately called their qualms "a fraudulent use of the Constitution."[15] The Republican governor of South Carolina continued to think that the rationale for the repeal "would seem to destroy the independence of the judges and cause them to depend for the tenure of their offices on the will (or caprice) of the legislature."[16]

The apparent bad faith of the Congress emboldened Federalists to protest the legislation. The Judiciary Act's formal repeal would not go into effect until July 1, 1802. The Supreme Court was scheduled to convene a month before that, and Federalists meant to ask it for a ruling on the constitutionality of the repeal before its implementation. The Republican Congress, to prevent this, canceled the next two terms of the Court, leaving the supreme bench idle for a year. James Monroe, of all people, complained of this move to Jefferson, saying it conveyed the message that Republicans were afraid to have the law tested.[17]

The Federalists were not willing to give up even now. They petitioned the Supreme Court justices not to ride circuit, and Justice Chase supported their motion. In a response that may have surprised Jefferson, John Marshall knocked that idea down. But the indomitable Federalists urged the ousted circuit judges to take their benches at the court time, and some did make the attempt. Senator Roger Griswold of Connecticut, soon to be a collaborator with Pickering, entered a motion in Hartford denying the authority of Supreme Court Justice Bushrod Washington to take the bench there. He was unsuccessful, as were similar attempts in Boston and Richmond.[18] Those making these gestures had little chance of repealing the repeal, but they did hope to discredit the administration's war on the judiciary and blunt its criticism of judges who were *not* "midnight appointees."

Patronage

Though the ouster of the sixteen judges was the most vivid of Jefferson's replacements, he was making a slower but equally decided replacement of presidential appointees if they were Federalists. James Bayard of Delaware, whom modern Jeffersonians call the noble "savior of the Constitution" in 1801, becomes a villain in 1802 when he accuses Jefferson of breaking the pledges he made to win the presidency. Bayard saw the dismissal of the sixteen judges as only the first and most egregious act in a continuing purge of Federalists. He asserted that Jefferson won the presidency not only by pledging not to engage in a purge, but by promising and delivering "places" to those who would support him.

Jefferson now had to face the consequences of the new party system he had helped create (initially as a temporary measure). It was the classic problem J.G.A. Pocock recognized in the very nature of the Republican ideology: "It was to be the recurrent problem of all Country parties that they could not take office without falsifying their own ostensible values."[19] It is customary to say that Jefferson, who did not want to use a party test for holding office, was forced to yield his principles by the partisanship of his allies, who could not bear to see Federalists remaining in ministerial posts. But Bayard saw Jefferson leaping to use the power of appointment even before he won his own office. In December of 1800, just when the probability of a tie vote in the election became clear, Jefferson offered to make Robert Livingston secretary of the navy (a place not yet his to give) while Livingston's brother Edward was crucial to the support for Jefferson over Burr.[20] Edward had been Burr's ally, the man Bayard thought he should go to for negotiating with Burr; but Edward's biographer says that Robert, now Jefferson's "placeman," wrote a key letter to his brother making him switch his loyalty to Jefferson.[21] And Robert Troup, the prominent New York lawyer, wrote after the election that Edward was rewarded for this service by being made district attorney for the state of New York. Rewards were in store for other key figures. Charles Pinckney, the Republican opponent of his Federalist cousin Charles Cotesworth, maneuvered skillfully to win electoral votes in the South Carolina legislature — and he was made minister plenipotentiary to the court of Madrid.[22]

Bayard no doubt exaggerated when he told the House of Representatives in 1803 that "every [Republican] man on whose vote the event of . . . [the 1800] election hung has since been distinguished by presidential favor."[23] But he did produce an impressive list of appointees who met this description. The list was embarrassing enough to Jefferson that he took energetic measures to oust Bayard from Congress. Dumas Malone himself wrote:

> He urged Caesar A. Rodney to run for Congress against James A. Bayard in the troublesome little state of Delaware. This action could be readily interpreted as one of personal revenge against the Federalist leader of the House of Representatives for what he had done and said in the judiciary fight and it was of doubtful political wisdom for that reason . . . Rodney defeated his personal friend and political rival Bayard by fifteen votes. The Federalists lamented that Delaware was disgraced by such trampling on talents and merit.[24]

The use of executive pressure for one's party is now an expected, indeed esteemed, part of a president's effective leadership. But it was new enough, and bad enough in repute, for Jefferson to disclaim he was doing in fact what he did. Though "the spoils system" is popularly thought to have come in only later, especially with Andrew Jackson, Henry Cabot Lodge saw its real birth in Jefferson's first term: "Jefferson's stealthy removals from office looked like the political proscription so unhappily familiar to a later generation."[25] This was just one of the things about the 1800–1801 election that revolted Timothy Pickering. First, it was carried by "the Negro vote." Second, it was the result of "violence even threatened during the doubtful pendency of the Representative election" — all that talk of Pennsylvania and Virginia militia action (P 47.54). Third, Jefferson rewarded those who elected him with places: "I meet with nobody who does not believe . . . that the last presidential election by the House of Representatives was effected by such *undue influence*" (P 14.76). "Had Burr been at the seat of government [instead of at his daughter's wedding in Albany] and made similar promises of appointments to office, he would have become the president of the United States instead of Jefferson" (P 47.57). And fourth, Jefferson carried out a purge of Federalists while pretending not to.

It was this last point that made people think Jefferson must be devious or hypocritical. He said that he would not remove men from office because of their views, even as his floor manager in the Senate, William Branch Giles, was calling for "a general expurgation."[26] The richest area for patronage was the extensive network of excise offices at ports under the control of the Treasury, so Albert Gallatin drew up a circular statement on his appointment policy, saying "integrity and capacity suitable to the station [will] be the only qualifications that shall direct our choice."[27] But Jefferson told him that it was not time to release such a statement, since key Republicans were demanding a more aggressive patronage policy and "we must not, even for this object [of objective appointments], absolutely revolt our tried friends."[28] It never became time to release the circular.

Jefferson quietly but quickly shifted his position on ideological tests for office. At first there were to be none. Then he said that the monopoly on offices established by the Federalists should not stand, with only one party represented — he would appoint Republicans until they made up half of the ministers.[29] That balance once struck, he would "return with joy to that state of things when the only questions concerning a candidate shall be: is he honest, is he capable, is he faithful to the Constitution?"[30] But then he decided that a fair balance should reflect the growing strength of Republicans in the populace at large, which he estimated at two-thirds to three-quarters.[31] He still maintained that he was not punishing Federalists for their views, since "real" Federalists — i.e., men who were not monocrats — would be retained; but as Robert Johnstone says, "There seems little doubt that to Jefferson the only 'real Federalists' were those who had turned Republican."[32]

It was not only the number of Republican appointments that bothered Federalists. It was the targeting of particular men to be removed or rewarded in order to accomplish Jefferson's purposes — the using of place for the goals of policy. As we shall see, patronage was deftly used in 1803 to affect the outcome of the Senate trial of the impeached New Hampshire judge John Pickering. The judge had gone insane while serving on the bench, and was therefore incapable of the "high crimes and misdemeanors" that were the only constitutional grounds for impeachment or conviction. But seven men from New Hampshire claimed that Pickering was not mad, simply a drunkard (which some would construe as a misdemeanor). All seven witnesses were Republicans, five had been appointed by Jefferson, and two of them were angling for appointments (which they got). One of these witnesses, a former student of Judge Pickering named John Samuel Sherborne, was chosen to replace him — prompting his rival, Jonathan Steele, to say that no man should fill a vacancy he had himself created.[33] Plumer wrote in his account of the proceeding: "This is the man [Sherborne] who advised and promoted, as far as he was able, the impeaching of Judge Pickering, rewarded by being appointed his successor" (PM 178–79). Sherborne would, while on the bench, become mad himself, and "many devout people of Portsmouth considered it to be the judgment of God visited upon him for his part in Pickering's removal."[34]

Jefferson's treatment of Burr was a clear example of the way patronage was withheld or bestowed on policy grounds. After Jefferson and Burr were elected, Jefferson rewarded Burr for what he considered his playing with usurpation by publicly snubbing his suggested appointments for a full three years. But when Burr, already in disgrace for having killed Hamilton in a duel, was about to preside over the impeachment of Justice Chase in 1804, Jefferson showered posts on Burr's friends and allies, hoping to win Burr's favorable conduct in the trial. Burr's stepson, J. P. Prevost, was made a federal judge in the southern unit of the Louisiana Territory. His brother-in-law, James Brown, was made the secretary of the northern unit. And Burr's old war comrade, James Wilkinson, became the military governor of the northern unit. All these appointments in the Louisiana Territory would come back to haunt Jefferson when Burr moved to the West with schemes of his own. But they all show that Jefferson was willing to do anything to please Burr in the run-up to the trial he would preside over. Jefferson had become a complete convert to the politics of "place."

III

Pickering in Congress

After President Adams dismissed Pickering as secretary of state in 1800, he began to farm again his lands in Pennsylvania. But Federalist friends wanted him back in Salem, to help them fight a rising tide of Republicanism in Massachusetts. They brought him back in 1802, to run for the House of Representatives. When he failed to be elected to that office, the legislature appointed him to the Senate. This began the twelve-year period Pickering spent in Congress — eight years in the Senate, mainly during the Jefferson administration, four years in the House, entirely during the Madison administration.

In Congress, he fought the protection and extension of the slave system. Although he sincerely abominated slavery, his energies against its system were not solely altruistic. The slave power damaged the political and commercial interests of New England. Each added slave territory, its power swollen by the federal ratio, diminished New England's standing in the government. Jefferson's war on the judiciary made it harder for northern interests to find protection in the courts. The Twelfth Amendment tilted toward the large states where Republicanism was making strides. The Louisiana Purchase, and the effort to acquire the Floridas, increased the realm of the plantation owners.

The Jeffersonian policies were continued under Madison, in renewed embargoes, a war with England, and the seizure of West Florida — actions that led New England to petition for redress of grievances at the Hartford Convention. Even after he left Congress, Pickering continued to oppose the slave power during crises like the Missouri controversy. His defiance of the slave power was carried on, beyond his death, by his young disciple, William Lloyd Garrison, and his old former rival, John Quincy Adams.

7

1803: The Twelfth Amendment

IN 1802, WHEN MASSACHUSETTS Federalists put up what
they considered two strong candidates for the House of Representatives — Pickering in his old Salem district and John
Quincy Adams in the Quincy area — they were both beaten, along
with two Federalist candidates from other districts. These men from
"the party of the few" would not deign to electioneer, though Republicans were proving the effectiveness of the new populist meth-
ods of campaigning. For the first time, Massachusetts sent seven
Republicans to the House of Representatives, out of a delegation of
seventeen members (PM 63).

Backers of Pickering and Adams had to deflect their aspirations
toward the Senate. Election to it was in the hands of the legislature,
which still had a Federalist majority. But which man should be
put in which seat? Early in 1803, the state could fill both Senate
posts at the same time, since Jonathan Mason was retiring after a
full six-year tenure and the other senator, Dwight Foster, did not
want to serve out the two years remaining in his term. A party
caucus met to decide who would get the longer term, who the
shorter. The pairing of Pickering and Adams was an uneasy one,
since Pickering was still chafing at his dismissal by Adams's father. Some men thought that Pickering, as the older man and a

"martyr" to Republican insults, should be favored for the longer term (JQ 27.8). Adams, who seemed to have a long career still before him, would be better able to "trade up" from the two-year Senate service. Others, however, thought that Adams could work better with the different factions in Congress.

Pickering had the strong support of John Lowell and Harrison Gray Otis, who hammered out an agreement that the caucus would support Pickering for the six-year term in the first two ballotings. If by then he had not won a majority, they would switch to Adams. Some in the caucus failed to keep this bargain and kept voting for Pickering on the third ballot, but they gave up on the fourth and chose Adams (JQ 27.9). The shorter term went to Pickering. The odd couple went to Washington together — though when it came time for re-election, Pickering would win a second term and Adams did not.

As soon as Pickering arrived in Washington he made his rooming house there (Coyle's) a center of fierce opposition to Jefferson. Members shared their quarters not only with men of the same region but of the same party and the same ideological stripe. Coyle's was a New England house, and strictly Federalist. Its residents threw themselves into the struggle with Jefferson's party, which in 1803 was pushing for the Twelfth Amendment and for the purchase of Louisiana.

The Twelfth Amendment

The amendment to prevent what had happened in 1800 — a tie between two men for the presidency — does not look like a party issue to modern observers. In fact, it seems such an obvious remedy for a constitutional problem that it is hard to imagine why men spent over two years fighting about it, and passed it only by a slim margin. To see what was at stake, we must remind ourselves of the oddities in the Constitution's plan for choosing presidents. The clumsy process had eight provisions, cobbled into uneasy coexistence with one another out of deference to states' distrust of each other. According to the plan:

1. Each state chooses a body of presidential electors (the number of electors equaling the state representation in Congress).

2. Each state sets its own method of choosing these electors — e.g., by the state legislature, by people voting for electors from their districts, or by people voting for candidates statewide.

3. Each elector votes for two men as president (and *only* for president), at least one of the two not from the elector's own state.

4. The person with the greatest number of resulting votes (provided these be a majority of all votes cast) becomes president.

5. The person with the second highest number of votes *for president* becomes vice president. This produces an anomaly. Though the president must be chosen by a majority vote, the vice president need have only the second highest count, which can be a minority figure (and, in a sufficiently spread-out vote, a relatively small minority), though he can succeed to the presidency on that basis.

6. If no one gets a majority of votes cast, then the House of Representatives, with at least a two-thirds quorum and with representatives from each state casting only one vote, chooses the president from among the top five vote-getters.

7. If two people get a majority of the votes cast, and get the *same* number, then the House of Representatives — again with a two-thirds quorum, and casting a single vote per state — decides which will be president and which vice president.

8. If two men tie for the second highest number of votes, the Senate chooses the new vice president.

At the Constitutional Convention, James Wilson had proposed direct election of the president by the people at large. But states wanted to keep control over their own populations. Small states would be over-represented in the resulting compromise, since they get two electors for their senators, even if — like Delaware — they have only one representative in the House. These small states have even greater power if the election is decided in the House, since each state has only one vote there, Delaware having the same weight as Virginia or Massachusetts, the two largest states. This regard for states' jealousies led to the initial deadlock of 1801, where an eight-to-eight tie among the sixteen states threatened to leave the country with no choice for president. Something, apparently, had to be done. But what?

The most obvious remedy might have been reversion to James Wilson's proposal; but the states were still not ready to cede their power (they are not ready to abandon the Electoral College even now). Gallatin and Jefferson thought some motion toward that position should be taken — namely an amendment taking away from states the power to choose their own method of voting. Gallatin wanted a popular vote by districts, Jefferson a winner-take-all popular vote by states.[1] Senator Jonathan Dayton of New Jersey argued that the problem of deciding who shall be president, who vice president, would be solved by getting rid of the vice presidency altogether. His motion for an amendment to that effect was warmly debated.[2] A different procedure for filling a vacancy in the presidency might be more efficient than having a man sit around for four years on the off chance of presidential accident.

Others proposed that in case of a tie in the House of Representatives, the resolution of the deadlock should be left to the Senate. But since states voted equally in that chamber, too, another tie vote might be the outcome. The solution to the problem was difficult, so long as one kept the electoral system. In one sense, the Twelfth Amendment did not solve the problem, since the House had to choose again in 1824 and the Congress chose in 1877, in the latter case with an extra-constitutional intervention by an ad hoc Electoral Commission. There were no ties in those cases, but leaders who each had a minority of the votes — still, the amendment does not prevent ties of two-man party teams, any more than the Constitution had prevented the tie of Jefferson and Burr as individuals. Some thought that the chance of a choice without genuine popular backing could be reduced by making the House consider only the top three vote-getters (instead of five) when no single person had won a majority — but the small states felt this would remove their chance of getting a candidate of their own into the larger pool of five candidates.

It was the objection of the small states that made the debate so protracted. Congress took up the question in 1802, but got nowhere toward a solution of the problem. The legislators returned to it in

1803, worried that there would not be time for the states' ratification before the 1804 election. It was hard enough to get a two-thirds vote in both houses — the amendment barely scraped by in the Senate, 22 to 10 (two-thirds of the senators present but not of the whole Senate), and 85 to 42 in the House. "A transfer of a single vote in either house of Congress would have defeated the resolution."[3]

Pickering entered this debate because the objection to great power for the large states meant, for him, more power for the slave-bonus states. Pickering's allies in this struggle were thus the Senate opponents of the three-fifths ratio — William Plumer from New Hampshire and, from Connecticut, Roger Griswold, Uriah Tracy, and Samuel Dana. They saw "designation" (of distinct offices) as the root of the problem. If, instead of voting only for the best men, any of which was considered presidential, electors chose a team of two, the second place would be filled with a party hack, unable to challenge the first man but able to bring in votes from a different state, preferably a large one. The executive branch would in this way become the monopoly of one party, without the inclusion of a man from another party — as Jefferson was included in the executive branch as Adams's vice president.

Even if a party wanted to put a man of distinction in the second place, it was argued, he might well refuse the offer, not wanting to serve in such a minor capacity. Only mediocrities would apply (P 14.81–83). As Roger Griswold said,

> The man voted for as vice president will be selected without any decisive view to his qualifications to administer the government. The office will generally be carried into the market to be exchanged for the votes of some large states for president; and the only criterion which will be regarded as a qualification for the office of vice president will be the temporary influence of the candidate over the electors of his state.[4]

Better a nonentity from, say, Virginia, than a stellar candidate from tiny New Hampshire or Delaware.

Pickering himself came from a large state, but in 1803 the Republican states of New York and Pennsylvania had been added to the slave-state bloc led by Virginia, with the prospect of large slave states being added in the West by the acquisition of Louisiana. Once more, according to Plumer, the federal ratio was behind the southern strategy, at the cost of the Union's future:

> Why should the four states of Maryland, Virginia, North and South Carolina be entitled for their slaves to more than thirteen electors and representatives, while all the wealth of New England does not give them a single vote, even for the choice of one of those officers? All the slaves give sixteen [sic] representatives and electors and are more than equal to the vote of four whole states . . . Thus it appears that the Negro electors exceed those of four states, and their representatives are equal to those of six states. (PM 67)

Pickering denied that there was any crisis sufficient to justify changing the Constitution. If it was feared that the House would be too partisan to make a fair choice in the future, he suggested that a man be chosen by lot from the top three vote-getters. Any one of those, under the old system, would be better qualified than any vice president under the new system. They would all have been chosen *to be president,* not simply to fill a ticket.

> All the difficulty, all the embarrassment, which had hitherto been experienced had arisen from a palpable departure from the plain constitutional rule, from the electors acting on the discriminating principle; not, indeed, by designating by name, but in their minds, which of the two persons voted for should be the president and which vice president — a designation forbidden by the spirit, if not by the letter, of the Constitution. If the electors, laying aside all attempts to give one of the candidates for president an advantage over the other, vote for two men, each possessing the qualifications requisite for that high office, it will then be a matter of much indifference as it respects the great interest of the nation, which becomes the president and which the vice president. The evil arising from the non-observance by the electors of this plain rule would, after a few elections, work its own cure.[5]

The new system would guarantee that some men will succeed to the presidency who would never have been chosen directly for that post, something impossible under the Constitution's first mode.

If the House failed to choose a president, the whole Congress could decide the matter by the same procedure it used in passing a law.[6] Pickering had, as well, some lawyerly objections to the language of the amendment. In case no candidate receives a majority, says the amendment as passed, the House must choose a president from "the persons having the highest numbers not exceeding three." The House could therefore consider only one candidate, or two, since neither would "exceed three." Pickering was admittedly coming up, at this point, with any excuse to fend off the amendment.

He was not alone in seeing it as aimed at promoting Republican electoral chances. Representative John C. Smith of Connecticut attacked it on those grounds, as did Senators James Hillhouse and Pierce Butler. Republican William Cocke of Tennessee blithely admitted this was the case.[7] Pickering held that the amendment would insure "that there would never be another Federal president or vice president" (P 12.297). That prediction came true, but partly because the Federalist party was in the process of undoing itself. But two other predictions of the men opposing the Twelfth Amendment were confirmed, and in interesting ways.

For over two decades after ratification of the amendment, the vice presidential candidates under the new system would be either superannuated men or nonentities. And they would all be from large states. The first two were the ancient George Clinton and Elbridge Gerry, both of them ill or absent much of the time, and both dead before the end of their term, the first two of seven vice presidents who would die in office, so little was vigor a priority for the post.[8] Clinton and Gerry were followed by the corrupt Daniel Tompkins, who was drunk or absent oftener than not. As Leonard Richards wrote of the vice presidency: "That office had some stature before 1800, but after 1800 the Virginians turned it into a dead-end job, and made sure that it always went to a political has-been."[9] The idea of geographical balance, with a man from a large state in the second spot, was used by the southerners in the Republican caucus to make a non-succeeding northerner fill the office of vice president, offering no threat to control by the slave power. This string of pathetic vice presidents was broken in 1824 only because, in the confused scramble of presidential candidates that year, John C. Calhoun was not really anyone's running mate. He was one of three slaveholding candidates, whose splintering of the southern vote let John Quincy Adams slip into office.[10] Pickering, for the rest of his life, tried "to restore the original mode of electing the president and the vice president, to prevent the election of a fool for the latter" (P 15.66).[11]

The fight over the amendment also confirms what Henry Adams treated as the "comedy" of Jefferson in power — that his efforts, and those of his followers, continually worked against their declared object. Jefferson came saying that he would reduce the power of the executive and the centralizing nationalism of the Federalists. But the Twelfth Amendment, by subordinating the vice president, increased the power of the president, who was able to run unopposed by anyone in his own party once he was nominated, and who was served by the man in second place. The creation of a "designated" ticket also made it possible for the president to run not as an individual but as a member of a team chosen for geographical spread and numerical inclusiveness. This can be seen as helping build national unity, but it undercut states' rights, as the small states argued in the debate over the amendment. (Delaware refused to ratify the amendment on just those grounds.) Even the reduction of the chances for a tie vote in the Electoral College took power away from the small states, since they had an equal vote in cases of a tie.

The opposition to Jefferson on patronage, the Judiciary Act, and the Twelfth Amendment were just minor skirmishes within the simultaneous and more serious fights over the Louisiana Purchase and impeachments. Those were the deeper concerns of those listening to Timothy Pickering at Coyle's Boarding House.

8

1803: Louisiana

B Y ONE OF THE MANY ironies running through Jefferson's career, he and Pickering were unwitting collaborators
in the sequence that led to the Louisiana Purchase. By helping Toussaint gain control of Saint Domingue, Secretary of State
Pickering (as he was then) alerted Bonaparte to the difficulty of
crushing this rebel. The First Consul therefore assembled a flotilla
at Brest, led by Leclerc, with orders to conquer Toussaint. President
Jefferson (as *he* was by then) aided this endeavor by promising
American aid to starve Toussaint out. But after Toussaint had been
taken into custody, the island did not submit to Leclerc's army,
which was dying of yellow fever. Napoleon at this point decided to
cut his Caribbean losses, including his plan to use Louisiana as
a base for further operations. His attitude was expressed with typical vigor: "Damn sugar, damn coffee, damn colonies!"[1] It was in
this mood that he offered all of Louisiana to Jefferson's emissaries, who were asking merely for West Florida. Napoleon would use
the money gained by selling Louisiana to accomplish his next goal,
the conquest of England. The offer of Louisiana was suspect at its
source, according to Timothy Pickering, who felt like Laocoon saying, "Fear sudden generosity of tricky men." Yet this particular gift
became available, at least in part, because Pickering himself had

worked to push Napoleon off from the Caribbean and Jefferson had
worked to pull him in.

New Slave States

Pickering felt that Jefferson's deal with Napoleon, increasing the latter's means for attacking England, was a betrayal of the cause of
freedom in Europe, now menaced by the Bonaparte tyranny. But
Pickering had a more pressing reason to resist the Louisiana Purchase, beyond his fear and hatred of France. New states in the
Southwest would increase the slave count in national politics. Jefferson's plan was to divide the vast new territory along the thirty-first
parallel.[2] Land to the north of this would be used for Indian reset-
tlement. By persuading tribes in states east of the Mississippi to
move there, Jefferson could sell the lands they left to pay part of the
price for Louisiana.[3] Land south of the thirty-first parallel was to be
processed into territories, and eventually into states, with slaves to
work the new plantations needed to make the area prosper.

This addition of slave states was widely denounced in New England. Josiah Quincy of Massachusetts argued against "the unnatural
junction of the new hotbed of slavery, Louisiana, to the United
States."[4] In Connecticut, a Hartford toast was given to "freemen"
who will "never be governed by southern slaves," and in Simsbury
a writer vowed that the Constitution must "suffer no further inno-
vation to increase the influence of Negro electors."[5] The Boston
Repertory (June 12, 1804) feared that the Purchase "had sealed the
vassalage of these states." Stephen Higginson said that the Purchase
proved "the Virginia faction have certainly formed a deliberate plan
to govern and depress New England" (P 26.333). Manasseh Cutler
claimed that adding new slave states "will lay the foundation for a
separation of the states."[6]

Uriah Tracy told his fellow senators in Washington: "The relative strength which this admission gives to the southern and western
interest is contradictory to the principles of our original union."[7]
In Boston, the *Columbian Centinel* (August 13, 1803) sounded a
note that would frequently be repeated, the complaint that electoral

power was shifting decisively to the South while economic contributions were expanding just as decisively in the North: "The money [for the Purchase] will be raised not on the gilt carriages of the Virginians, or on the whisky of Kentucky and Tennessee, but on the opulence of the middle, the industry and enterprise of the northern, states." William Plumer had earlier noted the growing disconnect between representation and financial worth: "The powerful states of the South have an increase of representatives and electors for their slaves, while the property of the eastern states gives them none" (PM 70).

Most treatments of the Louisiana Purchase pay scant attention to this form of opposition to it — Joyce Appleby covers them by saying that "some Federalists turned churlish" over Louisiana.[8] Objections are usually confined to constitutional arguments, and not even those are much dwelt upon. It is known that Jefferson considered aspects of the transaction unconstitutional — he made at least two drafts of an amendment to address the problem — but he quickly put his scruples aside. Yet Appleby maintains that "he [Jefferson] alone gave serious thought to the constitutional implications of adding such a vast area to the country."[9] The northerners by no means neglected constitutional matters, as we shall see. But those who had hitherto been most insistent on strict interpretation of the Constitution — men like John Randolph and John Taylor of Caroline — were quick to cast aside that concern when it was a matter of adding slave states to the Union. In this they were simply following their leader. Jefferson's attitude can be seen from this passage, in which he says that his principles are as strict as ever, and as strictly opposed to extending federal power; but that he will yield to his friends if they have other views. It is done in one easy slide:

> Our peculiar security is in the possession of a written Constitution. Let us not make it a blank paper by construction . . . I confess, then, I think it important in the present case, to set an example against broad construction by appealing for new power to the people [in an amendment] . . . If, however, our friends shall think differently, certainly I acquiesce with satisfaction; confiding that the good sense of our country will correct the evil of construction when it shall produce ill effects.[10]

The Republicans' volte-face on executive power is best exemplified in the role John Breckinridge played in the acquisition of Louisiana. Breckinridge was the cat's-paw Jefferson had used to introduce into the Kentucky legislature a resolution calling the Alien and Sedition Laws non-binding because unconstitutional. He played a similar role, but on the opposite side of the constitutional issue, in 1803. He was now in the national legislature, where he also introduced Jefferson's plan while keeping his source secret. Jefferson held that the executive should not usurp legislative functions. In his annual addresses, he usually called things to the attention of Congress while not saying what he thought that body should do. He preferred to act secretly (therefore unaccountably). In introducing the legislation to govern the Louisiana Territory Senator Breckinridge made two proposals, which were both carried, without revealing their source. One was written for him by Jefferson's adjutant at Treasury, Albert Gallatin, and the other by Jefferson himself.[11]

Constitutionality

It has been said that Jefferson put aside his constitutional doubts about Louisiana only because it was feared that Napoleon would withdraw his offer if Congress did not act at once on the treaty of purchase. But Jefferson envisaged the amendment as coming *after* the treaty of acquisition, in order to legislate a government for the territory (PM 262–63). That was the content of both his draft amendments, and they could have been adopted after the transaction with Napoleon was complete. Indeed, that is just when John Quincy Adams urged Secretary of State Madison to help him promote such an amendment in the Senate. Madison tried to discourage him. This could no longer be because of Napoleon's reservations, but because of objections in the Congress. Jefferson continued, when Napoleon was already committed, to want the process to be completed "with as little debate as possible, and particularly so far as respects the constitutional difficulty."[12]

The Louisiana Purchase is too often discussed as if it were a single act. But from the moment it was first rumored that France would sell, Jefferson foresaw that the procedure would have two stages. He wrote to Gallatin in January, 1803:

> You are right, in my opinion, as to Mr. L[incoln]'s proposition: there is no constitutional difficulty as to the acquisition of territory, and whether, when acquired, it may be taken into the Union by the Constitution as it now stands will become a question of expediency. I think it would be safer not to permit the enlargement of the Union but by amendment of the Constitution.

There were two things, then, separated by time as well as content — first, the acquisition of territory from France, and only then the mode of making the inhabitants, present and future, become citizens of the United States. Lumping the whole process together as "the Louisiana Purchase" puts two separate matters — the territorial acquisition and the political incorporation — under the heading of the former. That the two steps were distinct can be seen from the fact that some (like J. Q. Adams) supported the former but opposed the latter (short of an amendment), while others (like Timothy Pickering) opposed the former but supported the latter.

There was, admittedly, a connection between the two, since the treaty with France said, in Article III, that the inhabitants of the territory would become citizens of the United States "as soon as possible." France could not sell people as well as land, and it had to demand protection for the French subjects whose allegiance was being traded. But the stages and timing of this incorporation of the inhabitants were for Congress alone to specify, and almost all the constitutional arguments had to do with this process. Mere territorial acquisition was not very controversial, though some purists questioned Congress's right to collect money for it. There was in fact one sticky point even in this first step. Article VII of the treaty with France pledged that French and Spanish ships could use Louisiana ports for twelve years while paying no more duty than American vessels did. By giving that privilege to some ports but not others, the treaty contravened Article I, Section 9, Clause 6 of the Constitution (the no preference clause). But few people, in or out of Congress, wanted to make this a bone of contention.

The next step, however, raised a throng of constitutional objections. The Constitution gave Congress the power to form new states — but those were envisaged as coming from western territories already claimed by the federal government. Inhabitants of that land were not considered the subjects of foreign governments — none, at least, that Congress recognized as valid: Native Americans were vagrants, British soldiers and traders were interlopers. Jefferson's plan, relayed to Congress by Breckinridge, was for the inhabitants to be governed by executive authority during a formative period. This demoted free French and Spanish subjects to the role of an occupied people. John Quincy Adams said that the Breckinridge Bill was "forming a government for that people without their consent and against their will" (PM 143). Since customs would continue to be collected, there would be taxation without representation (PM 108). Some noted that the Constitution guarantees every state a republican form of government — which would not exist for the foreseeable future in the Louisiana Territory (PM 114, 136, 143).[13]

Congress was being asked to turn over all the powers of rule to the executive, in an exercise more "Federalist" than anything Jefferson's predecessors had attempted. No wonder Jefferson did not want to be seen as the originator of a plan that made him sole manager of the New Orleans territory. He alone would appoint its governor, secretary, council, and judges — the entire government, executive, legislative, and judicial. The Boston *Repertory* of March 6, 1804, protested: "The establishment of a monarchy over a large country appertaining to the United States is a gross violation of the spirit of the Constitution." When it was objected that the residents of the territory were not (yet) citizens, that they were living in an acquired colony, others responded that even the American colonies had representative assemblies — the British did not restrict all governmental power to themselves. Manasseh Cutler said:

> Look at the power given to the president by the provisional government of Louisiana. By one sweeping clause, he is made as despotic as the Grand Turk. Every officer is appointed by him, holds his commission during his pleasure, and is amenable only to him. He is the executive, the legislature, and the judicature. What clamor [there

was] a few years ago, lest the president should be vested with too much power, the department the most dangerous of all to be trusted.[14]

Defenders of the plan, on the other hand, said that territory purchased is like territory conquered — one could dictate the terms of its tenure by military, not civil, law (PM 136). In fact, the northern part of the new territory was put under military law, that of General James Wilkinson, though even Jefferson expressed some misgivings about combining civil and military authority in one office.[15] Jefferson justified his draconian rule of the territory by saying that the people there were not capable of self-rule. They had been formed in the ethos of foreign systems, French and Spanish, and they had to be accommodated to the quite different genius of the United States Constitution before they could be given the tools of their own government. He even proposed government subsidies to American citizens who would go and settle there, to provide a leaven of freedom.[16] "This would not sweeten the pill to the French but in making that acquisition we had some view to our own good as well as theirs, and I believe the greatest good of both will be promoted by whatever will amalgamate us together."[17] Plumer called this a feudal system of colonization.[18] *Pace* Professor Appleby, there were many people thinking long and hard about the constitutional implications of developing the West.

Much of that pondering had to do with slavery in the new territory, though that is not highlighted in most studies of the Purchase. The most heated arguments in Congress were over this aspect of the Breckinridge Bill. Senators James Hillhouse of Connecticut and William Plumer of New Hampshire tried repeatedly to exclude slavery from the new territory, but their motions were beat back with arguments from utility.[19] Even John Quincy Adams said, "Slavery in a moral sense is an evil; but as connected with commerce, it has important uses" (PM 114). Wealthy southerners would not move there to develop the land if they could not take their slaves. The new plantations could be worked only by slave labor (PM 111, 119–20, 128).

The divisiveness of this subject was so great that Samuel Smith of Maryland anticipated later gag rules, hoping that discussion of the matter could simply be avoided: "I am unwilling to think, much less to speak, on this subject" (PM 128). When the issue of slavery in the new territory is raised by modern historians, it is normally to say that Congress accepted Jefferson's plan to exclude foreign slave trade from the area. This looks enlightened now, but in fact the South had long been trying to block that, since it drove down prices on the surplus of blacks already in the country. All the southern states but South Carolina had already outlawed slaves' foreign importation — they wanted exclusive selling rights in Louisiana (PM 130). The protests from New Orleans were first and most vociferous on this head, since African slaves were much cheaper for the development of that area.[20]

Virginia was the state most interested in exploiting the cut-off in foreign slave trade, since it was the leading seller of slaves in the domestic market. Its soil was depleted by tobacco crops that leached important minerals from it, yet the slave population grew from the fecundity of its women — Jefferson said that a slave woman brought a higher price than a man since she was a capital-replenisher.[21] The way to make a profit from this capital was to sell excess slaves to states with soils not deteriorating, those that raised rice and indigo and (increasingly) cotton. Michael Tadman has documented that Virginia's domestic sales of slaves were almost doubling in just the decade when the Louisiana Purchase promised a rich new market for them.[22] This larger market would drive up prices on the slaves to be supplied by Virginia and Kentucky, the highest traffickers in it.

These economic facts undermine the myth of the patriarchal slave owner, who claimed that slaves in his "family" were more secure and cared for than "wage slaves" in the North, who were always uncertain about their jobs. According to this myth, the slave trader was an intruder in settled plantation areas, a man not respected or dealt with by responsible owners. But the number of slave sales belies this dream, and Tadman documents that there were Virginia slave traders honored in society and politics — Francis Everod Rives, for instance, a member of the Virginia House of Delegates and the federal House of Representatives.[23] Jefferson himself sold 85 of his slaves, a high number, since he owned 199 in 1810. He put 71 of those sold up for auction — that is, into the hands of slave traders.[24]

These bartered human beings would have gone where the prices were highest — that is, out of state, though he condemned the *international* trade for wrenching blacks out of their communities.[25] Louisiana looked like a bonanza to people anxious to unload their slaves at high prices — and it looked that way precisely *because* Jefferson excluded slave importations from abroad.

Ideology of "the Thirteen"

While Plumer and Hillhouse were sincere in their opposition to slavery as such, they also had an eye on the effect more slave states would have on representation in Congress and the Electoral College. The Louisiana debate prompted them to elaborate a new ideology, a theory of "the original thirteen." There grew up around this time a Federalist cult of "the good old thirteen" of the original Union. Some have attributed this to mere conservative nostalgia for the founding period. But it was actually critical of the founders, insofar as they had been forced by their circumstance to accept the federal ratio. The new analysis of the original founding circumstance was hardheaded, not softhearted. It advanced a number of tenets:

1. The three-fifths count of slaves was not a matter of constitutional theory, legal equity, or moral right. It was not an eternal principle meant to guide all just governing. It was a concession to an ultimatum, a necessary evil, the condition for forming a government at all. (See Chapter 3 above.) The raison d'être of the clause was balance, and the balance was worked out in a specific temporal and geographical framework — that of the contracting parties in 1789. Now that the federal ratio had become a cause of *im*balance, in a drastically altered geographical situation, it had lost its entire rationale. The Massachusetts legislature, reasoning from this position, adopted a resolution proposed by William Ely calling for a constitutional amendment to remove the three-fifths clause from the Constitution.[26] It instructed both its senators, Pickering and John Quincy Adams, to introduce this amendment in Washington (JQ 27.107). Pickering energetically promoted the Ely amendment,

though he was discouraged by the reflection that the slave count could not be removed until the next census had determined its size (P 14.117–18).

Nothing else in the Constitution demanded retention of the three-fifths clause. In fact, trying to perpetuate a condition that no longer existed would jeopardize the sound parts of the Constitution. The Salem *Gazette* of September 13, 1803, said that destroying the original balance would dissolve the Union. Pickering's notes for presenting the Ely amendment included this passage: "The inequality of representation which existed when the Constitution was formed has increased and is increasing by the gradual or entire abolition of slavery in one portion of the Union and by the importation and natural multiplication of slaves in the other."[27]

2. The ancillary argument for the federal ratio, offered in 1789, had by now proved its emptiness. It had been claimed, back then, that higher taxes would be paid by those states given additional representation. But that was based on the old requisition system of the Articles of Confederation. Indirect taxes had become the rule of government under the Constitution — mainly excise and duties. So the three-fifths clause was no longer counterbalanced with any justifying consideration. By Louisiana's acquisition, said Rufus King, "the present inequality arising from the representation of slaves [will] be increased":

> Going upon the maxim that taxation and representation are inseparable, and that the general government must resort to direct taxes, the states in which slavery does not exist were injudiciously led to consent to this unreasonable provision of the Constitution . . . I know of no one alteration of the Constitution of the United States which I would so readily propose as to confine representation and taxation to the free inhabitants. (P 14.319)

3. The original states had formed a fundamental social compact, for which — as Locke and other theorists maintained — unanimity of the parties is necessary. New states wanting admission to the Union were entering into the basic compact, and renewed the situation of its original acceptance. So unanimous consent must be given

to anything that so basically reformulates the contract — not the mere majority envisaged for creating new states out of the Louisiana Territory. Louisiana, with its mishmash of legal claims and practices, the residual legacy of alternating Spanish and French rule, was seen as outside the agreement system of the original thirteen. As William Plumer put it: "We cannot admit a new partner in the Union from without the original limits of the United States without the consent, first obtained, of each of the partners composing the firm."[28] Josiah Quincy argued that the people of New Orleans were "aliens who were not *parties to the compact*" (emphasis added).[29] According to the Boston *Repertory* (June 12, 1804), removing the federal ratio from the Constitution was a necessary step "to place the states in their primitive relation under the Constitution." Uriah Tracy made what Henry Adams called the best statement on this issue:

> We can hold [purchased] territory; but to admit the inhabitants into the Union, to make citizens of them, and states, by treaty we cannot constitutionally do; and no subsequent act of legislation, or even ordinary amendment to our Constitution, can legalize such measures. If done at all, they must be done by universal consent of all the states or partners to our political association.[30]

It will be remembered that Jefferson himself thought the French and Spanish subjects left in the territory were unfit for immediate self-government. That is how he justified his plan of benign temporary dictatorship. Opponents of the Purchase would turn that argument against him, saying with Josiah Quincy that this was "a population alien to it [the Constitution] . . . French and Spanish subjects whose habits, manners and ideas of civil government are wholly foreign to republican institutions."[31] Another northerner called the people in Louisiana "a Gallo-Hispano-Indian omnium gatherum of savages and adventurers." It was feared that the original states would be engulfed in something that was not in the spirit of the founding pact. Samuel White of Delaware said: "As to Louisiana, this new, immense, unbounded world, if it should ever be incorporated into this Union . . . will be the greatest curse that could at present befall us."[32]

4. In light of these considerations, now seemed the time to free the Constitution of the three-fifths clause. If that could not be accomplished, the agitation to amend might lead to one or other compromise — either that slavery be excluded from Louisiana (as Hillhouse proposed to the Senate), or that the three-fifths clause not be extended to the territory (since it was tailored *only* to the specific balance of the thirteen original states). These demands were dismissed as idle, but the issues they raised would come up again and again as the fight over slavery in new states was renewed across the decades, in Missouri, in Texas, in the Floridas, in Kansas.

Pickering entered fully into this ideology of the original thirteen. He reached the Senate in time to vote against the Purchase treaty. He was one of only five senators who did so, the others being Uriah Tracy and James Hillhouse from Connecticut, and Samuel White and William Wells of Delaware. John Quincy Adams did not reach the capital in time for that vote, but he professed that he would have supported the treaty (JQ 27.49). He would later demonstrate concern for establishing democracy in the territory, but he was not opposed to adding the territory. This was not the sense of priority felt by Federalists back in Massachusetts. As George Cabot wrote to Pickering, "I am not surprised, though I am mortified, to see your colleague assisting to accommodate the Constitution to the view of the party in power, when it is so obvious that the influence of our part of the Union must be diminished by the acquisition of more weight at the other extremity" (P 26.339). When Adams followed his approval of the acquisition with a proposed amendment on the form of representation, Fisher Ames derided him: "An amendment now is like getting a dentist to put an artificial tooth in a dead man's head. I think the funeral can proceed very decently without it."[33]

The gap between Pickering and Adams widened rapidly in the months after Louisiana was acquired. Since there was little hope of passing the Ely amendment, Pickering sounded out friends on a more radical response to the expanding slave dominion. The addition of a huge new realm in the Southwest should be countered by a withdrawal of the Northeast from the Union. As we shall see in the next chapter, those who consider Timothy Pickering at all give much of their scant attention to this scheme. Hardly anyone adverts to the ideology of the original compact that lay behind the scheme. (Clarfield does not treat it at all.) Yet that is far more interesting in its implications than the feckless separation effort, which went nowhere.

9

1804: Pickering and Burr

ONE OF THE TWO or three things historians tend to know about Timothy Pickering is this: he tried, in 1804, to separate the northeastern states from the Union. This was hardly known at all during his lifetime. He communicated his plans to a small circle of the like-minded, and the most influential Federalists in New England quietly urged him not to act on his scheme — at least not yet. The "conspiracy," as it has been called since the time of Henry Adams, was so little noticed that when a reference to it was published in the midst of the presidential campaign of 1828, descendants of those allegedly involved in the plot wrote a public protest, saying they had never even heard of it. If they knew nothing of it, then who could?[1] The scheme might have become more generally known at that point, because John Quincy Adams, with typical overkill, wrote a 230-page book to back up his allegation that it had existed. But he was wisely dissuaded from publishing it, and the story slumbered again for half a century.

In 1877, the Pickering plot entered the historiography of New England. In that year, Henry Adams and his Harvard graduate student, Henry Cabot Lodge, published complementary volumes. They had investigated Pickering's unpublished correspondence as part of the courses they jointly taught on the founding period. Adams's whole emphasis in his Harvard career was on the discovery and use of original documents. Adams asked Lodge, in teaching a course on the early republic, to defend the Federalist position while he spoke for the Republicans.[2] Lodge used his knowledge of the Pickering documents in writing a biography of his grandfather, George Cabot, who had been a sympathetic listener to Pickering but had discouraged the idea of disunion. Adams published the suppressed long harangue of his grandfather, under the title *Reply to the Appeal of the Massachusetts Federalists,* with a preface of documents explaining how it had come to be written, and a lengthy appendix containing correspondence pertaining to the plot. The whole of this volume he called *Documents Relating to New-England Federalism, 1800–1815.*

Some have taken the simultaneous appearance of Lodge's and Adams's works as a case of "dueling books," each man defending his own grandfather. But there was amity and cooperation in their preparation — so much so that Adams could write the Virginia historian, Hugh Blair Grigsby, from whom he had sought information on Virginians:

> I have ordered my publisher to send you by post a copy of the Life of George Cabot by H. Cabot Lodge. Please accept it from me as a slight acknowledgement of the trouble I have given you. Mr. Lodge is, or was, one of my scholars, and took under me the degree of Ph.D. at Cambridge last year. His book was written under my eye.[3]

Adams and Lodge read each other's manuscripts and made suggestions for their improvement. Then each reviewed the other's work — anonymously, and favorably — in *The Nation.*[4] They agreed on the main point shared by the books — that Pickering had tried to organize a secession from the United States. Lodge said that his subject, George Cabot, had tried to dissuade Pickering; and Adams published the correspondence that proved that point. Adams was not trying to defend John Quincy, who explained his support for President Jefferson's embargo — a decision Henry Adams considered wrong and motivated by ambition.[5] Besides, John Quincy's defensive rant is more than a little absurd, as his grandson knew. On these counts, at least, there is no reason to question the sincerity of Adams's prefatory note:

This volume has no controversial purpose. Under the ashes of half a century the fires of personal and party passion still glow in these pages; but only curious students in history care any longer to stir them. For such as these this volume is printed; not with a view to controversy, but to place before them historical matter which there is no further reason to withhold.

But if the Adams book did nothing to enhance his grandfather's reputation, it was deadly to what little reputation Pickering had in the 1870s. Adams did perpetuate the myth of an "Essex Junto" that obsessed both the Adams presidents. Both men had been renounced by parts of their own Federalist party, and both saw Pickering as a principal agent in that renunciation. When John Adams dismissed Pickering from his post as secretary of state, he accused him of conspiring with Hamilton to defeat his re-election bid. When John Quincy Adams, as senator, backed the Jeffersonian embargo, Pickering, as we shall see in Chapter 11, became the nation's most effective critic of the embargo. John Quincy was forced to renounce his Senate seat by the Massachusetts legislature, which chose his successor before his term had ended. John Quincy blamed the "Essex Junto," a group of like-minded men from Salem and its environs in Essex County.

Adams would complete the blackening of Pickering's name, a decade after he published *Documents,* when he prominently featured the "Essex Junto" in his *History of the Administrations of Thomas Jefferson.* David Hackett Fischer has demonstrated conclusively that Adams was too trusting when he accepted his grandfather's claim that there was a junto plotting against the Adamses. The men involved were old republican Federalists of some prominence, men who knew and liked each other, who agreed on some things and disagreed on others. Their public service was undertaken, individually, in different spheres and with different motives. They were not a coordinated or effective force in Massachusetts politics.[6] Their "Junto" is the product of a paranoia shared by the Adams presidents.

Henry Adams's own animus toward Pickering did not arise from a desire to defend his presidential forebears, but from a hatred of secession in all its forms and his desire to show that New England had entertained its own version of that perfidy. He was writing after the Civil War, in which his father labored to preserve the Union as a diplomat in London and his brother fought in the Union cavalry. When, in *The Education of Henry Adams,* Henry comes to the formation of the Confederacy, he calls his chapter "Treason." Similarly, in his book on the administrations of Jefferson, the chapter on Pickering is called "Conspiracy." In his review of Lodge's book for *The Nation,* Adams concedes that George Cabot and other supposed "Juntists" told Pickering his plot was impracticable; but he thinks they should have gone further in their criticism. He is disturbed that none of Pickering's correspondents "seems even to have thought of the objection that the scheme proposed was treason."[7]

Adams's view of Pickering was further darkened by the latter's connection with Aaron Burr. Adams had just done research in European archives that confirmed Burr's later efforts to become the agent of foreign governments, for a fee. Pickering's dealings with Burr were nothing less than criminal in Adams's eyes, though the only overt act in his "plot" with Burr was to support Burr for election as governor of New York in 1804. None of the supposed "Junto" was involved in Burr's later schemes, after he left office as vice president. In fact, Pickering denounced him as the murderer of Hamilton, and was the most eloquent in rejecting on the floor of the Senate Burr's request for lifelong franking privileges. Yet Adams found any dealings with Burr a compact with the devil.

> To bring New York to the Federalism of Pickering and Griswold, the Federalist party needed to recover power under a leader willing to do its work. The idea implied a bargain and an intrigue on terms such as in the Middle Ages the Devil was believed to impose upon the ambitious and reckless. Pickering and Griswold could win their game only by bartering their souls; they must invoke the Mephistopheles of politics, Aaron Burr.[8]

Adams was clearly right to link Pickering and Roger Griswold, the senator from Connecticut. They took most seriously the argument that the Louisiana Purchase, by advancing the slave power, had broken the regional compromise on which the three-fifths clause was based. They tried in secret to recruit people who would help them declare New England independent of a country they saw as ruled by the slave power. Neither got far in this effort. Griswold had a little better luck recruiting support for it among his colleagues in Connecticut than did Pickering in Massachusetts. The thickest cluster of men entertaining the idea of secession was not in Essex County, Massachusetts, but in the Connecticut Valley. Griswold got a warm response there from Samuel Hunt, Simeon Olcott, Caleb Strong, Uriah Tracy, James Hillhouse, and John Goddard.

But when Pickering sounded out his state's most important Federalist leaders, foremost among them Fisher Ames, George Cabot, and Stephen Higginson, they all told him his plans were impracticable. That did not mean they had any doubts about the evils wrought by the federal ratio. They deplored the addition of Louisiana and said that a separation might become not only desirable but necessary at some future date. The public, however, had not yet reached a consensus on that, and without public support Pickering's plan was doomed. George Cabot, in a long and friendly letter (P 27.53), spelled out the problem:

> The subject [of separation] is as important as it is delicate, and has often occupied my thoughts. All the evils you describe and many more are to be apprehended; but I greatly fear that a separation would be no remedy, *because the source of them is in the political theories of our country and in ourselves.* A separation at some period not very remote may probably take place. The first impression of it is even now favorably received by many. [emphasis in original]

Cabot thought some triggering event would have to prod people into recognition of the danger from the South — he gave, as an example, "a war with Great Britain manifestly provoked by our rulers" (something that would in fact prompt more serious thoughts of secession when the War of 1812 was declared). Short of such a catalyst, Cabot thought things would have to get much worse before they could get better.

> If, as is probable, we do not find ourselves strong enough now to act with success the part proposed, I am sensible of the dangers you point out, and see no way of escaping them. We shall go the way of

all government wholly popular — from bad to worse — until the evils, no longer tolerable, shall generate their own remedies.

A change in people's minds should first be worked, since that must precede action:

> By this time, you will suppose I am willing to do nothing but submit to fate. I would not be so understood. I am convinced we cannot do what is wished; but we can do much, if we work with nature (or the course of things), and not against her. A separation is now impracticable because we do not feel the necessity or utility of it. The same separation then will be unavoidable, when our loyalty to the Union is generally perceived to be the instrument of debasement and impoverishment. If it is prematurely attempted, those few only will promote it who discern what is hidden from the multitude; and to those may be addressed —
>
> > Truths would you teach, or save a sinking land,
> > All fear, some aid you, and few understand.
>
> I have said that a separation now is not desirable, because we should not remedy the evil but should bring it home and aggravate it, by cherishing and giving new sanction to the causes which produce it. But if a separation should by and by be produced by suffering, I think it might be accompanied by important ameliorations of our theories. (P 27.60)

Other leaders Pickering tried to interest in his scheme threw the same cold water on it. Stephen Higginson wrote on February 15:

> I have seen your letters to Mr. Cabot and Mr. Lyman on the question of separation, which is a very delicate and important one, considered in the abstract. We all agree there can be no doubt of its being desirable; but of the expediency of attempting it or discussing it now, at this moment, we all very much doubt. It is dangerous to continue under the Virginia system; but how to extricate ourselves at present we see not. (P 27.57)

Fisher Ames was just as discouraging, and this response from Massachusetts figures would be made even more strongly by Alexander Hamilton and Rufus King in New York.

Pickering's great plot looks, then, like an idle hope quickly struck down in the real world. But he tried to keep his scheme alive. Like most ideologues, he was so convinced of the evil he faced that he could not conceive its continuation. As he had written late in 1803, "There will be — and our children at farthest will see it — a separation. The white and black population will mark the boundary" (P 14.68). When Cabot told him that even New England was too corrupted at the moment by Republicanism, he tried to turn that very argument into a motive for action:

> [If] Federalism is crumbling away in New England, there is no time to be lost, lest it should be overwhelmed and become unable to attempt its own relief. Its last refuge is New England; and immediate exertion, perhaps, its only hope. (P 14.93)

The sluggish response from New England could be enlivened, he hoped, by the addition of two factors essential to his scheme, the recruitment of New York to the project, and help from England. These are the points on which Henry Adams thought that Pickering sold his soul.

> New York must be associated; and how is her concurrence to be obtained? She must be made the center of the confederacy. Vermont and New Jersey would follow of course, and Rhode Island of necessity. Who can be consulted, and who will take the lead? The legislatures of Massachusetts and Connecticut meet in May, and of New Hampshire in the same month or in June. The subject has engaged the contemplation of many. The Connecticut gentlemen have seriously meditated upon it. We suppose the British provinces in Canada and Nova Scotia, at no remote period, perhaps without delay, and with the assent of Great Britain, may become members of the Northern League. (P 14.95)

Why did he think New York could be brought into the new league? This is where Burr enters the picture. Pickering had admired Burr for the very actions that made Republicans distrust him. He thought Burr should have been chosen president in 1801. He believed that Burr conducted himself well when he voted to recommit the bill for repealing the Judiciary Act of 1801. He also knew that Burr was being frozen out of Jefferson's circle in Washington and would have to go back to New York to acquire an independent base.

Burr, it seemed, could rally both Republican and Federalist votes if New Englanders urged their party in New York to support him. Then he would return the favor by leading those New Englanders in their drive for a separate league. Burr was ambitious and always sought an independent course for himself — so why should he not become the leader of a force seeking independence from the slave power? Pickering hoped that the election of Burr in New York would change the equation of resistance to the slave power. Even if secession were not immediately in consequence, a new atmosphere might eventually make that more feasible:

> Were New York detached (as under his [Burr's] administration it would be) from the Virginia influence, the whole union should be benefited. Jefferson would then be forced to observe some caution and forbearance in his measures. And if a *separation* should be deemed proper, the five New England states, New York, and New Jersey, would naturally be unified. Among those seven states there is a sufficient congeniality of character to authorize the expectation of practicable harmony and a permanent union, New York the center. Without a separation can those states ever rid themselves of Negro presidents and Negro congresses, and regain their just weight in the political balance? (P 14.100)

Pickering and Griswold dined with Burr early in 1804, to sound him out on their purpose. They brought several of their senatorial allies along with them to the dinner, including James Hillhouse of Connecticut and William Plumer of New Hampshire. Plumer describes the meeting:

> Mr. Hillhouse unequivocally declared that it was his opinion that the United States would soon form two distinct and separate governments. On this subject Mr. Burr conversed very freely, and the impression that his observations made on my mind was that he not only thought such an event would take place, but that it was necessary that it should . . . I well recollect that, on my return to my lodgings, I carefully recollected every sentiment and even expression that were used by Mr. Burr upon that subject. And after critically analyzing his conversation, there was nothing that he said that necessarily implied his approbation of Mr. Hillhouse's observations. In after visits, I became more particularly attentive to the language of Mr. Burr,

and I found he possessed the talent of making an impression of an opinion upon the subject on the person with whom he conversed, without explicitly stating or necessarily giving his sentiments thereon. In everything he said or did, he had a design, and perhaps no man's language was ever so apparently explicit and at the same time so covert and indefinite. (PM 517–18)

The separatists continued to place their hopes in Burr; but he was too slippery for them. Griswold pursued the matter, meeting with Burr in New York while he was returning to his home in Connecticut. The most he could report were such Delphic sayings as this: "In respect to the affairs of the nation, Burr said that the northern states must be governed by Virginia or govern Virginia, and that there was no middle course."[9] Burr was right to fend off any solid commitment to these New Englanders. In the event, they had nothing to offer him. They were naïve in thinking that fellow Federalists in New York would take outside guidance in choosing their governor. In fact, Burr had not only forfeited his Republican support in the state by his bad relations with Jefferson, but he had a mighty foe among the Federalists waiting to exact revenge for the way Burr had won the 1800 legislative election in New York. He had outmaneuvered Hamilton then, and Hamilton could not wait to return the favor.

The campaign of 1804 became an electoral duel between Burr and Hamilton, to which the immediately succeeding actual duel formed a kind of logical climax. While Pickering hoped to get Federalists to vote for the Republican Burr, Hamilton worked to get Federalists to vote for the Republican Morgan Lewis — anything to block Burr. And blocked he was. It was in the heat of this showdown that Hamilton spoke the fatal words that he refused to recant.

Henry Adams, with a taste for melodrama, thus puts Pickering at the origin of a chain of events leading to the death of Hamilton. If Pickering had not urged Burr to run for governor, and if Pickering's plot had not alarmed Hamilton into excess, there would have been no electoral contest, and therefore no mortal sequel. In his review of Lodge's book on George Cabot, Adams described "the collapse of the plot of 1804 in the blood of Hamilton and the flight of Burr."[10] Neither of his initial assumptions is justified. Burr was not impelled into the New York election by Pickering and Griswold. It was an inevitable choice if he were to rebuild his support in conventional politics. Only after the failure of this move did he begin to invent more extravagant ways to regain lost power. And Hamilton did not see Burr as Pickering's surrogate, a man to be thwarted in order to prevent secession.

Adams again resorts to melodrama in describing the gubernatorial race:

> The obstinacy of Pickering and Griswold in pressing Burr on the party forced Hamilton to strain his strength in order to prevent what he considered his own humiliation . . . The struggle for control between Hamilton *and the conspirators* lasted to the eve of the election — secret, stifled, mysterious; the intrigue of men afraid to avow their aims, and seeming rather driven by their own passions than guided by the lofty and unselfish motives which ought to inspire those whom George Cabot emphatically called the best! [emphasis added][11]

Some modern admirers of Hamilton, going even further than Henry Adams, make him a martyr to the Union. In this view, Hamilton had to fight in order to keep his influence, which was needed for thwarting the Essex conspirators. Their evidence is that Hamilton wrote a final letter to Theodore Sedgwick, a friend of Pickering, saying that "Dismemberment of our empire will be a clear sacrifice of great positive advantages, without any counterbalancing good." The proponents of this interpretation go beyond Adams because he thought the Essex Junto had already collapsed in the election of Morgan Lewis over Burr — making Hamilton's "sacrifice" unnecessary as a means of defeating the defeated. The Essex Junto, so far as it ever existed, was dead. It is time for its myth to die as well.

There are many ironies here. Henry Adams thinks Hamilton was trying to oppose Pickering in his duel. But Pickering had always admired Hamilton more than Burr, and he would have no more dealings with the man who killed the Federalist champion. When Burr returned from the duel to preside over the Senate in his capacity as vice president, Pickering "withheld my hand from his, then reeking with the blood of the murdered Hamilton."[12] Burr, on retiring from the vice presidency, asked for franking privileges for the rest of his life — a thing that had been voted for Washington and John Adams on their retirement from office. That was a greater material advantage then, when postal service was so difficult if one had to make private arrangements for it — and abuse of franking was still a subject of concern even half a century later, when Twain made it the subject of satire in *The Gilded Age*.[13] Pickering rose to delay consideration of Burr's request until he should have left the chair of the Senate (PM 303). Then, when Burr was absent, he demanded that his request be refused:

> As there is no evidence of extraordinary services having been rendered by this man, and no evidence of extraordinary merit; and considering his late fatal conduct on the Jersey shore, which has inflicted a wound on our country which even the lenient hand of time for ages cannot heal, I shall therefore vote against the passage of this bill. (PM 307)

A further irony in the Pickering-Burr relationship is that each man's ideas became reciprocally more important to the other *after* they had severed the possibility of any direct cooperation. The claim that New England might separate itself was one that Burr dangled before the British as he tried to raise money from them for his own separatist schemes in the West. He was now taking more seriously — or feigning to — the prospect Griswold and Pickering had presented to him early in 1804. The British minister he approached, Anthony Merry, reported to his superiors in London:

> He [Burr] observed — what I readily conceive may happen — that when once Louisiana and the western country become independent, the eastern states will separate themselves immediately from the southern, and that thus the immense power which is now risen up with so much rapidity in the western hemisphere will, by such a division, be rendered at once [less] formidable; and that no moment could be so proper for the undertaking in question, and particularly for Great Britain, to take part in it as the present. (B 2.946)

Pickering, for his part, without actually plotting for Burr, or having any feeling but detestation for him, naturally hoped that he might break off parts of the Southwest from the bloc of slave states, cutting down the inequities caused by the federal ratio. In fact, he felt that a secession on the slave-power side would make unnecessary the withdrawal of New England. In that sense, his initial hopes for Burr to help secession in the North were replaced by hopes that Burr would *keep* the North from seceding. When Governor Sullivan of Massachusetts said that Pickering was backing Burr's separatist schemes to promote his own, Pickering replied that the two were not only not linked but that the one canceled any appeal the other might have. Taking away the tier of plantation states added by the Louisiana Purchase would restore "the good old thirteen" of the original compact.

> Who but your Excellency would have imagined that such a separa-tion would induce the Atlantic states further to diminish their strength by a division into a northern and a southern section? On the contrary, would not the northern and southern states then cling more closely together? These are the thirteen United States which, with half their present population, dared defy the power of Britain, and finally achieved their independence.[14]

Pickering no longer talked of secession. He hoped the slave power could be weakened by other means; and when the Embargo made Jefferson unpopular, he advocated resistance to the government, not withdrawal from it. Even later, during the War of 1812, when some men were hoping that the Hartford Convention would move to-ward secession, he said only that a temporary suspension of the Union should be used to bring the war to an end.

To complete in this chapter the treatment of Burr, we should no-tice the difference between Jefferson's reaction to the idea of north-ern secession and to the threat of a southwestern breakaway. John Quincy Adams assures us that he informed Jefferson in 1807 that some men in Massachusetts were plotting with the governor of Nova Scotia to withdraw New England from the Union.[15] Though Jefferson would later, after the War of 1812, refer to the alleged acts as treasonous, he did nothing at the time in response to Adams's alarm.[16] But the Burr effort to create an independent section of the country in the Southwest led Jefferson to frantic and illegal acts that have been justly criticized by Leonard Levy and others.[17] Why did

Jefferson treat attempted secession in the North with indifference while panicking over a similar attempt in the South?

I think some people tend, as I did when I first heard of Burr's plots in college, to think of his activity "in the West" as referring to the trans-Mississippi area brought in by the Louisiana Purchase. But the parts of the country Burr specified for independence in his dealings with the British minister were trans-Appalachian (B 891), and the most immediate ones were cis-Mississippi, in what is now West Virginia, Kentucky, Tennessee, and Alabama — territory that had for decades been sealed off from Atlantic ports by the mountains, and had therefore wanted closer vents to the world, through Mobile, Natchez, and New Orleans. This is the area Burr's ally, Andrew Jackson, was interested in.

We should remember that Burr was tried in Richmond because the overt act alleged against him was perpetrated in what was still the state of Virginia (at Blennerhassett's Island). To stir up this territory was to drive at Jefferson in the center of his political existence, where the federal ratio promised him the edge he needed to protect his agrarian culture. To lose the commercial Northeast would be a pinprick compared to this, which would be a mortal stab. Jefferson wanted to deter men who might be thinking of independence in that region (there had been some already, and would be others).[18] He therefore dearly wanted to see Burr hanged, and he took extreme measures to bring it about. When John Marshall would not do the hanging, he dearly wanted to see the Chief Justice impeached, and he tried to bring that about. "Jefferson sent a message to Congress which can only be read as an invitation to that body to initiate impeachment proceedings against Marshall."[19] Slavemasters cannot afford to be squeamish. A younger Jefferson had reflected, sadly, on the way owning slaves inevitably coarsens a man.[20] The older Jefferson exemplified that inescapable truth. The masters become ruthless not only to their slaves but to those who threaten their ownership of slaves. That, in Jefferson's eyes, was the real crime of Aaron Burr. He tried to endanger the slave power.

10

1804–1805: Impeachments

T HE REPUBLICANS who repealed the Judiciary Act in 1802 wanted to remove some of the judges who had not been created by that act. Their campaign culminated in the impeachment, trial, and conviction of Judge John Pickering in 1804 and in the impeachment of Justice Samuel Chase in 1804, followed by his trial and exoneration in 1805. The Republicans were acting from a belief that the Federalist-stocked judiciary had become illegitimate by virtue of the "Second Revolution." As one of Jefferson's party leaders in the Senate, William Branch Giles, put it:

> What concerns us most is the situation of the judiciary as now organized. It is constantly asserted that the Revolution is incomplete, as long as that strong fortress is in possession of the enemy; and it is surely a most singular circumstance that the public sentiment should have forced itself into the legislative and executive department and that the judiciary should not only not acknowledge its influence, but should pride itself on resisting its will, under the misapplied idea of "independence" . . . No remedy is competent to redress the evil system but an absolute repeal of the whole Judiciary [Act] and terminating the present offices and creating a new system.[1]

Removing the sixteen circuit judges would not sate this desire. John Marshall was another "midnight appointment" made by the outgoing President Adams — and the campaign against the judiciary was angling toward him from the outset.

Judge John Pickering

The first target was Judge Pickering, who had drafted New Hampshire's constitution and now was the state's chief justice, but who had gone insane. He was obviously unfit, and should be removed. Another judge could have stepped into his place under the Judiciary Act of 1801, had the Republicans not repealed it. It was the repeal, and the removal of the new circuit judge, that forced Pickering to hear cases again. In this situation, the only way to oust him was by impeachment; yet the Constitution gave no grounds for that action but "high crimes and misdemeanors." The bar was set so high in order to guarantee the independence of the judiciary. Thus the House members impeaching Pickering had to resort to hypocrisy, both as to fact and as to law — as to fact, by saying that the judge was not really insane, just drunk on the bench; as to law, by saying that drunkenness is a high crime or misdemeanor. When the defendant did not show up, the Senate tried him in absentia and without counsel, over the protest of John Quincy Adams and others. Timothy Pickering asked his fellow senators: "Suppose your sergeant at arms had found the accused chained in a mad house and had on the process returned the fact, would you in that case proceed against the unfortunate judge?" (PM 168).[2] But the Republicans pushing this forward were beyond embarrassment. Senator Robert Wright said: "If Judge Pickering was now here as mad as bedlam, it would make no difference — I would remove him. He holds his office during good behavior — madness surely is not good behavior" (PM 176). Others said that his mere absence was a confession of guilt (PM 165) or that mere misconduct is a "high crime and misdemeanor." According to Senator William Cocke of Tennessee:

> The Constitution says that a judge shall receive a compensation for his *services.* If this judge for any cause whatever fails to render services, he ought to have no compensation, for the omission of services are [sic] *criminal.* (PM 162)

Pickering was unable to travel because ill, and unable to appoint counsel because mentally incompetent. His son hired a famous lawyer, Robert Goodloe Harper of South Carolina, to present evidence of mental incapacity. The House managers prosecuting the trial said he could not speak since he did not directly represent the defendant. When Aaron Burr, presiding, turned this issue over to the Senate sitting in conference, the House managers withdrew in protest. Their allies had tried to prevent Harper's very appearance from being recorded in the minutes of the Senate (PM 157), as they would later refuse to print the proceedings of the trial (PM 19).

The Senate convicted, but with a bad conscience reflected in its weaseling formation of the judgment — "guilty as charged," not "guilty of high crimes or misdemeanors." The president had fobbed off the matter in a similar way during the trial. When Senator William Plumer, a longtime friend of Judge Pickering, asked if insanity is a valid basis for impeachment, Jefferson answered: "If the facts of his denying an appeal and of his intoxication, as stated in the impeachment, are proved, that will be sufficient cause of removal without further enquiry" (PM 100). The senators were so shamefaced about their action that eight of the thirty-four did not vote. Senator James Hillhouse of Connecticut asked his colleagues: "Can we lay our hands on our hearts and say, if this case was our own, it has been a fair trial?" (PM 172). John Quincy Adams wrote his father: "It was impossible to establish by a stronger case than [this] . . . the principle that *criminality* was not an essential ingredient of impeachable offenses."[3] Another New Hampshire judge remarked, sardonically, that the insane man had at least been judged by his peers.[4]

Timothy Pickering urged his colleague from Massachusetts, J. Q. Adams, to sign a joint letter of protest with him at the injustice of the conviction. Adams, though agreeing that the trial was unjust, refused to sign the protest because that would be "irregular" (JQ 27.303). Pickering wrote George Cabot that the Senate trial proved there was no limit to what the Jeffersonians would do now (P 14.93–95). He found his fears confirmed by Republicans in the Pennsylvania legislature. Egged on by the Republican paper *Aurora,* they removed one judge from the court of common pleas, impeached three judges of the state supreme court, and tried to add a fourth judge to the bill of impeachment when he sided with his fellows on the bench. Pickering wrote to George Cabot:

> By the Philadelphia papers I see that the supreme court judges of Pennsylvania are to be hurled from their seats . . . I presume that Shippen, Yates, and Smith are to be removed by the governor on the representation of the legislature. And when such grounds are taken, in the national and state legislatures, to destroy the rights of the judges, whose right can be safe? Why destroy them unless as the prelude to the destruction of every influential Federalist, and of every man of considerable property who is not of the reigning sect? (P 14.94)

Even some Republicans in Pennsylvania saw that this was going too far. Alexander Dallas, the Jefferson-appointed district attorney who opposed repeal of the Judiciary Act, defended the impeached judges, to the disgust of the *Aurora*.

Justice Samuel Chase

Republicans in Congress were quick to move on from the trial of Judge Pickering to their real target, the Supreme Court. On the very day when Pickering was convicted, John Randolph moved for the impeachment of the most vulnerable man on the Court, Samuel Chase. The case against Chase was even more ideological than that against Pickering. Chase's sin was that he had a) convicted men under the Sedition Act, and b) defended the rationale of the act in Federalist pronouncements from the bench. But a) the Sedition Act was the law of the land, passed by Congress, and b) punishing a judge for his views was what the Constitution had tried to preclude. Pickering gloomily predicted that this would make no difference, that Chase would go the way of Pickering, and that would seal the fate of the rest of the Court. He represented the thinking of John Randolph, in the impeachment hearings, this way:

> He says that the provision in the Constitution, that the judges should hold their offices *during good behavior,* was intended to guard them against the *executive alone,* and not by any means to control the

power of Congress, on whose representation against the judges the president should remove them. Such a removal of some would, or at least ought to, occasion the resignation of all the rest. (P 14.96)

Chase, like Pickering, would be tried in the Senate with Aaron Burr presiding. In modern impeachments, the Chief Justice of the Supreme Court presides. That was not the procedure then. Even if it had been, there would have been an insuperable impropriety in having one member of the Court conduct the trial of another member. Besides, the Chief Justice, John Marshall, was himself called as a witness in the trial — he conveyed a prudent disapproval of Chase's behavior (PM 291). And, beyond that, Marshall's brother William was also a witness — he had been clerk of the Court for the trial where Chase's misconduct was allegedly most pronounced, though William's testimony did not support the charge (PM 290).

At any rate, Burr had to preside at this trial, though he had by this time killed Hamilton in a duel and was wanted for murder in New Jersey. Despite or because of that fact, he was basking in unaccustomed blandishments, as I have noticed in Chapter 6. Burr was invited to the White House, and consulted by Republicans. His friends were hurried into office. Burr's stepson, J. P. Prevost, was made judge of the superior court of New Orleans; his brother-in-law, James Brown, became secretary of the Louisiana Territory; and James Wilkinson, Burr's friend from their Revolutionary War days, was made governor of that territory (an appointment that would come back to haunt Jefferson). As Burr's biographer puts it, "The Administration's wooing of the man they had long treated as a pariah was blatant to the point of being comic."[5]

When Chase was summoned to his trial, Jefferson might have concluded that his charm campaign with Burr had succeeded. At the request of the Senate, Burr had completely redecorated its chamber, to give it more majesty and to expand the gallery for attendees. While overseeing every detail of this redecoration, he removed the chair provided for the defendant, saying, "Let the judge take care to find a seat for himself" (PM 236). When Chase, on his appearance, asked for a chair, "Mr. Burr in a very cold, formal, insolent manner replied [that] he presumed the Court would not object to his taking a seat" (PM 236). The sergeant at arms brought a chair; but when William Plumer suggested to that official that a writing table be provided for Chase to place his notes on, he was told that Burr had expressly forbidden this. As Chase was reading his opening statement, Burr repeatedly interrupted him. It is not surprising that William Plumer, Chase's supporter from New Hampshire, thought that his friend was about to be railroaded. Plumer's notes at the time run: "This man [Burr] seems inclined to act the tyrant. What can be his motive now? He can neither intimidate his enemies or flatter his friends to any purpose" (PM 283).

But Burr's severity seems to have come simply from a determination to run a disciplined court. He may have been convinced of the need for this from the rather unseemly events at the Pickering trial. He rebuked senators for nibbling apples or cakes during the proceedings. One of the apple eaters, Robert Wright of Maryland, said "he never would submit to be schooled and catechized in this manner" (PM 285). One of the lawyers, Mr. Key, was instructed not to appear indoors wearing an outdoor coat. "Mr. Pickering observed to him [Caesar Rodney, one of the House managers] he was unwilling to see gentlemen controlled in their dress — ill health might render greatcoats necessary" (PM 283). Plumer and Pickering both resented Burr's schoolmasterly bearing: "Really, Master Burr, you need a ferule of birch to enforce your lectures on polite behavior" (PM 283, 285).

But the orderly manner of Burr did not hurt Chase's effort. On the contrary, it served to underline by contrast the undisciplined conduct of the prosecution, led by John Randolph with a flamboyant incoherence of vituperation. And in one of Burr's few substantial interventions, he ruled in favor of Chase's defense team: he admitted, over prosecution objection, a newspaper report written by one of the witnesses against Chase, a report that showed the witness had misrepresented facts in the case.[6] By the end of the trial, Plumer, who began by calling Burr treacherous, had to admit he had been fair: "Mr. Burr has certainly, on the whole, done himself, the Senate and the nation honor by the dignified manner in which he has presided over this high and numerous court" (PM 310). Of course, Plumer might have been softened by the fact that Chase was not convicted.

Chase, whatever his flaws, was a shrewd lawyer, who framed his own defense well, and called on great talents to help him, including Luther Martin of Maryland, an alcoholic but brilliant legal strategist who would return to harass Jefferson in the trial against Burr, where he would be speaking *for* the man he had spoken *to* as president of the court at Chase's trial. John Randolph, on the other hand, was not only spectacularly incompetent as a prosecutor. He had cut off any help he might have got from Republican senators or the president by attacking James Madison as a criminal in the settlement of disputed Georgia land claims.

Hopes for moving on from a conviction of Chase to the attack on other Supreme Court justices were dashed for a while — but only for a while. Before Jefferson left office, a number of those involved in the Chase trial would gather for another trial — Burr himself, Luther Martin, John Randolph, George Hay, and John Marshall. This was the trial of Burr for treason, with John Marshall presiding in Richmond, George Hay and Luther Martin as opposing counsel, and John Randolph as foreman of the grand jury. When Marshall's ruling made it impossible to convict Burr, Jefferson sent materials to the Congress to begin a new impeachment effort, this time against the Chief Justice himself.

11

1808: Embargo

PICKERING'S EARLY ASSAULTS on the slave power made little headway in New England, and none at all in the rest of the country. He had inveighed against Republican patronage, judicial impeachments, the Twelfth Amendment, the Louisiana Purchase, all to no avail. But in 1808 the unpopularity of Jefferson's Embargo gave him a new occasion for protest, and he won wide and enthusiastic support. He wrote a pamphlet that became an international best seller. He helped unseat the Republican legislature in Massachusetts, ended the Senate career of John Quincy Adams, nearly defeated the governor of his home state, and goaded Jefferson into attacking him as a traitor. At this stage he was no longer a separatist, since he thought resistance *within* the Union could succeed. For the first time in his experience, the slave power was losing. Pickering's old ally from 1804, James Hillhouse, now wrote him exuberantly of the prospect that "we may place our country in a better situation and our government in better hands" (P 28.237). George Cabot and Richard Peters congratulated Pickering on his mobilizing of resistance within the Union, rather than any attempt to end it (P 28.357, 14.72).

Jefferson unwittingly helped Pickering by eventually casting the Embargo in terms of two cultures — the agrarian South against the mercantile North. The president did not mean to do that at the out-

set. He adopted the Embargo out of frustration, from an inability to
find any other response that would look strong enough, in 1807, after the British ship *Leopard* fired on the U.S.S. *Chesapeake* just off
Norfolk, killing three and wounding eighteen. The *Chesapeake*'s
captain had refused to let the *Leopard*'s emissary search for desert-
ing British seamen on the American vessel. A wave of indignation
made Jefferson toy with the idea of a rapid buildup for war while
Congress was not in session.

Since England was engaged in its deadly conflict with Napoleon,
Jefferson thought that a quick march of militiamen could seize Canada while his gunboats staved off landings by any troops Britain
could spare from its continental war.[1] He ordered his secretary of
war, Henry Dearborn, to "classify" the militia — that is, to create
three different classes, one of which could be dispatched for service
outside the state. His secretary of the treasury, Albert Gallatin, had
to report to Jefferson that the nation lacked all three of the requi-
sites for war — men, money, and munitions. The states were not
even filling the ranks of militia for service within their boundaries,
and would certainly not create detachable bodies of men. Besides,
Jefferson had badly underestimated the British resources available
for war with America:

> I will only add that if the British Ministry is possessed of energy,
> and that we have no reason to doubt, we must expect [if we go to
> war] an efficient fleet on our coast late this autumn, with perhaps a
> few thousand land forces, for the purpose of winter operations in the
> South. Their great object of attack will be one of four places accord-
> ing to seasons and circumstances — New York, Norfolk, Charleston
> (or perhaps Savannah), New Orleans.[2]

Gallatin went on to show why each of these places was ill equipped
to resist invasion. He had earlier expressed his lack of enthusiasm
for the efficacy of Jefferson's gunboats.[3]

That left only embargo (a ban on all ship movement between nations) or non-intercourse (refusal to trade with targeted nations)
as responses to British insult. The difference between these was
well understood from congressional experiments with them in the

1790s.[4] Embargo was understood to be a temporary measure with two goals — defensive (keeping shipping away from foreign depredations) and threatening (using the limited time to prepare for more serious measures, whether commercial or military). Non-intercourse was open-ended and coercive — depriving a foreigner of goods until the lack of them brought compliance with the non-trading partner's demands. Jefferson rushed the Embargo through Congress, which understood it to be a temporary measure while a next step was being formulated. But Jefferson was soon treating the Embargo as essentially coercive, a course to be adhered to for as long as it might take to make England capitulate. He did not spell that out for Congress or the public, neither at the outset nor later on. "To Congress he stated, at most, half his thought, and that without elucidation."[5] He was papering over a real disagreement in his cabinet, between Gallatin and Madison, with Madison a firm believer in the coercive power of the Embargo.[6] Gallatin tried to warn Jefferson that this policy was suicidal. He wrote at the time of its imposition:

> The measure being of a doubtful policy, and hastily adopted at the first view of our foreign intelligence, I think that we had better recommend it with modifications, and at first for such a limited time as will afford all time for reconsideration and, if we think proper, for an alteration in our course without appearing to retract. As to the hope that it may have an effect on the negotiation with [British agent] Mr. Rose, or induce England to treat us better, I think it entirely groundless.[7]

Gallatin realized from the outset that the Embargo would involve the government in a vast police effort against its own citizens, anxious to trade and willing to do it illegally if necessary: "Governmental prohibitions do always more mischief than had been calculated; and it is not without much hesitation that a statesman should hazard to regulate the concerns of individuals as if he could do it better than themselves."[8]

The man put on the spot by Jefferson's policy was the great organizer of the Republican party's successes in Massachusetts, James

Sullivan, whom James Banner calls "one of the earliest professional
politicians in the nation."[9] After running for governor three times
unsuccessfully, Sullivan had finally prevailed, at his fourth try, just
as the Embargo was passed into law. He warned Jefferson that officials in his mercantile state would not prosecute men plying their
business, and neither judges nor juries would convict if prosecutions did take place. The Federalists he had just defeated would
thrive in such a conflict:

> They talk of a division between the southern and northern states as a
> matter of course, and are openly forming a party to be united under
> the protection of a British standard. You will not believe this until it
> shall be too late. Nothing but an alteration in the judiciary can save
> us from destruction in this way.[10]

A series of supplemental laws had to be passed in attempts to enforce the Embargo. At first, only vessels going to another country
were immobilized, but soon the coasting vessels had to be stopped,
too, since once they cleared harbor they were claiming that the
winds blew them off course to the West Indies (or wherever). But
since major shipments moved by water in 1808, the interdiction of
coasting trade led to vital shortages in some areas, especially of
foodstuffs like flour. Governor Sullivan, like his fellow governors,
asked for the power to exempt vessels in an emergency. Fighting for
his political life, Sullivan had to grant these exemptions liberally —
so flour was being shipped into Massachusetts and sold to Canada,
where scarcity had caused temptingly high prices.[11]

Jefferson called the merchants behind such activity killers of their
country, "parricides," and was furious at Sullivan for coddling them.
He ordered Secretary of War Dearborn, himself from Massachusetts, to move troops toward the state for enforcing the Embargo at
bayonet point. "I fear your governor is not up to the tone of these
parricides."[12] Gallatin reported that in just one week Massachusetts
had received shipments of 19,000 barrels of flour, 4,000 of pork, and
4,000 of naval stores.[13] Sullivan responded, when Jefferson rebuked
him, by baring what he felt was the real problem — the president's
cooperation with those who opposed on principle "the commerce
and navigation of the northern part of the nation," and he said Jef-

ferson could give the power to exempt shipment to some other hand than his own if he thought another could enforce his ban.[14]

More and more Jefferson found himself obliged to take over personally the details of enforcement. Even members of his own party did not want to implement so unpopular a measure. The president himself came to decide not only how much flour could be shipped and where, but what kind of flour and what its uses should be.[15] When Gallatin came to Jefferson with questions about which ships to prevent from sailing, he said that the presumption should always be against any of them sailing: "Where you are doubtful, consider me as voting for detention."[16] Gallatin should be especially strict against towns that had a history of defying the Embargo. Of Penobscot, Maine, he observed:

> A general disobedience to the laws in any place must have weight toward refusing to give them any facilities to evade. In such a case we may fairly require positive proof that the individual of a town tainted with a general spirit of disobedience has never said or done anything himself to countenance that spirit.[17]

Jefferson had been willing to have Virginia defy federal law because President Adams would punish seditious speech. Now he was trying to punish the *lack* of speech supporting the Embargo. When Nantucket pled genuine need, he refused its request for food: "Our opinion here is that that place has been so deeply concerned in smuggling that, if it wants, it is because it has illegally sent away what it ought to have retained for its own consumption."[18]

Gallatin, who had to enforce the Embargo at the ports under his jurisdiction, said that even the escalating laws had not kept up with the emergency. In an attempt to call off the madness, he said that only tyrannical measures would match the defiance:

> I am perfectly satisfied that if the Embargo must be persisted in any longer, two principles must necessarily be adopted in order to make it sufficient. First, not a single vessel shall be permitted to move without the special permission of the Executive. Second, that the collectors be invested with the general power of seizing property anywhere, and taking the rudders, or otherwise effectually preventing the departure of any vessel in harbor, though ostensibly intended to

remain there — and that without being liable to personal suits. I am sensible that such arbitrary powers are equally dangerous and odious; but a restrictive measure of the nature of the Embargo, applied to a nation under such circumstances as the United States, cannot be enforced without the assistance of means as strong as the measure itself. To that legal authority to prevent, seize, and detain, must be added a sufficient physical force to carry it into effect; and although I believe that in our sea ports little difficulty would be encountered, we must have a little army along the Lakes and British lines generally.[19]

Jefferson responded that "Congress must legalize all means which may be necessary to obtain its end."[20] Troops and gunships were deployed, with the result, as legal historian Leonard Levy wrote, that Jefferson became and remains the only president "to use an army for routine day-by-day execution of the laws."[21] He was "laying the whole country under military law," in what was "the most repressive and unconstitutional legislation ever enacted by Congress in time of peace."[22]

When a large raft smuggling timber to Canada was confiscated by authorities in Vermont, the owner hired sixty men to seize it back and conduct it to the buyers. When these men returned to their homes, Jefferson instructed the federal attorney to arrest them and try them for treason. As he had earlier longed to see Aaron Burr hanged, he now wanted these smugglers to pay that price. He knew it might be unpopular to execute them all, so he reserved to himself the right to decide which should die:

> If all these people are convicted, there will be too many to be punished with death. My hope is that they will send me full statements of every man's case, that the most guilty may be marked as examples, and the less so suffer long imprisonment, under reprieves from time to time.[23]

As in the Burr case, Jefferson's later reputation was saved by a judge who was not willing to give the treason clause a broad interpretation — this time by a Republican he had himself appointed, Henry Brockholst Livingston. In deciding the case (*United States v.*

Hoxie, 1808), Livingston said that it was wrong to compare "theft" of one's own property to levying war on the United States. Livingston also referred to President John Adams's conduct in a similar case.

In that episode, Pennsylvania Dutch farmers, protesting what they considered unfair taxes, had rescued men who were in jail for non-payment. A jury voted to execute them for treason, and Adams's cabinet opposed his pardoning them. But Adams wrote them a pardon, asking: "Is there not great danger in establishing such a construction of treason as may be applied to every sudden, ignorant, inconsiderate heat, among a part of the people, wrought up by political disputes and personal or party animosities?"[24] Judge Livingston was not the only Republican judge to decide against Jefferson on Embargo issues. Judge William Johnson of the Supreme Court also ruled, in *Gilchrist v. Johnson* (1808), that the executive had overstepped itself in forbidding a ship to sail. In fact, the only judge who ruled in accord with his views — John Davis, in *United States v. "The William"* (1808) — was a Federalist who believed in a strong executive. That is the measure to which Jefferson came to resemble his former enemies.

What made Jefferson so ferocious in his futile prosecution of the Embargo? In the best study of this matter, Burton Spivak argues that Jefferson gave vent to his hatred of merchants who do nothing but trade other people's goods, neither producing their own nor servicing their countrymen's products — the so-called carrying trade, which plied between foreign ports (mainly between the West Indies and Europe). One drawback to Jefferson's hostility is that the carrying trade was a principal source, not only of New England's prosperity, but of Republicans' progress in that region during the early years of Jefferson's presidency. The "re-exporting" trade had flourished, taking advantage of the war needs of the continental powers, putting much of this country's capital in the hands of the merchants who conducted it.[25] Over half the trade abroad was in the carrying trade, and this was to be the special object of Jefferson's wrath.[26] Earlier in his presidency, Jefferson had tempered his dislike of merchants while party men like James Sullivan won northern merchants to Republicanism. In these circumstances, it was politically

unwise for Jefferson to adhere to his original prejudices, the kind he
had expressed in 1785:

> I should wish them [the American states] to practice neither com-
> merce nor navigation, but to stand with respect to Europe precisely
> on the footing of China. We should thus avoid wars, and all our citi-
> zens would be husbandmen. (J 8.633)

> Cultivators of the earth are the most valuable citizens. They are the
> most vigorous, the most independent, the most virtuous . . . As long
> therefore as they can find employment in this line, I would not con-
> vert them into mariners, artisans, or anything else. (J 8.426)

Even in 1785 he admitted that not all men would stay on the farm.
But any drift toward other callings should be discouraged or minimized, and especially any engagement in manufacturing. "I should
then perhaps wish to turn them to the sea in preference to manufactures because, comparing the characters of the two classes, I find the
former the most valuable citizens" (J 8.426).

The Embargo made Jefferson reverse this preference. Since he was
now excluding Europe's manufactured goods (which he wanted to
rely on earlier), he began to praise native products: "Homespun is
become the spirit of the times."[27] But his acceptance of manufacture
went along with a revulsion to traders, who were defying the Embargo. He now took toward them the attitude of an Ezra Pound toward usury. They produced nothing themselves, nor serviced the
good farmers who were productive. They were sterile, un-natural,
parasites as well as parricides. They traded other people's goods to
other people, making their native country "a mere headquarters for
carrying on the commerce of all nations with one another."[28] Spivak
rightly observes: "During the last six months of his presidency, Jefferson could not contain his hatred of this commercial class."[29] In
the draft of his 1808 annual address to Congress, he wrote:

> The extent of this conversion [to native manufacture] is far beyond
> expectation and little doubt remains that these establishments will
> not be permanent and the mass of our future wants will be supplied
> among ourselves . . . The produce of the agriculturalist will soon find
> at his own door that exchange for his wants for which it has traversed

the ocean, exposed to the danger of that element as well as of the rapine practiced on it.

This passage horrified Gallatin, who called it "little less than a denunciation of commerce." He urged Jefferson (successfully) to trim back and rephrase the whole paragraph:

> This paragraph appears to me the most objectionable in the message. From the manner in which it is expressed, it might be inferred, as the President's opinion, that a positive benefit is derived from the introduction of manufactures caused by the annihilation of commerce . . . I would omit everything which looks like a contrast between commerce and manufactures, and exultation in the result.[30]

Jefferson's animus, though softened in the resulting address to Congress, had been made clear by his acts, his denunciations, his prosecutions, his military action against the "traitors" who defied the Embargo. Governor Sullivan had said Jefferson was allied with enemies of New England's way of life, and that feeling was widely echoed through town meetings and legislative gatherings in the North.

The anti-commercial passion of Jefferson connected, in a retrospective way, with his fear of the "anglomen" and "monocrats" he thought he had vanquished in the Revolution of 1800. He saw New England yearning back to Old England, and Pickering and others fed his obsession by their open agreement with George Rose, the British minister, in criticizing the Embargo. This was treason in Jefferson's eyes, though it was the whole point of his neutrality policy to say that we were not at war with England or any other country, and expressions of sympathy were no more treasonous than were Jefferson's expressions of regard for the French revolutionaries in the 1790s.

The merchants of the North found in Jefferson's outrage a high-sounding hypocrisy. He presented the Embargo as a great "experiment" to vindicate the ideal of neutral trade; but it was aimed primarily at England, whose shipping was most within its reach:

> Although the United States offered ostensibly the same package [for ending the Embargo] to each belligerent — revocation of its mari-

time restrictions in exchange for American trade and American cooperation in the European war — the offers were quite unequal in
fact because their maritime emphasis threatened England's entire
apparatus of commercial war but left unchallenged the heart of
Napoleon's commercial system, his control of the European continent.[31]

Jefferson presented his program as a *defense* of New England,
since *its* merchants were the ones whose ships were being harassed
by British vessels "impressing" deserters. Its vessels were being seized
as contraband by both British and French forces (mainly the former). Yet the profits from trade continued to be very high despite
this harassment. Most ships got through, and the northerners preferred pressing and capture to a suspension of such lucrative business. Even the 1805 *Essex* decision of the British admiralty court —
which decreed that the carrying trade must be "broken" to be exempt from seizure — had not blunted their enthusiasm for continued risk. The court had said that United States ships taking goods
from, say, the Caribbean must return to a United States port, unload
their cargo, pay duties, and be reloaded on different vessels before
proceeding to trade to Europe (or vice versa). The ingenious merchants found ways to fake the unloading and reloading, and to
shorten the time mandated for a stay in harbor.

In fact, it was the South that suffered more from the Embargo
than the North, since it did not have the ships, trading skills, and
smuggling experience to evade the laws. Nor did its manufacturing
capacity grow under challenge as did the North's. And, just to add
to the sectional nature of the conflict, the South had been the region that had called for an end to the carrying trade, since its representatives thought such re-exporting distracted from and endangered the direct trade taking its plantation goods to Europe.[32]
Merchants flouting the *Essex* decision, which technically did not affect direct southern exports, put even the non-carrying trade at risk.
As Congressman Peter Early of Georgia put it:

> Do not gentlemen ask too much when they require us to jeopardize
> the whole agriculture interest of the nation for the sake of that which
> in our opinion produces no benefit to that interest? Is it not expect-

ing too much to suppose that we will consent to surrender the certainty of good markets and high prices for our produce, and brave the danger of total stagnation for the purpose of embarking on a hazardous contest with Great Britain for the carrying trade?[33]

Thus it was the South that stayed true to the Embargo and kept voting for its extension, on the assumption that it was ending the carrying trade, even when it was clear that it could not be made an instrument to punish foreigners in any effective way. The poor were hurt most by the Embargo, and the poorest section was already the South. As Henry Adams put it:

> Tobacco was worthless [under the Embargo]; but four [actually seven] hundred thousand Negro slaves must be clothed and fed, great establishments must be kept up, the social scale of living could not be reduced, and even bankruptcy could not clear a large landed estate without creating new encumbrances in a country where land and Negroes were the only forms of property on which money could be raised . . . With astonishing rapidity Virginia succumbed to ruin, while continuing to support the system that was draining her strength. No episode in American history was more touching than the generous devotion with which Virginia clung to the Embargo, and drained the poison which her own president held obstinately to her lips.[34]

By the latter part of 1808, it was clear that the Embargo was hurting no nation as seriously as it did the United States. John Armstrong, the U.S. minister to France, wrote Secretary of State Madison of the Embargo: "Here it is not felt, and in England (in the midst of the more recent and interesting events of the day) it is forgotten."[35] Henry Cabot Lodge rightly described the Embargo's Alice-in-Wonderland quality:

> No civilized nation today would seek the possible injury of its enemies by its own certain impoverishment . . . The theory of the Embargo was wholly false, for it assumed that a great and powerful nation, mistress of the ocean, flushed with the triumphs of Nelson, struggling as she believed for very existence, would, by a partial injury to material interests and to a fraction of her mercantile population, be constrained to make concessions to an unarmed republic acting apparently in the interest of her most deadly enemy.[36]

Jefferson would believe, for the rest of his life, that the Embargo failed to reduce England to submission only because New Englanders defied it with their smuggling. Later, when he was out of the presidency, his hatred for "licentious commerce" would become so great that he joined the separatists, but from the other side, writing that "I would rather the states would withdraw which are for unlimited commerce."[37] But in 1808 he was determined to keep the rebels within the Union by crushing their resistance. That is why, when Timothy Pickering wrote the most successful attack on the Embargo, Jefferson compared him to Satan luring Adam and Eve out of the Eden ("Elysium") Jefferson had prepared for the nation. Addressing the Republicans of Pickering's own county of Essex, he wrote:

> But for the voice of faction and the bribery of Britain, but for the efforts of a party headed by a man outrageous in his passions and disgraced by his own friends, who to effect his purposes would ruin his country, and whose uneasy temper would disturb Elysium to gain the mastery — but for him and his friends, your exertions would have been crowned with the securement of the rights of our seamen and our merchants.[38]

12

1808: Pickering and Governor Sullivan

— a very malevolent and incendiary denunciation of the
administration
— Jefferson, of Pickering's "Letter to Governor Sullivan"[1]

JEFFERSON'S EMBARGO LASTED through the entire year 1808,
the last complete year of his second term. It was imposed in the
last month of 1807 and lifted in the third month of 1809. Reactions to it, especially but not exclusively in the North, went from bad
to worse, from dismissive to defiant, from a belief that it could not
be enforced to a belief that it could not be prolonged. Objections to
it were mounting to such an extent by March 9, 1808, that Timothy
Pickering's published attack on it had an electric effect, one that
John Quincy Adams described this way: "The government of the
United States needed the pulse of every heart, and the aid of every
head, in support of the interests of the country, when Timothy
Pickering hurled a firebrand upon the stage" (D 104). Henry Adams
would later write that Pickering's letter "was stamped with a touch
of genius."[2]

Pickering chose his strategy carefully. He did not make a direct
attack on Jefferson, but chose two surrogates whose position in
Massachusetts had become vulnerable. With a one-two punch he
went after the state's governor, James Sullivan, and its other senator,

John Quincy Adams. The more immediate impact was on Sullivan, the more lasting one on Adams. It has already been noticed that Sullivan was in a ticklish spot. As a Republican ally of the president, he had to observe the Embargo, if only in a perfunctory way. But if he wished to retain some control over his state, he had to make large concessions to the merchants who were going to defy the law with almost certain impunity. Pickering meant to drive a wedge between these contradictory obligations on Sullivan's part.

An outright attack on Sullivan would have been less effective than the means he used. Speaking as a member of the national legislature in Washington, he affected a delicacy about intervening directly in the affairs of the Massachusetts state legislature. Rather, in a long letter sent February 16, he asked the governor, who was the state official obliged to commune with the legislature, to relay to it Pickering's expression of concern about the Embargo. There was good reason for Pickering to want his views conveyed to the legislature. George Cabot had written him that the General Court was still holding off from a condemnation of the Embargo, even though "no man likes the Embargo, and nineteen in twenty detest it" (P 28.199).

By asking Sullivan to relay his message, he was presenting the governor with a trilemma. As one option, Sullivan could simply relay the letter to the General Court, which might imply that he agreed with its criticism of the Embargo. Or, second, he could send it on with comments, in which case, if they were (even mildly) approving comments, he would be pried some way apart from Jefferson; or, if they were opposing comments, he would be pushed uncomfortably close to Jefferson, as if defending (rather than merely observing) the Embargo. Third, he could simply refuse to send the letter on, in which case he could be seen as refusing a courtesy to the state's representative in Washington, or fearing to expose certain views to his legislators, or trying to cover up his own quandary.

Sullivan chose not to forward the letter to the General Court. He returned it to Pickering "not *read.*" Anticipating such a response, Pickering had already sent a copy of his letter to George Cabot, who was trying to push the legislature into action. He hoped for a response like the one he got from Cabot, dated March 8. After telling

Pickering that the governor had not yet sent the letter to the General Court, Cabot said:

> It is impossible your letter should be read throughout New England without producing great benefit. Indeed, if it could be read in the House of Representatives here by one who would do justice to the composition, it would for a moment electrify the members. It is decided to wait as long as decorum requires for a communication through the medium of the legislature, after which the press will give it to the people in a pamphlet. (P 28.219)

In a letter of March 10, Pickering left it up to Cabot whether to release the letter to the legislature or to the press.[3] But Cabot had already written him on March 9: "This day will come from the press a copy of your letter to the governor, which he dared not to communicate. Five thousand copies will be struck in a pamphlet form, and it will be printed in the newspapers" (P 28.219). The publication had the long title, "A Letter From the Hon. Timothy Pickering, a Senator of the United States From the State of Massachusetts, Exhibiting to his Constituents a View of the Imminent Danger of an Unnecessary and Ruinous War, Addressed to His Excellency James Sullivan, governor of the Said State."

The pamphlet had a prefatory note meant to goad Governor Sullivan:

> The following is a public letter. It is very properly addressed to the Governor, and through him to the legislature; by this channel it would have come most regularly to the eye of the whole people. It is not known to the publishers why it has not been already printed for the use of the public — whether it is only delayed, or intended to be entirely withheld. But a copy which was sent from Washington, after the original, to a private friend has been happily obtained for the press.

Just as this was published, Pickering sent a short letter to the governor, congratulating him on the announcement of a day of public fast for the state's troubles, calling this an admission of the crisis caused by the Embargo. Under the double provocation of the published letter and the ironic congratulation, Sullivan made a

double mistake — first, addressing an angry and repetitive letter to
Pickering, and second, releasing only part of that letter to the press.
Cabot wrote to Pickering about the released portion of the letter,
not knowing that Pickering had received a fuller version.

> When you see Governor Sullivan's letter in the newspaper, you will
> feel more of contempt than any other passion. Some of your friends
> here think you will answer him with some severity. I think the per-
> fect correctness of making the communication through him the only
> topic; and on this not much need be said, because no man doubts it.
> The inference that he has grossly violated his duty is sufficiently ob-
> vious not to need being much insisted on . . . Your [original] letter
> is read with avidity, and gives great satisfaction. Fifty thousand per-
> sons in New England will have read it before this month expires.
> (P 28.235)

Pickering hardly needed encouragement. He made a package of the
governor's complete letter, along with his own response to it, and
Cabot had it published as a pamphlet with this title: "An Interesting
Correspondence Between His Excellency Governour Sullivan and
Col. Pickering, in Which the Latter Vindicates Himself Against the
Groundless Charges and Insinuations Made by the Governour and
Others." This, too, had a great success, and an aftereffect on J. Q. Ad-
ams's career.

These results exceeded Pickering's hopes. As he wrote to his son,
"The public mind was in a state singularly fitted to hail its production."[4] The Salem *Gazette* (March 25, 1808) reported that seventy
thousand copies of the first letter were in print within two weeks
of its release. Charles Cabot wrote from Boston: "Your valuable letter has passed through so many editions that I have, at last, lost
my reckoning" (P 28.287). A Maryland newspaper editor distributed a thousand copies of the letter, and followed that up with another three hundred of the second pamphlet.[5] Delighted Federalists
spread it in every state. Nor were sales of the original text confined
to America. George Rose took a copy of it with him back to England, where "a sensation [is] produced in this country" (P 28.315).[6]
The Washington *Monitor* said that it was "all the rage" in London

circles, and the American minister there complained to Secretary of State Madison that he needed government materials to counter it.[7]

Jefferson's attorney general, Levi Lincoln, lamented to John Quincy Adams: "So copious and overwhelming was its issue, so extensive, sudden, and rapid its spread, that there was scarcely time or the means of a general counteraction."[8] Republicans in the Maryland legislature denounced "the infamous production of Timothy Pickering." The letter to Sullivan was denounced in both houses of Congress — by Joseph Anderson in the Senate, and by William Burwell in the House — for giving aid and comfort to the enemy (though there was no war on by Jeffersonian standards of neutrality). As Pickering noted, sardonically, "They have discovered that I direct the councils of the British Empire" (P 14.214). Jefferson himself fumed that "the author would merit exemplary punishment for so flagitious a libel, were not the torment of his own abominable temper punishment sufficient for even as base a crime as this."[9] The man who thought that expressing opposition to government was not seditious when Adams was president had certainly changed his tune.

The reception Pickering received on his next return from Congress, after publication of his two Sullivan pamphlets, was triumphal. Salem put on a banquet for him. A delegation picked him up at his farm and conducted him to the Wenham line, where a parade of carriages had been formed to escort him. When they reached the Essex Bridge, a salute was fired from a ship offshore. A reception was held at General Derby's mansion, where thousands greeted him. The day ended at Concert Hall, where Josiah Quincy delivered the banquet encomium. The Salem *Gazette* said, "We have seldom witnessed a scene of more rational gratification than that of Tuesday last, in tendering to an old and venerable patriot a public tribute of respect and gratitude."[10]

The First Letter

What did this letter, so powerful in its effect, actually say? Pickering dwelt on four themes in his attack on the Embargo — that it was unnecessary, that it was hostile to New England, that it was meant to bring on war with England, and that it was meant to benefit France.

1. It was unnecessary because the *Chesapeake* incident could have been settled without demanding an end to impressments. There was immediate and understandable outrage at the way the *Leopard* fired on the *Chesapeake* before it could even unlimber its guns. The British government had disavowed the acts of the *Leopard*, recalled its admiral, offered to free the Americans mistakenly taken off the ship, and pay reparations to the widows and children of the three men killed. But it would not give up the right to search American ships for British deserters. On those grounds, Jefferson and Madison refused the British offer.

Gerard Clarfield thinks that the charges this letter made in connection with the *Chesapeake* affair "seem insane" (C 234). If so, why did the letter score such a triumph? Were all those approving it insane as well? To understand what Pickering was saying, we must realize that northern merchants, those most affected by British impressments of deserters off their ships, took a view of pressing that was very different from that of the Virginians. They knew the most significant datum in this whole sequence, one that is rarely mentioned in treatments of the *Chesapeake* incident, and one that came as a surprise to Jefferson when he had Gallatin look into the matter: *fully half the able seamen on America's foreign-trade vessels were British subjects, mainly deserters from the British navy.*[11]

They supplied nine thousand of the eighteen thousand men working the ships of the carrying trade. New England could not do without these workers of their commercial fleet. But they also knew that England could not passively surrender so many of its seamen at a time when its navy had to expand to meet the threat of continental forces marshaled against them by Napoleon. The merchants therefore took their chances, submitted to searches when they had to, and maintained a brisk trade. The harassment of British impressments did not even drive up maritime insurance costs. The American merchants understood that for England to give up the search for deserters would encourage further desertion — it would be tantamount to surrendering to Bonaparte. In fact, the Embargo, by removing from the sea American vessels that might attract deserters, actually helped the British navy retain its crews. The attitude of England should have been clear after 1805, when James Stephen published in England the immensely popular book, *War in Disguise, or The Frauds of the Neutral Flags,* which claimed that America was fatally sapping the strength of the British empire by its seduction of sailors into "neutral" vessels.

Earlier in Jefferson's administration, Secretary of State Madison had offered to prevent the use of British subjects in return for an end to impressments. But now, faced with Gallatin's figures, he told Jefferson: "I fear that the number of British seamen may prove to be rather beyond our first estimate."[12] Jefferson responded:

> Mr. Gallatin's estimate of the number of foreign seamen in our employment renders it prudent I think to suspend all propositions respecting our non-employment of them . . . I am more and more convinced that our best course is to let the negotiation take a friendly nap.[13]

This confirms what Pickering was arguing at the time — that Jefferson was unwilling to settle the *Chesapeake* grievance because he was imposing a condition (the end of impressment) that England could not possibly observe.

Against this background, the firing on the *Chesapeake* — what George Cabot called "the supposed wrong in the affair of the *Chesapeake*" (P 28.199) — becomes a more complex matter than is often supposed. That is why Cabot and other leading Federalists — John Lowell, for instance, and Theophilus Parsons — did not join the outcry against the British action.[14] The *Leopard* was part of a squadron of British ships poised at the mouth of Chesapeake Bay to engage French ships as they left the American port. The privilege of putting in for refitting and revictualing was one that American neutrality guaranteed to both French and British ships (though the British took more advantage of this, since they had more ships in the area). Another ship of the squadron outside the bay, the *Melampus,* lost a landing boat's load of deserters during this wait. These and other deserters strutted about Norfolk mocking the officers of the navy they had left. Among them was Jenkin Ratford, who had deserted another British ship, the *Halifax*. The admiral in charge of ships in American waters heard that the *Chesapeake* was enrolling deserters for its departure. He had a list of deserters' names and of the ships they had left — four of them — and he ordered the squadron to search the *Chesapeake* when it cleared harbor.

The *Leopard* signaled the *Chesapeake* to stand by, sent an officer with a list of ships and names, and asked to search for them. Though the British ship had maneuvered to windward in what was considered a hostile move, Captain Barron of the *Chesapeake* did not prepare his vessel for action — yet neither did he grant the British the right to search. He said none of the men were on board. He knew, in fact, that three of his men were from the *Melampus*, but oddly that name was not on the list of four vessels presented to him. The three were also American natives who had enlisted on the British ship they deserted, but Barron did not know that — they told him they had been taken by a British press gang. Jenkin Ratford, from the *Halifax*, was also on the ship.

When Barron refused to let the British search his ship, he began, too late, to prepare for action. The *Leopard* fired three broadsides before Barron could clear his guns, and the *Chesapeake* struck its flag. Barron offered his ship as a prize of war, but all the British wanted was to retrieve its deserters. They took Ratford and the three from the *Melampus*, and offered to help Barron's wounded — an offer he rejected. Ratford was tried and executed, but the three Americans were held in prison pending the settlement of claims. Barron was tried by naval court and suspended from the service for not having his ship ready for action in a clearly menacing situation.

Pickering argues in his letter that this incident did not make the Embargo necessary. It could have been settled by the British apology and reparations. But Jefferson had a further goal — the end of impressments — that could not be extracted from Britain short of war, and then not successfully. All the misery imposed by the Embargo was therefore useless except in terms of hostility to England. Pickering accused the administration of exaggerating the warlike character of the *Chesapeake* affair:

The refusal of the British officer to receive the frigate *Chesapeake* as a prize, when tendered by her commander, is a demonstration that the attack upon her was exclusively for the purpose of taking their deserters and not intended as the commencement of a war between the two nations . . . Although Great Britain, with her thousand ships of war, could have destroyed our commerce, she has really done it no essential injury. (5, 10)[15]

Instructions to the U.S. minister in London, James Monroe, made abandonment of pressing a precondition of settling the *Chesapeake* grievance:

And it is now well known that such reparation might have been promptly obtained in London, had the President's instructions to Mr. Monroe been compatible with such an adjustment. He was required not to negotiate on this single transient act (which when once adjusted was forever settled) but in connection with another claim of long standing and, to say the least, of doubtful right; to wit, the exemption from impressments of British seamen found on board American merchant vessels. (6)

Pickering argues that the Embargo was rushed on Congress, in the absence of sure intelligence — points Gallatin had made to Jefferson when urging him not to proceed so hastily. One of the documents which Jefferson presented to Congress as justifying the Embargo was a clipping from a newspaper (4). The first, second, and third readings of the Embargo Law were passed, against required procedure, on the same day and in the span of four hours (4). Jefferson's attempt to classify the militia and other "bluster of war" was meant "to increase the public alarm, to aggravate the public resentment against Great Britain, to excite a war pulse" (5–6).

2. Pickering's second main point is that the Embargo was passed out of hostility to New England. Though Jefferson professed to be acting to protect merchants, he was in fact their longtime foe:

But seeing that we seldom hear complaints in the great navigating states, how happens there to be such extreme sympathy for American seamen in Washington? . . . Can gentlemen of known hostility to foreign commerce in our own vessels — who are even willing to annihilate it (and such there are) — can these gentlemen plead the cause of our seamen because they really wish to protect them? Can those deserve to protect our seamen who, by laying an unnecessary embargo, expose them by thousands to starve or beg? One gentleman has said (and I believe he does not stand alone) that sooner than admit the principle that Great Britain had a right to take her own subjects from our merchant vessels, he would abandon commerce altogether. To what will every man in New England, and of the other navigating states, ascribe such a sentiment — a sentiment which, to prevent the momentary loss of five [sic] men by impress would reduce fifty thousand to beggary? (7–8)

Pickering believed that the slave power held commerce to be somehow un-natural, not as legitimate as produce from slave-worked farms on the land. But he spoke for

those states whose farms are on the ocean, and whose harvests are gathered in every sea . . . Are our hundreds of thousands of farmers to be compelled to suffer their millions in surplus produce to perish on their hands that the President may make an experiment on our patience and fortitude? (9)

3. Pickering's third theme was that the Embargo was Anglophobe in effect, since its supposed neutrality affected France not at all but was meant to be coercive toward England. Why else was an attack on Canada meditated, but not on Spanish Florida, held at the mercy of France? The "bustle of war," the classifying of militia, was aimed at England, and it had produced an Embargo that was also making that power its target — though by 1808, after Napoleon had crushed Austria and Prussia, and been joined in league with Russia, England alone stood against the despot of Europe.

4. And that gave Pickering his fourth theme, "the towering pride, the boundless ambition, and unyielding perseverance of the conqueror of Europe." Pickering thought Jefferson was acting in accord with Napoleon — and the president was, in fact, trying to ingratiate himself with that ruler as a step toward winning the Floridas with French help. That is one reason he did not want to reveal his diplomatic correspondence with the American minister there, John Armstrong. Pickering struck at this secrecy where France was considered:

Why, in this dangerous crisis, are Mr. Armstrong's letters to the Secretary of State absolutely withheld, so that a line of them cannot be seen? Did they contain no information of the demands and intentions of the French Emperor? . . . Are they so closely locked up because they will not bear the light? (8)

Pickering was not alone in his suspicion that the Embargo was being used by the administration to help France in its fight against England. Congressman Gardenier of New York warned: "Do not go on forging chains to fasten us to the car of the imperial conqueror."[16] Going over the evidence later on with his teacher, Henry Adams, Henry Cabot Lodge would conclude:

The destruction of our navy had deprived our neutrality of any strength it might have possessed; and Jefferson now destroyed neutrality itself, by putting the country as far as he could, without actually engaging in war, upon the side of Bonaparte. One immediate result was to drive his opponents into an extreme support of Great Britain.[17]

Napoleon himself did not help dispel such suspicions. He let it be known that he was not only not harmed by this "neutral" measure but praised it for the way it defied the English despot. In a speech from his throne, October 25, 1808, he said: "The United States of America have preferred to give up commerce and the sea rather than to recognize a state of slavery upon those elements."[18] And he composed with his own hand a document to be released by his minister of foreign affairs, Champagny:

The Americans, that people which entrusts its fortune, its prosperity, and almost its existence to commerce, has given the example of a great and courageous sacrifice. It has forbidden itself, by a general embargo, all commerce, all interchange, rather than submit shamefully to that tribute which the English pretend to impose upon the navigators of all nations.[19]

It is not surprising that Pickering and others would think the Embargo not only pleased Napoleon but was meant to please him. Far from sounding "crazy," as Clarfield says, Pickering's letter made the Embargo look like the truly crazy act it was becoming. Pickering gave a structure of argument to house the less focused resentments that the Embargo had stirred in men. He connected the dots. And his basic concept and perception even Jefferson came to agree with in time — that the Embargo pitted the slave power against the commercial power.

13

1808: Pickering and J. Q. Adams

Neither of the senators [Pickering and J. Q. Adams] owned a temper
or character likely to allay strife. The feud between them was bitter and
life-long. From the moment of their appearance in the Senate they
took opposite sides.

— Henry Adams[1]

GOVERNOR SULLIVAN had the good sense, however
clumsy he was in other ways, not to respond to Pickering by
defending the Embargo. But Pickering's Massachusetts colleague in the Senate rushed in where Sullivan feared to tread. When
Pickering's first letter was published, John Quincy Adams could not
wait to write an attack on it, though Pickering had not mentioned
him in the letter, and the letter's popularity should have warned Adams not to engage it in direct competition. But Adams rose to what
he thought was Pickering's bait. He felt sure that Pickering was im-
plicitly contrasting his own stand against the Embargo with that of
Adams in its favor:

When one of the senators from a state proclaims to his constituents that a particular measure or system of measures, which has
received the vote and support of his colleague, are [sic] pernicious
and destructive to those interests which both are bound by the
most sacred of ties with zeal and fidelity to promote, the denuncia-

tion of the measures amounts to little less than a denunciation of the man. (3–4)[2]

Pickering's implicit contrast was, of course, with anyone who voted for the Embargo Act; but Adams, as usual, took the matter personally, and he responded, as usual, at great length. He always provided himself with plenty of rope for hanging himself.

Adams's unwise rush to combat with Pickering came from a long-standing hostility between the two. After they went to the Senate together in 1803, they rarely found it possible to agree. The opening days divided them on the Louisiana Purchase. They tried to coordinate their activities on the Ely amendment and the Judge Pickering Senate trial, but only halfheartedly. Adams would claim that Pickering hated him because he had won the six-term seat in 1803 while Pickering was given the two-year replacement one (D 155). It seems more likely that Pickering had an antecedent dislike for the son of the president who fired him as secretary of state. But, in any case, there was no love lost between the two. Pickering did not mock Adams in his private letters, but his correspondents did so, mercilessly. They apparently felt that he would like to hear that. In the early days of both men's Senate tenure, Pickering's old classmate at Harvard, Stephen Higginson, wrote Pickering that Adams would "build upon a third party of moderate, independent men," moving away from the Federalists who elected him, but would fail (P 26.307). Two years after that he found his prediction coming true.

> Mr. A. will continue to be, as was reputed, very erratic in his opinions and movements. Like a kite without a bob, he will be violent and constant in his attempts to rise; but like that, he will be impelled by every giddy wind, twist and pitch on one side and on the other . . . His dispositions, feelings, and habits are those of a very high-toned aristocrat, but in the present state of things he must rise by the democratic ladder or not make any progress in his pursuit. With such views and failings, etc., it is very natural for him at one time to court the Virginia democrats, to endeavor to conciliate his virtuous brethren of Louisiana; and at another to separate

himself from and perhaps affront both, to show his independence. (P 27.57)

This is eerily like the final judgment Henry Adams would make about his grandfather, and Higginson had not even seen, yet, the thing that made so many consider J. Q. Adams a turncoat, his vote for the Embargo.[3] That was the prehistory that prompted Adams to jump into the Pickering-Sullivan fray.

The Adams Pamphlet

It required some fancy footwork for Adams to find an addressee for his attack on Pickering. Since Pickering had not even referred to Adams, initiating direct combat with him would look like unprovoked aggression. Adams's own pamphlet would deny that he had the right to address the legislature, even (like Pickering) through the governor, so to whom could he send his own letter? He took up a public offer from Harrison Gray Otis to relay any communication from either of the state's senators if Governor Sullivan did not wish to do so.

So Adams claimed that if one side was already represented, then the other should be, too — even though he thought it improper for either of them to address the General Court. His maneuvering is reflected in the length of the title he gave his pamphlet: "A Letter From the Hon. John Quincy Adams, Senator in the Congress From Massachusetts, to the Hon. Harrison Gray Otis, a Member of the Senate of the Commonwealth, on the Present State of Our National Affairs, With Remarks upon Mr. Pickering's Letter to His Excellency, James Sullivan." There was a kind of loopy symmetry in this. Pickering, as a critic of the Embargo, had sent his epistle to the General Court by way of the Embargo's enforcer, Governor Sullivan. So, now, Adams, a defender of the Embargo, would send his missive by way of Otis, an Embargo critic.

Adams called Pickering's "alarming invocation" an intrusion of the national legislature into the local, reversing the proper order, by which the local should be represented to the general rather than vice versa (2). Later, in a longer attack on Pickering, Adams spelled out his argument more thoroughly:

> The letter of Mr. Pickering was unexampled, and in principle uncon-
> stitutional . . . Its principle was itself a dissolution of the Union, a
> transfer of the action of the national government to that of the sepa-
> rate states, upon objects exclusively delegated to the authority of the
> Union. (D 195–96)

Governor Sullivan had said that Pickering was guilty by association with Burr of undermining the Union. Adams says he was dissolving the Union simply by virtue of writing his letter to the legislature — and he wrote his own letter to the legislature to prove that point!

Adams says he voted for the Embargo as a temporary measure while the nation built a navy (6). But the Embargo did not prove to be temporary, and no navy was being built. He derides Pickering's fear of "the imaginary terrors of Napoleon" (6) — so the navy he wants must be constructed for use against England — which was Pickering's point. Adams says that the Embargo was an experiment worth trying, even though it might not produce the desired effects: "Still believing it a measure justified by the circumstances of the time, I am ready to admit that those who thought otherwise may have had a wiser foresight of events, and a sounder judgment of the then existing state of things, than the majority of the national legis-lature and the President" (7). He praises the Embargo for prevent-ing the capture of ships that were forbidden to sail: "it has dashed the philter of pillage from the lips of rapine" (16) — a sentence that prompted this from Henry Cabot Lodge:

> In other words, to sacrifice all our shipping and all our commerce, to
> throw our whole seafaring and shipbuilding population out of em-
> ployment, and to awaken hatred and distrust of the national govern-
> ment, was wiser than to risk the loss at the hands of England and
> France of a portion of our vessels, and to rouse thereby a general
> spirit of national resistance. If the Embargo is defensible on such
> grounds, it is useless to argue about it.[4]

But the three main arguments against Pickering are that he mis-represented two reasons for the Embargo — the *Chesapeake* affair, and the demand for an end to impressments — while he neglected the main reason for it, the British Orders in Council of 1807. On the *Chesapeake*, that "atrocious deed" (14), Adams claims that the administration was right not to accept the British offer of reparations because it was vague and insufficient (13), though that was not the reason offered by the administration — it refused to accept the terms without a formal abandonment of impressment. As Henry Cabot Lodge has remarked, "Since Mr. Madison, five years later, accepted the very same kind and amount of reparation for the *Chesapeake*, I feel authorized in calling it 'sufficient.'"[5]

On impressment, Adams admits Pickering's claim that it has been accepted throughout colonial and national times, but says that it should not have been. He says that Britain did not accept a reciprocal right of Americans to search British vessels (14), though America had not offered that — there were few deserters of American vessels for the harsher discipline of the British navy, so there would have been no point to such an offer. Adams makes the astonishing claim that three-quarters of the men seized from United States ships were American (9). He does not say that only half the men on our ships were American to begin with — leaving the British half practically undisturbed, an absurd position. Pickering had said that the United States had done nothing to register American and identify British seamen, a move that would have obviated mistakes.

Adams's main justification of the Embargo is that it was a response proportioned to the affront of England's 1807 Orders in Council, which forbade American ships from using any port closed to the British. But the Embargo Act was passed in December, 1807, and notice of the Orders in Council did not reach America until January, 1808. The rumor of such a British offense was deliberately excluded from the terms of the Embargo Act. Jefferson had included it in his first draft, but: "Unfortunately, no official document could be produced in proof of the expected British interdict . . . To avoid this difficulty, Madison wrote in pencil another draft which omitted all direct mention of the expected British order."[6] After promulgation of the Orders, the question became the efficacy of the Embargo as a response, and even Adams admits that those who projected a failure of effect may have been right.

Adams had admitted in the secret Committee of Inquiry, on the day when the Senate hurried the Embargo Act through, that there seemed insufficient declared grounds for the Embargo Act. But then he made a statement that Pickering, serving in the same committee, would remember and report, to Adams's great damage. The occasion given for this comment was not Adams's own pamphlet but an indiscreet comment made by Governor Sullivan when he finally answered Pickering's first letter. The Adams and Sullivan texts crossed each other. Sullivan's letter was dated March 18, though Pickering did not release it to the public until April 22. Adams's letter to Otis was dated March 31. Pickering would wisely answer Sullivan, not Adams, hitting at Adams indirectly. To follow the sequence we must consider this Sullivan-Pickering exchange.

Governor Sullivan's Letter

When James Sullivan acted under the double goad of Cabot's release of the Pickering letter and Pickering's congratulations on the fast-day proclamation, he took pride in the fact that he had returned the letter not *read* (he italicizes the word at each mention), and explains that

> I have *read* your letter in print since I returned the manuscript. It was printed, I find, before I received it by the mail. Had I *read* it on receiving it, I should, independent of your extraordinary claim, have refused to lay it before the legislature of this state as a public document. [4, italics in original].[7]

The charge that the letter was printed before Sullivan received it was easily refuted by chronology. Cabot had been careful to observe a delay called for by "decorum" before printing it.

Sullivan is careful not to praise the Embargo himself.

> No government is always right. You may take it for granted if you please, that the Embargo Act was an error, yet it was a constitutional act . . . I do not go into the question whether the Embargo Act, which you make (or would make) the apple of discord to set this commonwealth in an uproar against the general government, is right or

wrong; it is enough for me that it is a constitutional act of the supreme power of the nation. (4, 6)

As a governor, Sullivan says, he is just following the law, which does
not imply, necessarily, that he agrees with it. (He leaves that burden
to Adams.) But he says that for Pickering to criticize the law is to
advocate breaking it — Pickering carefully avoided that (the merchants of Massachusetts did not need encouragement in any case)
— and breaking the law amounts to secession from lawful authority.
Sullivan revives old talk of Pickering's 1804 secessionism, and con-
nects that with Francisco de Miranda's 1806 "filibuster" to revolu-
tionize Venezuela and Burr's 1806 schemes in the West to suggest
that Pickering is part of an ongoing conspiracy, the obvious conduit
for money that went from New England to Burr. This is a farrago of
charges offered with no evidence whatever. Sullivan even says that,
given Pickering's questionable loyalty, it was "profane" of him to
praise the fast-day proclamation. The tactics of the letter were those
Sullivan had been using in Boston to smear his opponents as disloyal Americans. Cabot had informed Pickering of this strategy on
January 20:

> Before this reaches you, our governor's speech will show you that
> no great good is to come from him; for, although he dares not praise
> the Embargo, yet he has taken from some of Jefferson's parasites the
> hint to attack the Boston writers. The truth is those writers are not to
> be answered, and therefore must be silenced by threat of popular
> clamor; but the attempt evidently fails. (P 28.169)

To Pickering, in this vein, Sullivan writes: "We are wrong if we quarrel with our own political existence" (6).

But the great mistake Sullivan makes in this letter is to expose his
ally on the Embargo, J. Q. Adams, to a Pickering riposte. Sullivan
asks why he should forward Pickering's attack on the Embargo to
the legislature, any more than he would Adams's defense of it. They
were both senators from Massachusetts. If the governor had to relay
the views of both senators, why not, as well, those of the state's seventeen representatives in the House? (3–4). This would make him
little more than a busy post office. Here Sullivan made his worst
move, saying: "Mr. Adams, our colleague, is quite opposed to you in

his opinion of the Embargo. He voted for it, and still considers it as a wise measure, and as a necessary one. I have his letters before me upon it" (6). Pickering, who felt it more dignified to refrain from a direct assault on his fellow senator, took this chance to explain *to Sullivan* why Adams approved the Embargo — and he could quote Adams's very words on the matter.

Pickering's Second Pamphlet

Sullivan almost pleaded with Pickering not to answer him — a sure way of getting him to answer: "I request that this may close our correspondence. I have not time to waste in this way" (5). Actually, Sullivan's letter had given Pickering the perfect excuse for a public response, since Sullivan had published only part of it, the moderate part. Pickering could publish the whole in the name of openness, and convict Sullivan of hypocrisy along the way:

> Those who will be at the trouble to compare the paragraphs you have chosen to publish as extracts with the letter itself, will see that they are so compounded, and with such alterations and additions, as to be in fact a studied imposition on the public. (7)

He notes that Sullivan left out of the public extracts the claim that Pickering's letter to Sullivan was printed before it reached him. That was too easily refuted for Sullivan to give it a public airing. But for Pickering to print it gave it a double debility.

The charge of an ongoing collusion with Burr is also easily refuted. Miranda's expedition was not related to Burr's western schemes, and was not aimed at dismembering the Union, and Pickering had nothing to do with it in any case (13). For Sullivan to bring up Miranda at all was a red herring. Nor did Pickering have anything to do with Burr's 1806 adventure, since his last dealings with him had been as a supporter of his 1804 campaign for governor of New York. That election led directly to the duel with Hamilton, for which Pickering denounced Burr as a murderer, one whose bloody hand he would not shake. Pickering's Senate attack on Burr's attempt to get the frank for life was well known. If anything, Burr's scheme in the West would have solidified the unity of the original thirteen, not torn them apart, as Pickering plausibly said in a passage I quoted earlier (16).

Faced with this attempt to establish guilt by association with a "Catiline" like Burr, Pickering gives a long account of his services to the Revolution: "I am now, sir, far advanced in life; I have children and grand children who, when I am gone, may hear these slanders repeated, and not have the means of repelling them" (17). This final section of the letter goes on too long; but even with its faults, the demolition of Sullivan's letter was complete. It was not mere diplomacy that made George Rose write from England:

> Your unfortunate correspondent is a mere child in your hands. It has not been often that I have seen so unequal a conflict; and the dignified yet simple gravity with which, as it were without meaning to ridicule him, but by the force of the thing, you bring him into absurd positions, has afforded me extreme satisfaction. (P 28.255)

But the real impact of the letter was not on Sullivan but on J. Q. Adams. Sullivan's mention of Adams's vote for the Embargo gave Pickering the chance to recall damaging words he had heard Adams use in the Committee of Inquiry:

> True — he did vote for the Embargo; and I must now tell your excellency how he advocated that measure . . . In my first letter I informed your Excellency of the haste with which the Embargo bill was passed in the Senate. I also informed you that "a little more time was repeatedly asked, to obtain further information, and to consider a measure of such moment, of such universal concern; but that these requests were denied" — and, I must now add, by no one more zealously than by Mr. Adams, my colleague. Hear his words — but even your Excellency's strong faith in the President's supreme wisdom may pause, while independent men will be shocked, at the answer of my colleague to those requests — "The President," said he, "has recommend the measure on his high responsibility. I would not consider, I would not deliberate, I would act. Doubtless the President possesses such further information as will justify the measure." (9)

Modern Americans have become used to the argument that classified information gives a president the knowledge that mere citizens cannot challenge. But this idea was new enough to look like a monarch's claim in 1808. Pickering called it the doctrine of passive obedience that Sullivan was endorsing when he said, "We are wrong if we quarrel with our political existence."

Adams had sent his own pamphlet off before he saw Pickering's, but he had to respond to this damaging quotation. He did so in an appendix to a new edition to his own pamphlet printed in Baltimore. He used the classic claim that he was quoted out of context, and not exactly — though Adams's grandson, no admirer of Pickering, believed Pickering in this case.[8] J. Q. Adams explained himself thus:

> In assigning to the Senate, very briefly, my reasons for assenting to the bill, and for the belief that it ought to pass without delay, I admitted that the two documents transmitted with the message would not have been of themselves, to my mind, sufficient to warrant the measure recommended in it; but referring to the existing state of things of public notoriety, and denominated in the message "the present crisis," I observed that *the Executive, having recommended the measure upon his responsibility, had doubtless other reasons* for it which I was persuaded were satisfactory; that with this view, convinced of the expediency of the bill, I was also impressed with the necessity of its immediate adoption; *that it was a time, not for deliberation but for action;* and that I wished the bill, instead of lingering through the dilatory process of ordinary legislation, might pass through all the stages of its enactment in a single day. (D 174, emphasis added)

Pickering rightly remarked that Adams was just trying to soften a statement he could not deny. The explanation was perhaps worse than the accusation, and Henry Cabot Lodge concludes from it: "Mr. Adams, when he supported Jefferson, was compelled to support him without asking any reasons, and was obliged to advance the measures of the chief — measures which involved the fate of the country — without knowing why or where they were framed."[9]

In his letter to Otis, Adams had said that he would leave it to the voters of Massachusetts to decide between him and Pickering (4). They were quick to take him up on that pledge. I described in the previous chapter how Pickering was greeted when he returned from the Senate session to Salem. When Adams came back to Quincy at the same time, he was openly insulted on the street and even at church.[10] He was scheduled to make his inaugural lecture as a professor of literature at Harvard during this time of obloquy, but he felt so unsettled that he at first postponed his appearance and then took his personal physician along with him to meet the challenge.[11] The Federalist state senate, just elected with the boost given by Pickering's letter, issued a vote of no confidence in him by selecting his successor ten months ahead of time. That could not, of course, deprive him of his seat for the remainder of his term. But the senate applied the screws to him by issuing an instruction that all their representatives must vote for repealing the Embargo. Having taken his stand on this matter, Adams felt obliged to resign.

George Rose wrote from London of his amusement at "Professor Adams's downfall" (P 28.344). And Henry Adams would conclude of Pickering: "Single-handed he had driven John Quincy Adams from public life."[12] Adams's crime, in the eyes of the Massachusetts voters, was that he had sided with the slave power against the commercial power, the underlying issue as Jefferson had established it in the Embargo. And the Virginians, who had been wooing Adams, gave him what his grandson called the appropriate recompense for his losses among the Federalists. President Madison appointed him minister to the court of Tsar Alexander I, and President Monroe made him secretary of state.

14

1809–1815: Pickering and Madison

IN NOVEMBER, 1808, the election of Madison to succeed Jefferson deceived the latter into thinking that the nation had accepted the Embargo — all but a few traitorous Federalists. In December, these traitors were targeted for swift punishment by the Enforcement Act. Its measures, according to Jefferson's great admirer, Merrill Peterson, "clearly violated guarantees of personal liberty (the searches and seizures clause of the Fourth Amendment, for instance) and, overall, so vast was the concentration of power in the President, in minor functionaries, the measure mocked every principle Jefferson held except the one principle, that of the Embargo itself."[1] The Massachusetts General Court declared the Enforcement Act unconstitutional and non-binding. New England port officials resigned their posts, unable to enforce the Enforcement — as collectors had done during the Stamp Act crisis. Jefferson, who had always praised local initiative, had to watch as, "all along the coast, town meetings passed defiant resolutions in an awesome display of grassroots democracy."[2] Gloucester, Newburyport, Beverly, Plymouth — these called for resistance, or for committees of correspondence or public safety, or called the law unconstitutional and its enforcers lawbreakers. Towns in the district of Maine did the same — Bath, Wells, Alfred.[3] Pickering, says Henry Adams, had prevailed — "his temper infused itself through every New England town."[4]

In Massachusetts, Governor Sullivan, whose life had been made so difficult by Pickering, died on December 10, just as the Enforcement Bill was about to be passed. He was succeeded by Levi Lincoln, the lieutenant governor (and Jefferson's former attorney general). When Lincoln tried to call out the militia to enforce the Embargo, he was disobeyed and received death threats. He wrote to Jefferson that he could not manage a state whose General Court was in league with "smugglers, speculators, usurers, foreign hirelings, men corrupted with a thirst or a glut of meretricious gain."[5] He would be voted out before the end of the year.

Instead of breaking the final resistance to the Embargo, the Enforcement Act broke its final defenders. Joseph Story, a freshman Republican representative from Pickering's own county of Essex, Massachusetts, reached Washington in November of 1808 prepared to support the Embargo — he even voted for the Enforcement Act in December. But by January he realized that he could escape the fate J. Q. Adams had suffered six months earlier only by teaming up with Pickering against the Embargo. Jefferson, with his tendency to personalize defeats, blamed the whole repeal on Story:

> The Federalists, during their short-lived ascendancy [itself caused, he does not say, by the Embargo], have nevertheless, by forcing us from the Embargo, inflicted a wound on our interest which can never be cured, and on our affections which will require time to cicatrize. I ascribe all this to one pseudo-republican, Story. He came on (in place of Crowninshield, I believe) and stayed only a few days; long enough, however to get complete hold of [Massachusetts representative Ezekiel] Bacon, who, giving in to his representations, became panic-struck, and communicated his panic to his colleagues, and they to a majority of the sound members of Congress. They believed in the alternative of repeal or civil war, and produced the fatal measure of repeal. This is the immediate parent of all our present evils.[6]

A year after this, President Madison was hard pressed to find a New Englander for the Supreme Court and he considered Story, a legal scholar, for the appointment. Jefferson objected strongly, writing to Madison on October 15, 1810: "His treachery to us under the Embargo should put him by forever." Madison hesitated, but could find no qualified person from New England who had not opposed the Embargo. This choice thus takes its place — with the need to replace Judge Pickering and the presence of John Marshall at the district trial of Burr — as one of the ironic consequences of Jefferson's repeal of the Judiciary Act of 1801. But for that, Madison would not have been compelled to confine his choice to a New Englander — i.e., to one who could preside in his own circuit.

In January of 1809, preliminary votes in Congress showed the Embargo could not survive. The true reason for repeal was not Story's "panic" but grim reality: "The nation plunged from unparalleled prosperity into an economic decline from which it would not fully recover for a quarter of a century."[7] The administration pleaded for Congress to keep the Embargo in effect, at least until June, hoping it would at last have its desired effect on England. But Pickering and others called for an immediate repeal (D 380). By the end of February, the date of repeal was set for Jefferson's last day in office, March 4. That was later extended to March 15, to allow time for harbor officials to receive their directives; but Jefferson had the humiliation of signing the repeal, in one of his last official acts, on March 1. Even then, he could not understand why people had deserted his noble experiment, abandoning it in a "sudden and unaccountable revolution of opinion."[8] When Madison took the country into the War of 1812, Jefferson wrote that "a continuance of the Embargo for two months longer would have prevented our war."[9]

Pickering, who had voted against every bit of Embargo legislation, at last had the satisfaction of seeing a majority of both houses join him in repudiation of it. But his satisfaction did not last long. The day the Embargo expired, Madison became president. Madison had been an even more fervid supporter of the Embargo than Jefferson. Deprived of it, he came up with a substitute — commercial non-intercourse with both England and France (though aimed mainly at England). This disturbed Pickering, but not as much as the Embargo had, mainly because he did not have the visceral hatred of Madison that he nurtured for Jefferson. Just before Madison's election, Pickering feared only that he would *not* be president: "Indeed, if Mr. M were to be president, Mr. J might be expected still to direct, or at least mischievously to influence, the affairs of the nation" (P 14.200).

But Pickering was happily surprised when Madison, a month after his inauguration, announced that the British were lifting their Orders in Council and full trade could be restored with England. Pickering was now the administration's friend, enjoying White House dinners and Dolley Madison's afternoon salons with a grateful surprise. This honeymoon ended abruptly when the British minister, David Erskine, who had conveyed the message that the Orders were being repealed, was recalled to London for not negotiating extra conditions to be met before that could happen. In a decided affront to the United States, England sent a man infamous for war crimes to replace Erskine. Francis James Jackson was the diplomat who had been sent in 1807 to demand that Denmark turn over its entire fleet to the British for use against Napoleon. While Danish authorities hesitated over what to do, the guns of the British fleet pounded Copenhagen into rubble, killing half its inhabitants. Jackson was ever after known as "Copenhagen Jackson." When he arrived in the United States, two years after the Copenhagen atrocity, he lived down to his reputation for arrogance, telling people that Erskine's blunder in presenting the offer to repeal the Orders in Council was Madison's fault. The president had seduced Erskine into misrepresentation of his instructions. Madison, embarrassed enough by precipitate action on the supposed repeal, refused further communications from Jackson, who went north to consort with unwise Federalists. Pickering, who had always enjoyed warm relations with British representatives in Washington, made the grievous mistake of championing Jackson against Madison. At a Boston banquet given in Jackson's honor, Pickering offered the toast, "The world's last hope — Britain's fast-anchored isle" (P 55.266). As in the last days of his service under President Adams, he was letting his Anglophile bent carry him into indefensible excesses.

He was on more solid ground when he opposed Madison's attempted seizure of the Floridas. This was a project that had long been dear to Jefferson's heart, and to that of the slaveholding states in general. Not only would it open up the ports of Mobile and

Pensacola to southern exporters, but it would add new states with the slave bonus. Accordingly, in the summer of 1810, Madison dispatched William Wykoff with government funds to be used for inciting a rebellion against Spain in West Florida, so that the administration could step in. "Secretly the administration had authorized an agent to foment revolution in the territory of a friendly nation."[10] When that effort succeeded and rebels declared part of the region liberated, Madison, acting on his executive authority without informing Congress, sent a proclamation on October 27 declaring that area annexed to the United States (M 2.595). He did not release the proclamation outside Florida, since he meant to present Congress with a fait accompli when it returned to Washington. He informed Congress on December 5, and Republican members, supposedly the champions of limited government, tried to rush through a resolution approving of Madison's usurpation of authority.

Pickering rose to the challenge of this latest attempt to augment the slave power. Madison was arguing that he could occupy Florida since it had become American territory as part of the Louisiana Purchase. To refute this, Pickering referred to a document from the time of the debates over the Purchase. In that paper of 1804, the French minister Talleyrand, who conducted the sale of Louisiana, expressly denied that the Floridas were included in the package. Its contents had been openly discussed five years earlier, in Senate debates over the Purchase. But the document itself, part of a package submitted confidentially to the Senate, had never been formally released. When the accuracy of Pickering's reference to Talleyrand was challenged, he produced the document.

In order to derail Pickering's assault, Senator Samuel Smith of Maryland rose to ask if Pickering could show that Talleyrand's letter had been "publicly communicated." Pickering was quoting from what would now be called a classified document, and Henry Clay introduced a motion to censure Pickering for this "palpable violation of the rules of this body." Debate over that motion changed the subject. Several senators opposed the motion, and William Crawford of Georgia softened it to get a favorable vote. He removed the adjective "palpable" before "violation," and the censure was voted through. Even Gerard Clarfield, in his hostile book on

Pickering, admits that this was done only because Pickering "was striking too near the truth."

> The vote of censure, as Pickering himself remarked, was a "put up affair" and was perhaps designed to distract the public's attention from the more important yet embarrassing Florida question. Pickering had violated Senate rules, to be sure. But he had certainly not infringed on their true spirit, since the original reason for insisting upon the confidentiality of the Talleyrand letter — the fear that its revelations might jeopardize negotiations taking place in 1805 between France and the United States over Florida — had long ago ceased to pertain. But in 1810 Senate Republicans were not only anxious to avoid drawing public attention to the French diplomat's letter, they were even more touchy about the constitutional issues raised by Madison's authorization. Indeed, they were so sensitive on these points that after Pickering's censure, rather than renew the debate on the resolution and thus risk further public discussion, they let the entire matter drop. (C 247)

But though the Republicans wanted to end public debate on the matter, Madison was pressing forward. On January 3, 1811, he sent a secret message to Congress asking for $100,000 to stir up a rebellion in East Florida to match that in West Florida, so it could be annexed as well. Pickering opposed, of course; but his Senate days were numbered. The Republicans retained the Massachusetts Senate in that year, and they would surely oust him, though his longtime friend and admirer, Chief Justice John Marshall, hoped not. He wrote on February 22, 1811: "Events have so fully demonstrated the correctness of your opinions on subjects the most interesting to our country that I cannot permit myself to believe the succeeding legislature of Massachusetts will deprive the nation of your future services" (P 29.411).

He was, in fact, stripped of his Senate seat in 1811. But his Essex constituents sent him right back to Washington as their representative in the House — at a time when moving to that chamber from the other one was not considered a demotion, so much more constant was the action of the House on American politics. In fact, Henry Clay this same year resigned from the Senate so he could be elected to the House, where he was immediately chosen Speaker. It may have daunted Pickering to see the man who moved his censure in the Senate now presiding over his new home in the House. It did not help, either, that John Calhoun was another of the "freshmen" representatives. Pickering, now sixty-six, was entering what Clay would fashion into a nest of young "War Hawks" supporting Madison's War of 1812 against England.

In this nest Pickering's wings were clipped. He would have nowhere near the influence against the war, in this chamber, that he had exerted against the Embargo in the other one. Nor would his epistolary urgings be as effective, back in New England, as before — not because he was out of step with Federalists there but because they outran him. The town resolutions, the militia balkings, that had infuriated Jefferson during the Embargo, were repeated on a far grander scale against "Mr. Madison's war." Governors and legislatures in four northern states unconstitutionally refused to release their militias to federal service. When some in Congress wanted to indict the governor of Vermont for refusing to deploy his militia, the governor of Massachusetts — Harrison Gray Otis, who had been too cautious to back Pickering in 1804 — said that the people of his state would support Vermont "with their whole power."[11]

Secretary of State Monroe wanted to move in federal troops to quell the local insurgents.[12] But Madison knew the unrest was too great to be put down. He repeated what Jefferson had said of New England authorities in 1798, that they represented a "reign of witches"[13] — yet he prudently refrained from pressing things to a showdown. His administration did, nonetheless, cut off the money sent to those states to arm their militia — one of the grievances that made the resisting states consult with each other at a convention in Hartford.

Henry Adams claimed that Pickering renewed his disunion plan at this period. But Henry Cabot Lodge, with the relevant correspondence before him, refutes this claim.[14] It is true that Pickering urged friends in Massachusetts to take the lead in opposing the war, but by the means already being used — resistance to federalization of the militia, civil disobedience, and petitioning for redress of grievance. In 1804, he had envisaged a large and permanently separate country of the North, one including New York and parts of Canada. The most he would say in 1811 was that the New England states should separate themselves from Washington's action for the duration of the war with England — something their governors were, in varying degrees, already doing. He wrote to Gouverneur Morris in October, 1814:

> I have even gone so far as to say that a separation of the northern section of states would be ultimately advantageous, because it would be temporary, and because in the interval the just rights of the states would be recovered and secured; that the southern states would earnestly seek a reunion, when the rights of both would be defined and established on a more equal and therefore more durable basis. (P 15.55)

He was aiming to change the government, not withdraw from it: "To effect a peace, our rulers must be changed, and men less proud and less haters of Great Britain be employed as negotiators" (ibid.). Pickering looked to the Hartford Convention of representatives from five northern states to accomplish the reforms he sponsored. Clarfield claims that he had "little enthusiasm" for the convention (C 258), but this is what he wrote to a convention delegate:

> I consider the destiny of New England and, in the result, of the United States to be placed in the hands of the proposed convention . . . The forlorn condition of the general government, and the destitute and helpless situation of the states south of the Potomac, will render your victory easy and complete. That victory will be used not to destroy but to recover and confirm the union of the states on more equal, solid and durable bases. (P 15.63)

Despite these words, Henry Adams and others are sure that Pickering felt that the Hartford Convention did not go far enough, since it confined itself to suggesting reforms in the federal government rather than withdrawing from it. It is true that Pickering expressed a fear beforehand that George Cabot, the leader of the Massachusetts delegation to the convention, might be too pessimistic to adopt energetic measures:

> I observe that Mr. Cabot is at the head of the list of the Massachusetts delegates for the convention at Hartford, and I am glad to see

him there. His information is extensive, his experience and observation invaluable. I do not know who has more political sagacity, a sounder judgment, or more dignity of character with unspotted integrity, and perhaps no man's advice would go further to save a nation that was in his view savable. But does he not despair of the commonwealth? (P 15.64)

Pickering wrote to John Lowell, who would be attending the convention, that perhaps the only way to save the Union would be to contemplate risking it: "Like you, I have uniformly disclaimed every idea of a separation of the states while the liberty and safety of the parts can be maintained in a union of the whole. At the same time, I have considered that there may be evils more to be deprecated than a separation" (P 15.66). This is a very important letter, because Pickering goes on to list all the steps he hoped the convention would take — and these were, almost all of them, adopted by the convention. Pickering put first on his list, just as the convention did, the rescinding of the three-fifths clause, the very basis of sectional division (P 15.66). He called for reform in the election of the president, beginning with repeal of the Twelfth Amendment and continuing with the addition of amendments to make it impossible for a president to serve a second term or be succeeded by a man from the same state. These too were in the convention's petitions dispatched to Washington. Both Pickering and the convention called for a mandatory two-thirds vote in Congress on going to war or raising taxes.

How could Pickering be disappointed in a convention that did almost exactly what he called for it to do? The answer is simple. He was not disappointed. He wrote to John Lowell, to whom he had addressed his own suggested measures:

I believe that some of my very cautious friends and acquaintances think me too ardent in whatever pursuits of a public nature my attention becomes engaged, and hence it may have been supposed that I was not quite satisfied with the doings of the Convention. The fact, however, is otherwise; and, as you have been pleased to ask my opinion, I will express it with my habitual frankness. I think the report of the Convention bears the high character of wisdom, firmness, and dignity . . . In their proposed amendments of the Constitution, I have the satisfaction to find that all, save that which regards the admission of new states into the Union, were among those which I took the liberty to intimate to you in my letter of the 28th of November. (P 15.87)

When he expressed the same feelings to James Hillhouse, the latter replied: "I was much gratified to find that the doings of the Convention met general approbation, and more especially of a friend whose judgment and opinion I hold in such high estimation" (P 30.378).

It is true that, toward the end of the war, Pickering, like many others, thought that the large naval force investing New Orleans was bound to win an English victory there. He looked on this development with equanimity, since he thought it would just advance something he also thought inevitable, the separation of the western country from the Union (P 15.67). But he looked forward to this as *strengthening the ties of the original Union.*

> I, with many others, felt disposed to let the western states go off, leaving "the good old thirteen," as John Randolph called them, to themselves; and so left, it is natural to suppose they would be more firmly united; for the southern states, conscious of their separate impotence, would cling to the strength of the North. (P 15.66)

When the British did not take New Orleans after all, thanks to the brilliant defense mounted by Andrew Jackson, Pickering was not only pleasantly surprised but immensely proud of this American victory. Memories of the Revolution, in which he too had fought the British, came back to him as he expressed pride in Jackson's feat (P 16.255). This pride was so great he supported Jackson for the presidency in 1828, though Jackson was a southerner and slaveholder (P 16.223).

Not that Pickering ever lost his hatred of slavery and the slave power. He and Jefferson both disapproved of the Missouri Compromise, but for opposite reasons, Pickering because it spread slavery into Missouri, Jefferson because it banned slavery above that territory. Pickering's abolitionism was as strong as ever in his declining years, and it made him see through the hypocrisy of the slave colonization movement. He had supported that movement earlier, accepting its stated goals of moving slaves to a place where they could be self-governing, as a first step toward general emancipation. But now he excoriated the hypocrisy of southerners, who claimed these goals were theirs, though they worked with all their energy to create new states where slaves could not be self-governing. In 1820 he wrote to Charles Mercer:

> When it will be seen that nearly all the members of Congress from the slaveholding states vote for the unlimited admission of slaves into the vast regions west of the Mississippi, what inference will be drawn from the sentiments of many (and the zeal of some) citizens of those states in favor of the colonization plan, but this — that they considered it as the best means of ridding themselves of troublesome and dangerous inmates, the existing free people of color? After which, the chains of their slaves would be forever invincibly riveted. If I mistake not, the few people of color in Philadelphia, in protesting against the administration [colonizing] plan, suggested that one of its objects or effects was or would be in confirmation of the slavery of their brethren. (P 15.200)

One of the lessons being learned at this time by William Lloyd Garrison was to reveal colonization as a fake humanitarian scheme. Garrison, who knew Pickering from his childhood, was fifteen when the letter to Mercer was written.

Pickering made wild charges at times, and had strange ideas, but he was always shrewd in identifying the self-interest of the slave power, whenever it added states with a bonus of power derived from the three-fifths clause. What had been true of Louisiana, the Floridas, and a hoped-for Cuba, was also true of Missouri and beyond.

> Do gentlemen imagine that the six states of New England, with the states of New York, New Jersey, Pennsylvania, Ohio, Indiana, and Illinois — composed entirely of free men — can acquiesce in the boundless increase of rulers representing slaves . . . especially as they do not even now receive any equivalent for the admission of the existing proportion of such rulers. (P 15.200)

By the time of the Missouri Compromise, Pickering had been out of public office for four years. He lost his House seat after serving two terms there, largely because he supported an unpopular bill for increasing congressional pay. Ever since his quartermaster days,

Pickering had seen that office holders made low pay an excuse for graft. Congressmen especially chafed at receiving a per diem and travel expenses in lieu of fixed salary, which led to complicated accounting in that time of irregular sessions. The new Compensation Bill gave them an annual salary, of the sort received by members of the executive and judicial branches. The salary was not high, but it offended a nation wanting to revert to prewar "normalcy," and it received disproportionate attention, displacing Pickering in the process.

Jefferson and Pickering were born within two years of each other, and died within three years of each other, Jefferson first at eighty-three, then Pickering at eighty-four. After their years of public service, they ended their days back on their respective farms, Pickering's small place in Wenham, Jefferson's large but debt-encumbered fields at Monticello. Pickering knew that the real difference in their holdings lay not in size or beauty but in the fact that Jefferson's farms were worked by slaves, Pickering's by himself, by his sons, and by wage-earning freemen.

IV

The Pickering Legacy

A fter Pickering's death in 1829, his fight against Jefferson's position on the slave power was continued by William Lloyd Garrison as well as by various abolitionists and Transcendentalists (Theodore Parker, for instance). But the most direct champion of his old view was his old foe, John Quincy Adams, who renewed most of Pickering's assaults on the slave power, even introducing another constitutional amendment to end the three-fifths clause and threatening northern secession if it were retained. He did this in Pickering's former arena, as a member of the House of Representatives from Massachusetts.

After a distinguished period as secretary of state (1817–1824) and a less distinguished term as president (1825–1829), Adams entered the House for the first time in 1831. He would spend the last seventeen years of his life there, and die in the Speaker's chamber, after being felled at his desk by a stroke at age eighty-one. Some thought a seat in the House too lowly a post for one who had been senator, foreign minister to several countries, secretary of state, and president. But the House was a more powerful body then, and he used his seat to very good purpose. In fact, he reversed the trajectory of Pickering, who had been more influential in the Senate than he became in the House. Adams, who had been thwarted in the Senate by Pickering, became in the House a spokesman for all of Pickering's old causes. Some think of this as his most honorable period. Ralph Waldo Emerson, watching as Adams caught fire with new zeal, wrote of him:

> Mr. Adams chose wisely and according to his constitution when, on leaving the presidency, he went into Congress. He is no literary old gentleman, but a bruiser, and loves the melee. When they talk about his age and venerableness and nearness to the grave, he knows better. He is like one of those old cardinals who, as quick as he is chosen pope, throws away his crutches and his crookedness, and is as straight as a boy. He is

an old roué who cannot live on slops, but must have sulphuric acid in his tea.[1]

Adams was drawn by cautious steps into the fight against the slave power, led on by his opponents' disregard for constitutional protections of free speech. This, said John Ludlum, was the first lure that engaged him: "This was the honey that attracted the dangerous old bear, John Quincy Adams, whose lunges and embraces so mangled his victims."[2] But, once involved, he was radicalized by the absurdity of the arguments mounted to defend the slave power. When southerners tried to reduce the moral issue of slavery to a mere point of parliamentary protocol, he brilliantly reversed their strategy, and made the rights of petitioners undermine the whole rationale for slavery. His opponents made a dreadful mistake when they chose procedure as an escape from moral debate. This was a man whose diplomatic prowess was well developed. He had been minister to three countries. As secretary of state, he had finessed the Floridas problem and created the Monroe Doctrine. No one could dance around him on procedural niceties. Fending those off, and turning them against their invokers, he made himself such an international champion of freedom that Charles Dickens, on his visit to America, exempted him from the acidulous treatment he gave many Americans. He described him in action on the floor of the House: "Adams is a fine old fellow — seventy-six years old, but with most surprising vigor, memory, readiness, and pluck."[3]

Finally, in 1844, Adams defeated the gag rule that had been imposed in 1840 only by virtue of the margin provided in the House by the federal ratio. It would, I suppose, be asking too much from the generosity of the human spirit to hope that Adams realized he was just fulfilling the aspirations of his old Massachusetts rival, Timothy Pickering, when he put the slave power first on the defensive, and then on the run. The clash of Pickering and Adams had been such that it is surprising to see them in a kind of final agreement. But Adams's grandson realized that there was one bond between them, running throughout all their other differences, that gave a common basis for their actions. Both distrusted Thomas Jefferson. Henry Adams wrote to the Virginia historian, Hugh Blair Grigsby:

> Now, if you ask why men like Tim Pickering and J. Q. Adams, with their ugly tempers and their fear of neither man nor devil, bowed to Washington and despised Jefferson, the answer is simply that they

thought Jefferson a moral coward. Justly or unjustly, they thought he did not tell the truth. And that idea is ineradicable here [in New England] and will always prevent Jefferson from standing on a plane with Washington or Marshall.

Let me give an amusing instance. On May 8, 1791, Jefferson writes to Washington about his endorsement of Paine's pamphlet: "That I had in my view the discourses on Davila [by Adams] is certain." On August 30, he writes to John Adams: "I had not even in view any writing which I might suppose to be yours, and the opinions I alluded to were principally those I had heard in common conversation" [meaning with Hamilton].

Now if J. had changed the address of those letters and sent to Adams the one inculpating him and to Washington the other, he would have done what a New Englander would have respected, a brutal, rude, ungentlemanly thing — but the truth.[4]

15

J. Q. Adams: The Federal (Slave) District

IT SEEMS AN UNLIKELY development for Adams to have emerged, late in life, as an enemy of the slave power. His was not a shining record on slavery before this. In 1804, he had voted against Pickering and Hillhouse on the motion to bar slaves from the Louisiana Territory (PM 114), a vote he later tried to explain away. As secretary of state under Monroe, he realized the dream of Jefferson and Madison by bringing the Floridas into the Union as a quarry of new slave states. During the Missouri controversy, he advised New England congressmen to vote for admitting Missouri as a slave state, since Maine was being added as a free state (JQ 34.270) — though Missouri had the potential for supplying more votes, including slave "votes," than tiny Maine. Even when Adams took his seat in the House of Representatives in 1831, he felt, at first, that submitting anti-slavery petitions to Congress just stirred up trouble while accomplishing nothing.[1] It is no wonder that Garrison and other anti-slavery men did not like or trust Adams.[2]

Adams had trimmed and tacked on slavery, like politicians from all regions, while seeking higher office. As Leonard Richards judged, "Whenever there was a conflict between liberty and the law, or liberty and his position in government, or liberty and his political career, the cause of liberty was abandoned."[3] Don Fehrenbacher concurs: "In four decades of public service, this former diplomat, senator, cabinet member, and president had never lent any open encouragement to the antislavery cause."[4] The important and exhilarating thing about his years in the House was that they liberated him, freed him to indulge a conscience put on hold for too long. Even so, he arrived at his anti-slavery post by a back door, as it were, not singling out slavery as evil — not initially, anyway — but protecting the free speech of others who criticized it. He voiced his support for the right to petition under the First Amendment. The perversity of the arguments used against this freedom made him progressively more aware of the hold slavery had upon the South, and — through the South — upon the nation. He was radicalized by the nine-year struggle over petitions, led to ever bolder stands, against slavery itself, in defense of the rebel slaves on the ship *Amistad,* and in favor of giving women a role in the abolition movement.

But it all began with freedom of speech. By the 1830s, southerners had decided that a slave society cannot afford the luxury of free speech. We generally think that the condoned terror squads of the South arose after the Civil War, with the raids of the Ku Klux Klan and its congeners. But vigilantism was organized and deadly in the antebellum decades, when critics of slavery were silenced, beaten, tarred and feathered, driven out of their state or out of the South. There were three hundred such "lynchings" of white abolitionists in the time leading up to the Civil War.[5] In 1835, the South went further to cut off discussion. It was not enough to gag live voices within a state. Even printed matter dealing with the topic had to be banned, whether it originated in the state or was sent into it.

When the postmaster in Charleston discovered a packet of anti-slavery pamphlets delivered by mail boat in the harbor, he refused to deliver the pamphlets to their addressees. That was not good enough for some citizens, who broke into the post office, seized the offending material, and made a bonfire of it on the city parade ground, to the gratification of an exigent crowd. The authorities, far from reproving this unlawful act, formed a committee of prominent citizens to make sure that South Carolina's soil would not be tainted by the reception of such thoughts. The committee examined mail boats as they arrived, and destroyed anti-slavery writings before they could be offloaded. As Robert Remini says, "An illegal elite, appointed by a mob, now ruled a terrorized city."[6] Mobs in other southern cities also seized and destroyed the mails.[7] And mobs were not alone in this activity. William Wertenbaker, the librarian of the University of Virginia, a school founded by Jefferson to be a bastion of free thought, publicly burned an abolitionist newspaper.[8]

The postmaster general in Washington asked President Andrew Jackson what he should do about states that impounded the federal mails. Jackson, while expressing horror that anyone could be so vile as to stir up trouble for the South, said that the mail must not be destroyed, but it could be withheld until an addressee asked for it, after which the names of all those asking for it should be "exposed through the public journals," so they could be shunned by all "moral and good citizens."[9] At his next annual message to Congress, Jackson called for legislation to "prohibit, under severe penalties, the circulation in the southern states, through the mail, of incendiary publications intended to instigate the slaves to insurrection." These mailings, of course, were not addressed to slaves, who could not read them (though one newspaper had one page of pictographs). They were addressed to adult white citizens of the United States, who were free to disagree with it after giving it a hearing. John C. Calhoun thought Jackson's proposed legislation insufficient. He would have Congress urge all the states, northern as well as southern, to ban such works.[10]

John Quincy Adams, looking on this and other actions by Andrew Jackson, the man who had defeated him eight years earlier, saw all too well the ability of the slave power to compel cooperation from its Democratic allies in the North. Jackson had to support his fellow slaveholders, and northerners had to support Jackson, if the party was to maintain its ascendancy. Adams, the foe of the three-fifths clause, had to be aware of its role in his defeat by Jackson:

Thanks to the mechanics of the electoral college and the three-fifths rule, Jackson's 200,000 southern supporters provided him with far more help, man for man, than some 400,000 northerners [for Adams]: 105 electoral votes as compared with 73.[11]

Adams's election in 1824 had gone to the House of Representatives for settlement only because the South had split its votes among three men, Andrew Jackson, Henry Clay, and William Crawford — slaveholders all — and he felt that, after his election, they had combined as "the sable genius of the South" to thwart and unseat him.[12]

Adams would devote his second congressional career to battling the slave power, and nine of those seventeen years focused on the gag rules banning congressional discussion, especially petitions concerning slavery in the District of Columbia. Southerners had long maintained that Congress could not even consider the question of slavery in southern states, since only the state legislatures had jurisdiction in the matter. But abolitionists soon identified the chink left open in that argument. Congress *did* have jurisdiction over the District, where slavery existed without any legislature *but* the Congress to protect it. Article I, Section 8 of the Constitution decreed: "The Congress shall have power . . . to exercise *exclusive* legislation in *all* cases *whatsoever* over such district, not exceeding ten miles square, as may, by cession of particular states and the acceptance of Congress, become the seat of the government of the United States" (emphasis added). It was concern over this power that made some southern states reluctant to ratify the Constitution until the capital had been fixed in slave territory.

In 1835 it became a matter of surpassing urgency for southerners to proclaim, in defiance of the Constitution's plain sense, that Congress had no power to interfere with slavery in the District — or even to discuss the matter. John C. Calhoun identified this in the Senate as the "all-momentous question."[13] The ingenuity of the arguments involved went beyond extravagance. And the more absurd the resistance became, the more abolitionist petitions were showered upon both chambers asking for abolition in the District — thousands of petitions in the nine-year period when Congress was gagged, with over a million signatures appended to the petitions. In the 1838–1839 session, Adams himself presented 693 petitions.[14]

For Congress to discuss slavery in the area of its own authority was characterized as an act of treason. It was said that members of Congress should be censured, or even remanded to prison, simply for bringing the matter up.[15] Representative Benjamin C. Howard, who lived just across the District line in Maryland, said he could no longer leave his children in safety, "surrounded by slaves" as they were, if blacks in the capital were free.[16] Petitioners were called the murderers of southern women and children. According to James Garland of Virginia, these petitioners had "the blood reeking from the bosoms of our wives and children, pouring from wounds inflicted through the instigation of these disturbers of our peace, and enemies of our lives and liberties."[17] James Henry Hammond of South Carolina said that if such incendiaries were caught in his state, they should expect "a felon's death," expressing "the indignation of offended Heaven."[18]

Congressman Henry Wise of Virginia said that if Congress began to discuss ending slavery in the District he would "go home, never to return." Allow freedom to blacks in the District, he claimed, and they would soon be in the Congress itself, with a new Toussaint to lead them in a black takeover of the government.[19] Several southern contingents withdrew from the chamber when petitions were mentioned, not letting their ears be poisoned with such talk.[20] Others said that the petitions should be not merely ignored or tabled but burned in the chamber.[21] This was, literally, a matter of life and death. It is no wonder that Adams's war to present the petitions brought him a string of death threats.[22]

Slavery at the Seat of Government

What arguments could the southerners make to deny the federal government's authority over its own domain? Most of the arguments were fanciful. It was said that petitions were for "redress of grievance," and those outside the South could not petition because "slavery was not a grievance to northerners who lived where it did not exist."[23] Or that the Constitution forbade passing *laws* against the right to petition, but that a gag rule was only a rule of the House, not a law.[24] Or that the Constitution guaranteed the fulfillment of contracts, and purchase of a slave was a contract.[25] Or that compensation for freed slaves would call for Congress raising money for a specific locale, which it was forbidden to do.[26]

But one argument, weak in law, became increasingly popular with southerners. The federal city, they claimed, had been formed on land ceded by two slave states, Virginia and Maryland, which would never have yielded this territory but on an understanding that slavery would be protected there. Indeed, Congress had initially recognized the laws of both states as applying to the District.[27] Although there was no such stipulation in the deeds of cession, it was retrospectively read into the "intent" of the deeds. A congressional committee said that ending slavery would be "impolitic, if not unjust, to the adjoining states."[28] Another committee went beyond that, recognizing a commitment to preserving slavery as a bond of "faith reposed in Congress" by the ceding states.[29] The Maryland Senate lent its authority to the argument, declaring in 1837 that freeing the District's slaves would be "a violation of the terms and conditions upon which the cession of the District of Columbia was made to the Federal Government."[30]

There is a neglected truth behind those retroactive legalisms. The capital *was* purposely embedded in slave territory. It is one sign of the way slavery has been downplayed in our history that its role in the placing of the federal city is almost never noted. The swamp by the Potomac was an unlikely place to be chosen. It lagged, at the outset, behind more obvious locations, near the great harbor city of New York, or near the center of American civilization at the time, Philadelphia, or near the birthplace of the Revolution, Boston. It was only a fierce drive on the part of Washington, Jefferson, and Madison that carried the seat of government into plantation territory.

The customary explanation for this move is given in a famous story Jefferson told (J 17.205–7). He had just returned from Paris to become the first secretary of state. In the temporary capital, New York City, he found the new administration already stalled over its basic financial plan. The secretary of the treasury, Alexander Hamilton, had a clear program that involved centralizing debts and payments in the federal government. But the South opposed this consolidation of financial power. Jefferson invited Hamilton and

Madison, the leader in the House of Representatives, to dinner at his house in New York, where his guests struck a deal. Madison would find the necessary congressional support for the Treasury's assumption of responsibility for state debts, if Hamilton would support moving the capital to the Potomac. Historians have found this story misleading. Like many of Jefferson's accounts of past events, it gains in clarity by economizing on the truth. But if we accept the story for a moment, it raises an obvious question: What made the site of the capital so important that Jefferson and Madison would yield to Hamilton on something so important to the South? Jefferson said he later regretted what he had given away, which still makes one wonder why he thought the capital's site was important enough at the time to make him yield.

What problems do historians have with this story? There are at least four.

1. Jefferson's story leaves out the key figure in negotiations over the capital site — President Washington.[31] The caustic Pennsylvania senator, William Maclay, saw what was going on at the time: "It is, in fact, the interest of the President of the United States that pushes the Potomac. He, by means of Jefferson, Madison, [Charles] Carroll and others, urges the business."[32] Congress chose the Potomac site only because Washington made it clear that he was determined to get it. This has only recently been realized, because "Washington's concern for discretion, and Madison's and Jefferson's willingness to honor it, mask his exact role."[33]

2. Jefferson's dinner, so far as it contributed to congressional agreement, was only one node in a network of negotiations, bargains, and tradeoffs going on in the summer of 1790. Though Jefferson presents the dinner party as his solitary intervention in the residency issue, he and Madison had already negotiated on it with Pennsylvanians.[34] And after the dinner Madison could still write that "the business of the seat of government is become a labyrinth" (M 13.252).

3. Hamilton was not in a position to make others vote for the Potomac site. He had tried to negotiate with backers of a Philadelphia site, and had not succeeded because he did not have the required

muscle. Madison, with the help of Washington's pressure, already had the votes for the Potomac. What little Hamilton could contribute at this point was an agreement not to meddle with the negotiations already secured.[35]

4. Insofar as a real bargain was struck at the Jefferson dinner, it had more to do with fixing Virginia's liability under Hamilton's assumption plan than with the capital site. Madison agreed to win others' open support (but not his own) for Hamilton's proposal if Hamilton would jigger the figures so that Virginia did not lose financially by passage of the Assumption Bill. Hamilton's creative accounting awarded Virginia a credit equal to its supposed obligation in payments. As Jefferson put it, "Being therefore to receive exactly what she is to pay, she [Virginia] will neither lose nor gain by the measure" (J 17.269).

It is clear, then, that Jefferson's account, written several years after the event it records, had as much to do with what had happened since the dinner as with the details of the actual meeting. In the interval, Jefferson and Madison had become more panicky over what Hamilton was doing, and regretted their cooperation with his plan for assumption of the debts. The South, too, was disturbed by Hamilton's financial efforts, favoring commerce over agriculture. But Jefferson could assure his fellows that, bad as things were, at least he had secured the southern capital out of the bargain. That was obviously meant to weigh very heavily in his favor — and it did.

The real story of the capital's location is a tale of three resolute Virginians working together. Jefferson and Madison relied on the prestige of Washington to get a first agreement to honor his preference, and then they worked to keep all further discussion out of Congress, granting Washington executive authority over each step in the planning and implementation of the scheme. Washington even labored to make the site's development as self-financing as possible — funded by local proprietors' donating half their land, to enhance the value of the other half — so that moneys would need as few congressional appropriation hearings as could be arranged.[36]

Each of the three men involved had to bend his own standards of conduct to bring this about. Washington shied from even slight hints of dictatorial powers. He did not want to trade on his immense prestige as leader of the Revolution, or give opponents a chance to portray him as power-hungry. But here he was eager to take an entire disposition of things into his own unanswerable hands. Jefferson resented executive privileges of all sorts but this one. He also resented at times what he considered the martial glory of Washington's reputation, though for this purpose he was willing to use it to its full extent. Madison was a champion of the legislative power he was currently wielding in the House, yet he deferred to Jefferson's secret strategy of keeping Congress from the exercise of its proper authority.

Jefferson, the guardian of states' rights, was also willing to suppress any action on the part of the state authorities involved in the site, deciding that "it would be dangerous to rely on any aids from Congress or the assemblies of Virginia or Maryland, and that therefore measures should be adopted to carry the residence bill into execution without recourse to those bodies" (J 17.461–62). Crucial choices about the nation's capital must be "subject to the President's direction in every point" (ibid.). This, the real reason why the Potomac site won out, just intensifies the question raised by all other alleged reasons. Why was this point so important to the Virginians that they would stretch the new powers of the government, in a manner they themselves had called dangerous, in order to get their way? Why did the capital's site matter so much?

We are normally told that they wanted the boost in prestige and influence for their region. Washington was even accused of wanting to enhance the value of his own Potomac holdings.[37] Joseph Ellis thinks that Jefferson wanted the rural site because he disliked cities — though Jefferson himself said that the area would profit by commerce brought to it, and Washington clearly had a large imperial city in mind, the plans for which he elicited from L'Enfant.[38] Do such motives explain the Stakhanovite effort of these men to secure the capital? We need to go back again to the idea of Washington's "discretion." Harder but unconfessable considerations were at play. As usual, slavery was exerting its vast but invisible influence.

Southerners knew what difficulties and embarrassments they suffered when acting outside their own arena. Though the Constitution guaranteed them the return of escaped slaves from any state in the Union, it was difficult to exert this "right."[39] Washington would not even advertise for an escaped slave "north of Virginia."[40] When one of Washington's slaves, named John Cline, escaped from the president's house in Philadelphia, he did not try to retrieve him.[41] When he did try to retrieve slaves escaping to the North — like Opey and Hercules — he did it by stealth, and in one case by using government agents. Opey was one of Mrs. Washington's most valued slaves, and Washington had his secretary of the treasury, Hamilton, alert port officials to be on the lookout for her and spirit her onto a ship without causing any public stir. When the agent who spotted her in Portsmouth said that she had support from the local opponents of slavery, and could not be secretly shipped back, Washington had to give up the hunt for her.[42] Hercules was a different matter. Great effort had been given to training him as a cook. Washington had to send Hercules back to Virginia, for fear of his being emancipated in Philadelphia. But Hercules ran away from Mount Vernon and returned, Washington was sure, to Philadelphia, where all the president's efforts to find him were baffled.[43]

Philadelphia, with its Quaker heritage of opposition to slavery, was an especially trying site for slaveholders. When Patrick Henry went to the first Continental Congress in Philadelphia, to deliberate on a course to pursue with Great Britain, the city's admired humanitarian, Anthony Benezet, asked Henry if he expected God to bless his efforts while he still held slaves.[44] But a more serious threat had arisen by the 1790s. Philadelphia had passed a law that any slave brought into the city could be held for no longer than six months, after which he or she was automatically manumitted. Pierce Butler lost one of his slaves to this law while serving in the Senate, and Attorney General Edmund Randolph alerted Washington to the problem of keeping their slaves in the city. Washington thought his office should exempt him from this law, but just to be safe he warned his secretary, Tobias Lear, to send slaves back, on some other pretense, as their six-month period approached. Washington was on a presidential tour of the South, but he wrote urgently from Richmond:

I wish to have it accomplished under pretext that may deceive both them [the slaves] and the public; and none, I think would so effectually do this as — Mrs. Washington coming to Virginia next month, toward the middle or latter end of it, as she seemed to have a wish to do — if she can accomplish it by any convenient and agreeable means, with the assistance of the stage horses, etc. This would naturally bring her maid and Austin; and Hercules, under the idea of coming home to cook whilst we remained there, might be sent on in the stage . . . I request that these sentiments and this advice may be known to none but *yourself* and *Mrs. Washington* [emphasis in original].[45]

Jefferson, too, had to worry about keeping his slaves while he served as secretary of state in Philadelphia. He had just brought his own cook, James Hemings, from Paris, where he had been trained to prepare French cuisine. Even in France, according to James's nephew, Madison Hemings, James had threatened to run away, though he did not know the language of that strange country. As a matter of fact, he was already free without knowing it, under the new legislation of the French revolutionary government. Jefferson, who had begun paying him a salary in Paris, continued to do so on their joint return to Monticello. Perhaps that was an inducement to keep him in service. But Philadelphia posed new and far more acute dangers. Hemings would find fellow blacks speaking English there, and a city with strong anti-slavery sentiment. The Pennsylvania Abolition Society, if it learned of James's time in France, could legally declare him free.[46] So Jefferson drew up an affidavit, properly witnessed, promising to free Hemings in the future if he stayed with him in Philadelphia and returned with him to Monticello:

Having been at great expense in having James Hemings taught the art of cookery, desiring to befriend him and to require from him as little in return as possible, I do hereby promise and declare that, if the said James shall go with me to Monticello in the course of the ensuing winter, when I go to reside there myself, and shall there continue until he shall have taught such person as I shall place under him for the purpose to be a good cook, this previous condition being performed, he shall be thereupon made free, and I will thereupon execute all proper instruments to make him free. Given under my hand and seal in the county of Philadelphia and state of Pennsylvania this fifteenth day of September, one thousand seven hundred and ninety three.

Th. Jefferson
Witness: Adrian Petit.[47]

Problems of this sort could only be compounded if the government stayed in a locale unfriendly to slavery. Aedanus Burke of South Carolina said on the floor of the House that Philadelphia was "a bad neighborhood for the South Carolinians," and Madison said that Virginia might not have ratified the Constitution if it had been clear then that the government would be in Philadelphia.[48] John Maclay remarked of the two senators from South Carolina: "These men have most settled antipathy to Pennsylvania, owing to the doctrines patronized in that state on the subject of slavery."[49] Washington was alarmed that, just when residency was about to be decided, anti-slavery petitions from Philadelphia Quakers were submitted to Congress. He called this "very mal-apropos."[50] He did not want open discussion of the relationship between the capital and slavery.

That these considerations were important to the Virginians is made clear by one of Washington's most risky moves. We have seen that he and Jefferson did not want to let Congress reconsider the capital's site, and kept the implementation of their scheme out of public debate. But Washington disobeyed the act of legislation creating the District, and asked for retroactive approval from Congress, for one purpose only: to move the site even farther south than he had been authorized to do.

Finally, on 24 January, he issued a proclamation announcing the chosen site. Washington not only included Alexandria — four miles south of the lower limit specified in the seat of government act of 1790 — but also named a point within the town as the starting place for the survey of the district's boundaries. In a letter to Congress, Washington suggested that it pass a supplemental act to enable him to complete the full ten mile square to his liking by taking in Alexandria and land south of the Anacostia in Maryland . . . By his placement of the district and his request for a supplemental act, Washington courted not only renewed sectional tensions and a confrontation between Congress and the president, but also attacks upon himself.[51]

The attacks upon him came quickly. He was said to be acting from greed, to enhance the value of his own property. His own vice president, John Adams, observed caustically that it had boosted his land's value "a thousand percent."[52] Was Washington really ready to risk his reputation and support for the capital from mere greed? A more probable reason for this venture is Washington's desire to insert the capital even more snugly into a thriving slave community, where the existence of slavery would be least challengeable. That was a public policy he felt required to entrench. Southerners were so concerned that official activities be associated with their own institutions, including the most controversial of them, that one reason for their strong resistance to the Bank of the United States was that its charter established it in Philadelphia, not at the national capital.[53]

Washington's coup was successful. He incorporated into the federal district the entire slave city of Alexandria, and a portion of Virginia making up a third of the whole District. This land was not retroceded to Virginia until 1846. Furthermore, during the ten years of the city's construction, before it was formally taken over by Congress, slavery was allowed to flourish throughout the former Maryland portion as well as the former Virginia portion of its domain. When the government moved down to the Potomac, over a fifth of the District's residents were slaves, "many of whom were undoubtedly the property of public officials."[54] The District was, moreover, a busy center of slave trading, where slaves were paraded in chains to the auction block.[55] James Talmadge, a congressman who tried to block the extension of slavery into Missouri, said on the House floor that he and his fellow legislators could see from the windows of their building "a trafficker in human flesh" driving chained men, women, and children "under the guidance of the driver's whip."[56]

Many people have noticed that the United States differs from most other countries by having its capital city separate from the financial, intellectual, fashionable, and commercial centers of the nation. Paris, London, Rome, and other central cities are where the great schools and banks and social life thrive. But Washington was placed where a diverse cultural life would pose no challenge to its sleepy southern folkways. No professors from a major university, no benevolent Quaker merchants, no sophisticated financial operatives would rub up against the Maryland and Virginia slaveholding natives. No major harbor would give a cosmopolitan air to the place. All visitors to the city in the first half of the nineteenth century described its hick-town atmosphere. Few went there for anything but politics — office holders, bureaucrats, lobbyists. The short sessions, the hard traveling conditions, the primitive accommodations — these tempted few families to accompany members of Congress there. The congressmen lived in close boarding-house quarters, and had the male environment of boys' schools, naval vessels, or prisons, with their louche subcultures of hangers-on and prostitutes. There was little cultural life, no fashionable shops, no literary circle. For those one had to go to New York, Philadelphia, Boston, perhaps Baltimore — or even to a thriving port city like Pickering's Salem. The social climate was sluggish, not challenged by outside values.

In this city there would be no escaping Hercules, no need for Jefferson to bargain with his own slaves to keep them in service, no uproar if a runaway slave were smuggled onto a ship. Here president after president would preside without embarrassment over an executive mansion maintained by slaves. Can one imagine a succession of twelve slaveholder presidents if the capital had remained in Philadelphia? The southerners got what they wanted, a seat of government where slavery would be taken for granted, where it would not need perpetual apology, excuse, or palliation, where the most honored men in the nation were not to be criticized because they practiced and defended and gave privilege to the holding of slaves.

It was for this all-important symbol of a slave capital that the whole petition battle of 1835–1844 would be waged.

16

J. Q. Adams: Petition Battles

THE POINT OF the debates that consumed endless days in both houses of Congress between 1836 and 1844 could not have been clearer. The First Amendment of the Constitution says: "Congress shall make no law . . . abridging the freedom of speech or of the press, or the right of the people peaceably to assemble and to *petition the government* for a redress of grievances" (emphasis added). The Constitution could hardly omit a right of petition — the Revolution itself had begun with a series of petitions to the king for redress of colonial grievances. How could the nation that arose from that rebellion deny its own path to power? Accordingly, most petitions were welcomed by Congress with polite acknowledgment, if not always with serious consideration. Petitions against slavery were the only ones systematically ignored, rejected, or dishonored — and, after 1835, when abolitionists began to target slavery in the District, those mentioning that area were treated with the most savage resentment.

Adams's first engagement was minimal. Barely a week into his first term as a member of the House, in 1831, he presented his first anti-slavery petitions. He was not concerned that they were ignored, since he thought outsiders protesting conditions in the District were "meddling with what did not concern them."[1] But four years later, in the congressional session of 1835–1836, he was put on alert by the overkill operation against the petitions. Henry Wise of Virginia said that all petitions on slavery must be tabled without further consideration:

> Sir, slavery is interwoven with our very political existence, is guaranteed by our Constitution, and its consequences must be borne by our northern brethren as resulting from our system of government, and they cannot attack the system of slavery without attacking the institutions of our country, our safety, and our welfare.[2]

But that was not enough for the southern hardliners. The pivotal years in the petitions struggle — 1836, 1840, 1844 — were all presidential election years, when, as William Freehling puts it, trial probes were made to test "whether southern extremists could pressure moderate Southern Democrats to pressure Northern Democrats into lining up behind the slave power."[3] The hardline demands in 1836 were made, as so often, by South Carolinians, by James Henry Hammond in the House and by John C. Calhoun in the Senate. For both of them, it was not enough to ignore petitions — like the mails in Charleston harbor, they must be blocked before arrival. Congress should have no jurisdiction to deal with the petitions in any way, not even to table them after reception. They should have no reception, no standing, no official existence. Only this could meet the danger "at the door," or "at the frontier." Calhoun topped the metaphors by calling the point of repulsion "our Thermopylae."[4] Hammond believed that treason was not a ground for petition, and opposition to slavery was treasonous. Calhoun, clever lawyer that he was, shaped a more procedural approach. Criticism of slavery was a personal insult to each senator who possessed slaves, so he could make it a matter of members' privilege to have no such insults countenanced.

In 1836, Martin Van Buren, who had run Jackson's successful campaigns of 1828 and 1832, was put forward by Jackson as his own successor. In order to hold the party together, Van Buren had to steer it away from the hardliners' extreme demands, while showing himself a determined foe of abolition. He therefore put up his allies — Henry Pinckney in the House and James Buchanan in the Senate — to create a "gag rule" that was not so clearly unconstitutional as a refusal even to receive them. Committees were formed to create a policy for rejecting the petitions. The Speaker of the House, James K. Polk, stacked the House committee with pro-slavery men of more moderate temper than Hammond. It reported that slavery in the states was off-bounds for Congress on constitutional grounds. As for slavery in the District, discussing it was not clearly unconstitutional, but it would be impolitic and unjust for Congress to interfere with it in any way. All anti-slavery petitions should therefore be automatically tabled and denied further notice.

In the Senate, Buchanan's motion for automatically tabling the petitions won out against Calhoun's determination not to receive them at all. Henry Clay proposed that they be remanded to a committee that would kill them.[5] It will be noticed how many of these men trying to retain while modifying the slave power's maximum demands were angling for the presidency — Van Buren, Calhoun, Clay, Buchanan, Polk. Three of the five would make it. This shows how central to politics was the use and management of the slave power.

Adams strenuously opposed the Pinckney gag, the first gag rule; but Polk in the Speaker's chair kept denying him the floor, or cutting him off. When the vote was taken on the Pinckney gag, he did not answer Aye or Nay, but began, "I hold the resolution to be a violation of the Constitution of the United States . . ." He was gaveled down by Polk. Only on the next day was he able to complete his sentence: ". . . of the Constitution of the United States, of the rights of my constituents, and of the people of the United States to petition, and of my right to freedom of speech as a member of this House."[6] Once the gag was voted in, Adams had to resort to various ploys to get around it. He would, for instance, present petitions that did not mention slavery, but obviously had that in mind — e.g., a petition to remove the seat of government to a more northern location, or to reaffirm the constitutional provision of a republican form of government in all states, or to ask that the bloodlines of all office holders be examined to make sure they were "of pure Anglo-Saxon blood."[7] He also used the attacks southerners made on him to argue for a point of personal privilege having to do with his petitioning. Slavery got in by many side doors when he rose to speak.

Besides, the gag was a House rule, not a standing order, so it had to be renewed at each session. Adams was quick to insert petitions before the House rules were debated and adopted, and then use them to oppose adoption of the old rule. The more outrageous his petitions seemed, the more they were guaranteed to evoke southern indignation, giving him new grounds for personal defense. It became a game to see what new devices he could come up with, as he made the gag rule a laughingstock in much of the North. Adams would get enough of the petition in to pique curiosity before a motion to table could be made. After adoption of the House rule, he would raise an objection that his petitions were made before the rule was re-enacted, so they should be considered, after all, as having prior standing.

There was no end to his inventiveness, which provoked responses on which he could hang further discussion. (He liked to point out that he could have read his interrupted petitions in far less time than the debate over their reading had consumed.) He named the petitioners before giving the subject of the petition, so his opponents could not at first move to table it until he named the grievance being identified for redress. In 1827 he introduced a petition from "nine ladies in Fredericksburg, Virginia," and said that he hesitated to name them because of reprisals they might suffer in their state. The petition was tabled, but John Patton from Virginia went over to the table and read the names. He said there was "not a single one of them of decent respectability," and one "was the name of a free mulatto woman of the worst fame and reputation." That prompted this exchange:

Adams: The gentleman from Virginia says he knows these women, and that they are infamous. *How* does the gentleman know it? [Laughter in the chamber]

Patton: I did not say that I knew the women personally. I knew from others that the character of one of them was notoriously bad.

Adams: I am glad the gentleman now says he does not know these women, for if he had not disclaimed that knowledge, I might have asked who it was that made these women infamous — whether it was those of their own color or their masters. I have understood that there are those among the colored population of slave-holding states who bear the image of their masters. [Sensation in the chamber][8]

Adams argued that even the lowly — indeed, especially they — have the right to petition for relief in their unhappy condition. "I shall forever entertain the proposition that the sacred right of petition, of begging for mercy, does not depend on character any more than it does on condition. It is a right that cannot be denied to the humblest, to the most wretched."[9] In fact, he had a case in hand — a petition from twenty-two slaves. Before raising the subject of the petition, he asked the House if petitions could be received from slaves. This was not yet a violation of the gag, since the petition did not necessarily deal with slavery, though the petitioners were slaves. The point on which he asked clarification was not the subject of the petition but the persons petitioning. He could not more deftly have shown that the real problem was racism, not parliamentary rules. There were cries of "Expel the mover!" Dixon Lewis of Alabama rose to say that if Adams were not "punished, severely punished" for the insult of bringing up such a petition, representatives from the slaveholding states would have to leave the House and leave Washington. Waddy Thompson of South Carolina formally moved for Adams to be censured for "a flagrant contempt on the dignity of this House."

Adams responded that he had not presented the petition, but only asked for a ruling of the House. And, besides, the subject of the petition was not touched by the gag rule, which dealt with petitions for "interfering" with slavery in the District. These slaves were petitioning that slavery *not* be interfered with. The southerners were now doubly infuriated, angry at being duped. Waddy Thompson asked whether it is "a light thing, for the amusement of others, to irritate, almost to madness, the whole delegation from the slaveholding states."[10] A new count was added to the censure motion, saying that Adams had "trifled with the House." All that this motion did was guarantee Adams's possession of the floor, where he could exercise his right to defend himself.

Adams was far better at these skirmishes than Pickering had been in his assaults on the slave power, since he had humor as one of his weapons, ridicule, and a skilled diplomat's eye for maneuver. And his enemies just gave him more ammunition. Defending his censure motion, Waddy Thompson said: "I can tell him [Adams] that there are such things as grand juries, and if, sir, the juries of this District have, as I doubt not they have, proper intelligence and spirit, he may yet be made amenable to another tribunal, and we may yet see an incendiary brought to condign punishment."[11] To threaten a member with penal law for privileged speech in the chamber was going too far even for the southern firebrands. Adams turned the tables, and demanded to know why the Speaker had not stopped or rebuked the person making such a threat. Thompson was the one who deserved censure.

Thompson replied that he was basing his motion on Adams's actions outside the House, since he must have met with the slaves before bringing their petition to the House, which "was evidence, in law, of collusion."[12] The motion to censure got swallowed up in the question whether one could meet slaves to receive petitions. For five days debate raged on this issue. It was decided that slaves could not submit petitions, by a vote of 224 to 18.[13]

Another presidential election arrived in 1840, and this time the southern hardliners were able to put their extreme gag — the one first raised by Hammond four years earlier — in the place of the mere tabling gag. This one was moved by William Cost Johnson of Maryland, a border state, as part of a loyalty test for the Democratic party. The Johnson gag won, but only by the margin of the federal ratio. Adams had been whittling away at northern support for the gag rule. It was becoming an embarrassment to some northern Democrats. Roughly 80 percent of them had voted for the Pinckney gag in 1836. But only half that number voted for the Johnson gag in 1840.

Adams would have won except for his parallel hate, the three-fifths clause. In a House apportioned on the one-white-man, one-vote basis, southerners would not have had the 19 representatives received for black non-citizens in 1840. The slave power needed most of those 19 boosts in power to pass the latest gag rule by six votes.[14]

Not only was the Johnson gag the harshest one that had yet been imposed. It was also passed as a standing order of the House, not a mere rule; so it did not have to be renewed in future sessions. Adams could and did argue repeatedly for its repeal — three times in the session of 1841; but unsuccessfully. He further angered southerners that year when he came to the defense of the blacks who rebelled on the slave ship *Amistad* and took command of it. The ship was seized off Long Island, and the blacks were imprisoned in New Haven. Adams devoted much of his defense before the Supreme Court to denunciation of the Van Buren administration for trying to smuggle these self-freed people back to their Spanish owners.

In 1842, still laboring under the Johnson gag, Adams escalated his war on the slave power. He had been elected, over some resistance, to be chairman of the Foreign Relations Committee. This seemed an obvious if belated move. He had, after all, been a successful diplomat and secretary of state. But his hatred of slavery made him "untrustworthy" to southerners. Adams had received a copy of a letter from Representative Henry Wise, directed to his Virginia constituents, that said Adams would not be firm enough in blocking diplomatic recognition of "the Negro government of Haiti."[15] Others feared, with good reason, that he would oppose the annexation of Texas. Adams determined to bring all such fears into the open and address them. To do this, he introduced a petition from Georgia asking that he be replaced as chairman of the committee. He then demanded the privilege of answering the petition he had himself introduced — and made his defense an eloquent attack on the gag rule and slavery. He was not removed from the committee, though five southerners resigned from it rather than sit with him, and the Speaker found it hard to find five other southerners who would.[16]

That was only the first salvo in his 1842 barrage. He next did what he had condemned Pickering for doing — raised the specter of northern secession. He presented a petition from forty-six residents of Haverhill, Massachusetts, asking that Congress either return to free debate or else consider "measures peaceably to dissolve the Union."[17] The petition evaded the gag by not specifically mentioning slavery. But once again some called for it to be burned, and the demand that he be censured was repeated. This was the most serious attempt to silence Adams. He had become a dagger in the entrails of the South. To find some modern equivalent, we might have to suppose that Jane Fonda were in the House during the Vietnam War, forever bringing in petitions from Southeast Asians. There had been earlier attempts to bridle or extrude Adams. It was even suggested that he be given some honorary new post for an ex-president, on the condition that he leave the House.[18] Another presidential aspirant, Millard Fillmore, tried to smother the conflict by tabling the censure motion.[19] But Adams voted against tabling it. He *wanted* to face censure. It gave him a fresh platform from which to air his principles.

After the opening speech had been made in favor of his censure, one that accused him of "high treason," Adams said that he could not respond until the clerk of the House read the opening of the Declaration of Independence. Against objection, that was done — down to the clause that says "it is the right of the people to alter or abolish it . . ." The clerk looked up here, but Adams said, "Proceed! Proceed! Down to 'the right and the duty.'" The man read on: "'it is their right, it is their duty, to throw off such government.'" Adams then said he hoped that the Haverhill petition would not become a second Declaration of Independence.

The spirit of Timothy Pickering was in the chamber at that moment, the Pickering who quoted the Declaration against Jefferson over the recognition of Haiti's revolution. Adams continued:

> If the right of habeas corpus, and the right of trial by jury are to be taken away by this coalition of southern slaveholders and northern Democracy, it is time for the northern people to see if they cannot shake it off, and it is time to present petitions such as this. I can say it is not yet time to *do* this . . .[20]

For two weeks the censure of Adams was debated. Adams recited his services to the country, recalled his friendship with the founders, reviewed the oath of office he had taken and observed in so many high places of trust. He said that he had material for another week of defense if the House desired it. The other side, recognizing the folly of this effort to humiliate a former president, agreed to table the censure, as it had tabled so many of the man's petitions. The vote was 106 for tabling and 93 against.

At the next session, of 1843, he introduced a resolution passed by the Massachusetts legislature for the repeal of the three-fifths clause in the Constitution. He returned to the days of the Ely amendment, when he and Pickering were instructed by their state to call for that clause's removal. The motion went nowhere, but gradually Adams was gaining ground. In the very next session, during another presidential year, he won a vote to end the Johnson gag. This did not mean that the slave power was giving up. It simply found this battle no longer the favored one. Adams had made the gag a vulnerability.

Priority now shifted to other matters, and especially to the annexation of new slave territory in Texas. Meanwhile, removing the gag on discussion of slavery in the District of Columbia did not mean that slavery was any less deeply rooted there. In 1850, when Henry Clay tried to cobble together the Compromise of 1850, giving concessions to both the North and the South, he proposed the Fugitive Slave Law as one to the South, while offering emancipation in the District as a boon to the North. The Fugitive Slave Law was enacted by Congress, and Daniel Webster became a villain in the North for supporting it. But the District Bill was defeated, and its southern opponents were celebrated for their success in killing it. The slave power won again. Slavery, with some restrictions, would continue to exist in Lincoln's capital throughout the Civil War — it was not included in the provisions of the Emancipation Proclamation. Only the Thirteenth Amendment at last freed the city.

Adams and Texas

In the presidential race of 1844, candidates or would-be candidates circled around the annexation of Texas as warily as they had around the gag rule in 1836. The slave power desperately wanted this new territory, where slavery had been abolished by the Mexican Republic, only to be reimposed if it were annexed to the United States. Missouri senator Thomas Hart Benton, when he was still an expansionist, became positively giddy at the prospect of carving anywhere from five to nine new states out of the former Mexican territory.[21] Tyler, Polk, Buchanan, and Calhoun were for immediate annexation. Clay and Van Buren hedged, speaking of eventual annexation. James Birney, of the new Liberty party, opposed annexation. Birney drained votes from Clay in the North, winning 62,000 votes there, 16,000 of which in New York denied Clay that state's 36 electoral votes.[22] The slave power went with Polk, who won. This strengthened the hand of outgoing president Tyler, who hoped to achieve annexation during his last months in office. But a vote on the treaty of annexation would require a two-thirds majority in the Senate, and the combined Clay-Birney numbers showed widespread opposition.

Adams, of course, was opposed to the annexation, though he could not vote on the treaty, since he was not in the Senate. This was not, however, a new fight for him. Even before he raised the specter of northern secession in 1842 he had threatened it in 1836, prompting another rebuke from Speaker of the House Polk when he had said that admitting Texas to the Union might be an occasion for some states to withdraw from it.[23] The Tyler forces tried to raise a fear that Britain would adopt the revolutionary Republic of Texas if the United States did not. This did not disturb Adams at all, since he was now as Anglophile as Pickering had been. Where Pickering defended even the *Chesapeake* boarding, Adams defended even Britain's Opium War.[24]

In fact, since Britain had freed all the slaves in its holdings, alliance with it would mean that Texas would have to support the abolition of slavery that Mexico had decreed for the area in 1829. American abolitionists therefore worked with their cohorts in England to bring about an alliance of a free Texas with England rather than with the slaveholding South of the United States. The wealthy Lewis Tappan, a backer of the American Antislavery Society, consulted with Adams on a plan to trade land for freed slaves in Texas, under English sponsorship. Adams told Tappan: "I believe the freedom of this country and of all mankind depends upon the direct, formal, open, and avowed interference of Great Britain to accomplish the abolition of slavery in Texas."[25]

In the Senate, Tyler not only failed to get a two-thirds approval for his treaty. He could not even get a simple majority. He decided to abandon the treaty route and try another device. This went against the obvious model for annexation, the Louisiana Purchase, which had been consummated by treaty. But Tyler claimed that Louisiana had involved a third entity, France, and no treaty would be needed where such a third party was lacking. There were only the two political bodies, one acquiring, one to be acquired. Tyler therefore proposed that the annexation be achieved by ordinary legislation. This not only took away the two-thirds requirement in the Senate, but involved the House, where the federal ratio gave the South an edge. After tremendous pressure was exerted in the Senate, the Annexation Bill passed by one vote only. The House passed it by twenty-two votes, nineteen of which had been provided by the counting of blacks. Adams wrote that the slave power had won again, which meant that the Constitution had become "a menstruous rag" (JQ 12.171). The Massachusetts legislature agreed that this proceeding violated the Constitution, and again threatened a dissolution of the Union.[26]

The appetite for Mexican territory was not sated but whetted by the annexation. Southerners wanted the whole southern tier of the West — the future sites of New Mexico, Utah, Arizona, and California — and James K. Polk, who had gaveled down Adams's attacks on the slave power a decade ago in the House, was now president, a slaveholder who meant to seize this territory. He invented the occasion for the Mexican War in 1846, and Adams, now in his eightieth year, opposed it. The old man was serving in the House with young Abraham Lincoln, who also opposed the war, but did not run for reelection after his single term.

Adams was now untouchable and could speak his mind. He supported the proposal of his young colleague David Wilmot, which would have excluded slavery from the acquired land. That proviso went the way of Hillhouse's attempt to exclude slavery from the Louisiana acquisition — but Wilmot gave Adams the opportunity to reverse his position on Hillhouse. This put him in good company, not only that of Lincoln but of Ulysses S. Grant, who served in the war but saw how wrong it was.

He wrote in his memoirs:

> The acquisition, separation, and annexation were, from the inception of the movement to its final consummation, a conspiracy to acquire territory out of which slave states might be formed from the American Union . . . Nations, like individuals, are punished for their transgressions. We got our punishment in the most sanguinary and expensive war of modern times.[27]

Adams died in the House in 1848, so he did not see and could not oppose (as surely he would have) later victories of the slave power — the Kansas-Nebraska Act (1854), the Dred Scott decision (1857). In the first of those he would have seen another victory for the federal ratio. What William Freehling calls this "most notorious pro-southern law" was passed in the House by a margin of only thirteen votes:

> The slave power's extra representatives aided Northern Democrats in securing the minority's legislation. Because every five slaves counted as three votes in apportioning House representatives, southerners received 19 more seats than a one-white-man, one-vote egalitarian republic would have provided. The slave power needed a third of those extra votes to pass Kansas-Nebraska. Anti-Nebraska forces had yet another reason to denounce the rape of republicanism.[28]

The slave power, when driven to its last ditch, always had that private mound to rise up on and make a stand.

Epilogue: Farewell to Pickering

God never made a more honest man than Timothy Pickering.

— James Madison, 1801[1]

I FEEL ALWAYS a reluctance to leave a subject of study, if only temporarily. That is especially true of this book. Thomas Jefferson I already knew, in some measure; and to him, for an American, there is no saying farewell. As Henry Adams said, Americans learned to think, for better or worse, with Jefferson. Though Jefferson will figure largely in my next project, I do turn now from the one aspect of the man I have been considering in this book — his protection and extension of the slave power. He is, of course, not the worst offender in this line. He did not defend slavery itself, like John Taylor of Caroline, or John Calhoun, who argued that the system was actually benign. Jefferson belonged to that large class of southerners — including the best of them, men like Washington and Madison — who knew that slavery was evil, but felt they could not cut back on the evil without cutting the ground out from under them. They knew, as well, that they would lose their influence over other southerners if they went against the system off which they lived. It is that influence, and not any evil intent on his part, that makes Jefferson's defense of the system so important. What he did about it mattered, because he was a president and the adviser to presidents — to Washington before him (especially on the site of the capital), and to Madison after him (especially on things like acquiring the Floridas). Other men intended worse, but could do little about it. He could and did do a lot.

No doubt, Jefferson persuaded himself, or tried to, that "agrarian virtue" was such a good thing that it counterbalanced the ancillary bad thing it nurtured and was nurtured by, plantation slavery. But this "virtue" never did or could counterbalance the evil of slavery, an evil for which we are still paying the price. The usefulness of Timothy Pickering for the purposes of this book lies in the unblinking way he stated, over and over, that nothing the South did could make slavery tolerable. Since that is the single point I have dwelt on in Pickering's life, I depart more absolutely from him now, but with a lingering interest in other aspects of the man, who was unknown to me until recently.

Students who spend time with people who are the objects of their work tend to become either exasperated with them, as Gerard Clarfield clearly did with Pickering, or fond of them, as Hervey Putnam Prentiss did. While I cannot claim any fondness for Pickering — I suspect I would have found his company irksome — I have grown in respect for him, the more I learned about him. In certain respects, he resembled the greater men he quarreled with, Adams and Jefferson.

He was as self-absorbed as John Adams. Both seem at first convinced of their own virtue — until we notice how much time they spent trying to convince themselves (and others) of it. Each was caustic and outspoken, often to his regret. Each had a prickly honor that separated him, in some degree, from others. It is touching to see how Pickering, when he discovered Boswell's life of Johnson, consoled himself with the thought that Johnson, too, was said to have a self-wounding candor. He wrote to his wife:

> It [the biography] deserves the more attention and study to understand Johnson's profound reflections on human life and manners. Perhaps I read it with the greater pleasure because, on every page almost, I met with those frank expressions of his opinions and feelings (the opposite to flattery and suppression of sentiments) which some

would call rude or at least imprudent; and for which, you know, my friends sometimes censure me. We are always pleased to meet with a congeniality of sentiment in persons of consideration, whose characters for discernment and knowledge give weight to their opinions. (P 3.153)

Adams could have written that, and it is typical that Pickering used his discovery of Johnson to make excuses to his wife, the beloved Rebecca, who was always in his mind, as he shows in the constant stream of correspondence whenever they were separated. In fact, the greatest point of resemblance between Pickering and Adams is their total devotion to and dependence on strong wives, John on Abigail, Timothy on Becky.

Pickering, however, had better luck than Adams with his sons, to whom he remained devoted as they became respectable, indeed admirable, citizens. Though Pickering was a stickler for discipline, his sons and daughters thrived under his affectionate guidance. It was Adams who broke down his sons' self-respect: "His confused and unhealthy sons cracked beneath his overbearing expectations."[2] Adams felt he had to renounce all his sons but one, though that one went on to greater fame than any that a Pickering could acquire. Still, Pickering's oldest son, John, after diplomatic service abroad, became a prominent Boston lawyer and the city's leading linguist, publishing the Greek-English lexicon that would not be replaced until Liddell and Scott produced the lasting standard.[3] He was also an expert on Native American languages — such that Jefferson, who shared that interest, consulted him, leading John to reply politely to his father's old enemy.[4] Pickering's son Timothy, named for him, died when *his* son, Charles, was only two, and the grandfather raised Charles, who became a famous anthropologist and naturalist.[5] The scientific interests of his sons were stimulated by Pickering's own. He had been part of the debates of his time on medicine and agriculture and languages. He joined his friend Dr. Benjamin Rush in well-meant though mistaken recommendation of treatment by "bleedings."

The main personal quality that Pickering lacked and Adams possessed was a sense of humor. On this point Pickering resembled, rather, the humorless Jefferson, but without the latter's philosophical wit (a quality quite different from humor). Each of these two men considered politics a realm for testing virtue. Each admired his father, in both cases a farmer of rugged enterprise, though Pickering came to see the merits of the merchant class into which he married — something that would never happen to Jefferson. Though Pickering did not have what Jefferson called his own "canine appetite" for reading, he was a bookish man, one who spent a large part of his little money on law books ordered from England. He and Jefferson exchanged books and documents on occasion (P 27.24, 30, 33, 38). Pickering had, like Jefferson, an Enlightenment interest in scientific farming.[6] His lifelong efforts for education had been sharpened by his friendship with Samuel Phillips, the founder of Phillips Academy in Andover, with whom he corresponded on school curriculums (P 5.369–71). While he was secretary of state, Pickering was given honorary degrees by Princeton and Brown universities (P 23.173, 25.323). He would have received one from Harvard, but Fisher Ames had to block that, reluctantly, in order to keep a degree from being given to Elbridge Gerry — a maneuver Pickering approved of, since he shared the dislike of Gerry as a turncoat Republican (P 24.243–44).

Coming from a Puritan background, Pickering achieved, by a harder effort than was required of the more sophisticated Jefferson, a similarly rational religiosity — a fact each recognized in the other. In 1821, when both were in their seventies, Pickering sent Jefferson a sermon by the liberal Unitarian, William Ellery Channing, with some reflections on his own upbringing and the way he gave up belief in miracles and the Trinity:

> There are some doctrines taught in Protestant churches, in Europe and America, so repugnant to the ideas I entertain of the perfect wisdom, justice, and benevolence of the Deity as to authorize the opinion that they could not be the subjects of a divine revelation ... They constituted parts of parental and school instruction, from my earliest remembrance; but I never taught them to any of my children. (P 15.243–46)

Jefferson answered amiably. He admired the Channing sermon and agreed with Pickering on the basics of belief:

When we shall have done away with the incomprehensible jargon of the Trinitarian arithmetic, that three are one and one is three; when we shall have knocked down the artificial scaffolding reared to mask from view the simple structure of Jesus; when, in short, we shall have unlearned everything which has been taught since his day and got back to the pure and simple doctrines he inculcated, we shall then be truly and worthily his disciples. (P 15.247)

It is strangely comforting to take leave of these two as they write each other, both with an old man's clear handwriting still, to affirm their agreement on important matters.

America was a better place for the labors of all three of these men; and if Pickering's contribution cannot be weighed in the same scale with that of the other two, his words still have something to teach us that the larger messages of his betters left unspoken. Pickering has not yet received his due.

NOTES

ACKNOWLEDGMENTS

INDEX

Notes

Prologue: Coming to Terms with Jefferson

1. *Inventing America: Jefferson's Declaration of Independence* (1978).
2. *Mr. Jefferson's University* (2002).
3. Most (though not all) of these appeared in the *New York Review of Books,* "Uncle Thomas's Cabin" (Apr. 18, 1974), "The Strange Case of Jefferson's Subpoenas" (May 2, 1974), "Executive Privilege: Jefferson and Burr" (July 18, 1974), "Jefferson's Jesus" (Nov. 24, 1983), "Jefferson the Aesthete (Aug. 12, 1993), and "Storm over Jefferson" (Mar. 9, 2000).
4. Pauline Maier, *American Scripture: Making the Declaration of Independence* (Alfred A. Knopf, 1997).
5. Conor Cruise O'Brien, *The Long Affair: Thomas Jefferson and the French Revolution, 1785–1800* (University of Chicago Press, 1996).
6. Recent readers of David McCullough who canonize John Adams should read the classic account of Federalism's demise, Stanley Elkins and Eric McKitrick, *The Age of Federalism, 1788–1800* (Oxford University Press, 1993). Though their account of Federalism is sympathetic, they come to judgments like this (p. 735): "[Adams] thereupon gave himself over to a torrent of rage whose after-effects, by the end of the year 1800, were to leave the ruins of Federalism in even smaller fragments than they were in already."
7. Ibid., pp. 751–52.
8. Paul Finkelman argues that Jefferson could have and should have freed his slaves, since other Virginians did. But the men he names either had no important electoral career or — like Washington and John Randolph — freed

their slaves only after their death and hid their intent to do so while in politics. See Finkelman, *Slavery and the Founders,* second edition (M. E. Sharpe, 2001), pp. 134–47.

Introduction: The Three-Fifths Clause

1. But in fact, Jefferson had declined, while in Paris, an invitation to join the Société des Amis des Noirs. See David Brion Davis, *The Problem of Slavery in the Age of Revolution, 1770–1823* (Cornell University Press, 1975), p. 944.

2. The number of extra votes given by the slave population is variously computed, because raw population numbers have to be rounded down to fit the rate of delegates to inhabitants (one to every thirty thousand). The number of "slave votes" in 1800 has been estimated as low as twelve and as high as sixteen (for the sixteen number, see PM 67). Then, to reach the number of those given to Jefferson, one must subtract the black population in the few slave-state districts — in states still voting by district rather than general ticket — where Adams won. The most respected figure currently given for 1800 is that of William W. Freehling in *The Road to Disunion,* Vol. 1 (Oxford University Press, 1990), p. 147, a book that generally uses census statistics in a sophisticated way. Freehling sets the number of "slave votes" at fourteen, of which Jefferson received twelve. Leonard L. Richards sets the number even higher: "In winning nationally by just eight electoral votes, he [Jefferson] had the benefit of at least thirteen of the fourteen slave seats; some pundits thought he had all fourteen. In any event, without the so-called slave seats, he would have lost the election and John Adams would have served a second term. Many historians, celebrating the virtues of the master of Monticello, forget this fact. New England Federalists never did." Richards, *The Slave Power* (Louisiana State University Press, 2000), p. 42. It is significant that Republicans did not try to refute the Federalists' claim. For them, the only numbers that mattered were the ones reached by constitutional process — which undermines Jefferson's boast that 1800 was a triumph of majority will. The Democrats' attitude is summed up by Albert F. Simpson: "The South was standing firmly on the Constitution, the three-fifths rule being a part of that document; her congressmen and leaders felt that it was not necessary to defend it." Simpson, "The Political Significance of Slave Representation, 1787–1821," *The Journal of Southern History* 71 (1941), p. 341.

3. Simpson (op. cit., p. 321) provides a fine survey of Federalist denunciations of the role of the federal ratio in Jefferson's election.

4. In 1803, John Quincy Adams understood exactly what was meant when conversing with a man who attacked "the Negro vote" (JQ 27.338).

5. William Plumer to Edward Livermore, Dec. 23, 1803, cited in Lynn W.

Turner, *William Plumer of New Hampshire, 1759–1850* (University of North Carolina Press, 1962), p. 137.

6. George Gibbs, *Memoirs of the Administrations of Washington and John Adams, Edited from the Papers of Oliver Wolcott,* Vol. 1 (New York, by Subscribers, 1846), p. 409.

7. "Impartialis" [William Plumer], *An Address to the Electors of New Hampshire,* 1804, cited in Turner, op. cit., p. 146.

8. Noble Cunningham, "Election of 1800," in Arthur M. Schlesinger, Jr., et al., editors, *The Coming to Power: Critical Presidential Elections in American History* (McGraw-Hill, 1972), p. 66. Cunningham does not mention the slave count.

9. Daniel Sisson, *The American Revolution of 1800* (Alfred A. Knopf, 1974), and Bernard A. Weisberger, *America Afire: Jefferson, Adams, and the Revolutionary Election of 1800* (William Morrow, 2000).

10. James Horn, Jan Ellen Lewis, and Peter S. Onuf, editors, *The Revolution of 1800: Democracy, Race and the New Republic* (University of Virginia Press, 2002), p. xv. None of the references is made the basis of discussion; though none of them, it should be said, challenges Freehling's claim that Jefferson would have lost without the slave count.

11. Page Smith's two-volume biography *John Adams* (Doubleday, 1962) does not mention the slave count, and David McCullough's *John Adams* (Simon & Schuster, 2001) makes only a fleeting (one-sentence) reference to it (p. 556). Dumas Malone dealt with the election of 1800 in two volumes of his six-volume biography of Jefferson without mentioning the slave bonus in either one. In *Jefferson and the Ordeal of Liberty* (Little, Brown, 1962), the only reference made to a vote margin is this (p. 493): "The margin of his party in the electoral vote was small, but it was larger than that of the Federalists in 1796." In *Jefferson the President: First Term, 1801–1805* (Little, Brown, 1970), he castigates the Federalists (pp. 113–14) for lack of "proper sportsmanship" in not "bowing to the obvious will of the American electorate" — with no mention of the fact that the electoral mandate depended on slaves, who had no will in the matter. Milton Lomask's two-volume biography *Aaron Burr* (Farrar, Straus & Giroux, 1979) does not refer to the slave margin.

12. Edmund Quincy, *Life of Josiah Quincy* (Ticknor and Fields, 1856), 308–16.

13. Seth Ames, *The Works of Fisher Ames,* Vol. 1 (Da Capo Press, 1969), p. 128.

14. Thomas Green Fessenden, *Democracy Unveiled, or Tyranny Stripped of the Garb of Patriotism,* by "Christopher Caustic" (Boston, 1805).

15. Paul Finkelman, *Slavery and the Founders,* second edition (M. E. Sharpe, 2001), p. 203. Others less plausibly argue that it was a factor in Madison's victory of 1812.

16. Richards, op. cit., p. 62.

17. Ibid., pp. 56–57.

18. Ibid., p. 9.

19. Ibid., p. 96.

20. Paul Finkelman, *An Imperfect Union: Slavery, Federalism, and Comity* (University of North Carolina Press, 1980), p. 239.

21. Richard H. Brown, "The Missouri Crisis, Slavery, and the Politics of Jacksonianism," *The South Atlantic Quarterly* 65 (1966), p. 55.

22. The ten pre-war slaveholders were: Washington, Jefferson, Madison, Monroe, Jackson, Van Buren, William Henry Harrison, Tyler, Polk, Taylor. Buchanan, the last president before the war, bought his brother-in-law's slaves and made them indentured servants; but he was served by the slaves of the plantation owner he lived with for a decade, William Rufus King (J. Mills Thornton III, "King, William Rufus," *American National Biography* (Oxford University Press, 1999). Johnson once owned eight slaves, but had freed them all by 1864. Grant briefly owned one slave, but his wife owned four, and he used on his farm those owned by his father and his father-in-law: William S. McFeely, *Grant* (W. W. Norton, 1981), pp. 62–63, 65, 69.

23. Richards, op. cit., p. 121.

24. Don E. Fehrenbacher, *The Dred Scott Case* (Oxford University Press, 1978), pp. 311–14.

25. Philip H. Burch, Jr., *Elites in American History: The Federalist Years to the Civil War* (Holmes and Meier, 1981), pp. 236–37.

26. Sidney H. Aronson, *Status and Kinship in the Higher Civil Service* (Harvard University Press, 1964), p. 115.

27. Richards, op. cit., pp. 92–96.

28. "Address of the Hon. J. Q. Adams to His Constituents . . . at Dedham, October 21, 1843," Boston *Atlas*, Oct. 26, 1843. Josiah Quincy claimed that even fewer large plantation owners set the national agenda — only a thousand of them: Quincy, *Address Illustrative of the Nature and Power of the Slave States and the Duties of Free States* (Ticknor and Fields, 1856), p. 25.

29. Richards, op. cit., p. 49.

30. Douglas Southall Freeman, *George Washington*, Vol. 6 (Charles Scribner's Sons, 1954), p. 344.

31. Jefferson to Joseph Cabell, Jan. 31, 1821.

32. Davis, op. cit., p. 184.

33. Michael Zuckerman, *Almost Chosen People* (University of California Press, 1993), pp. 196 ff.

34. *Mississippi Valley Historical Review*, 1921, pp. 113–80.

35. Russel B. Nye, "The Slave Power Conspiracy: 1830–1860," *Science and Society*, 1946, p. 273.

36. The pervasiveness of conspiratorial views, and the place of Lincoln's thought in this context, is well handled by David Zarefsky in *Lincoln, Douglas, and Slavery* (University of Chicago Press, 1990), pp. 68–110.

37. David Brion Davis, *The Slave Power Conspiracy and the Paranoid Style* (Louisiana State University Press, 1970).

38. David Brion Davis, *The Fear of Conspiracy: Images of Un-American Subversion from the Revolution to the Present* (Cornell University Press, 1971), pp. 104–5, 111–12. It is an embarrassment to the Hofstadter-Davis thesis that, according to later findings, there *were* some Communist conspirators in the federal government.

39. Finkelman, *Slavery and the Founders*, pp. 7–9.

40. Josiah Quincy, *John Quincy Adams* (Phillips, Sampson, 1858), p. 106.

41. Richards, op. cit., pp. 116–20.

42. Leonard L. Richards, *"Gentlemen of Property and Standing": Anti-Abolition Mobs in Jacksonian America* (Oxford University Press, 1970).

43. Seventh Debate with Douglas, *Abraham Lincoln: Speeches and Writings*, Vol. 1, edited by Don E. Fehrenbacher (Library of America, 1989), p. 809.

44. Theodore Parker, Speech of Jan. 29, 1858, in Frances Power Cobbe, editor, *The Collected Works of Theodore Parker*, Vol. 6 (Tübner, 1863–1876), p. 283.

45. Charles Neider, editor, *The Autobiography of Mark Twain* (Harper Collins, 1969), p. 30.

46. Edmund Wilson, *Patriotic Gore* (Oxford University Press, 1962), pp. 532, 535–36, 541–46.

47. Theodore Parker, Speech of May 12, 1854, in Cobbe, op. cit., Vol. 5, pp. 311–12.

1. Pickering vs. Jefferson: The Northwest

1. J. C. Levenson et al., editors, *The Letters of Henry Adams*, Vol. 6 (Harvard University Press, 1968), p. 435.

2. Ibid., p. 624.

3. For Adams's exaggeration of Pickering's role as the head of an "Essex Junto," see Chapter 9 below and David Fischer, "The Myth of the Essex Junto," *William and Mary Quarterly* 21 (1964), pp. 191–235.

4. Octavius Pickering and Charles W. Upham, *Life of Timothy Pickering* (Little, Brown, 1862–1867). Henry Cabot Lodge shrewdly said of the four volumes that "when a biography proves to be incomplete or insufficient, but it is elaborate and extended, there is but little chance that it will ever be rewritten, or at least within any reasonable time." Lodge, *Studies in History* (Houghton Mifflin, 1884), p. 184. Henry Adams called the four volumes "nearly worthless" (*The Nation*, July 5, 1877, p. 13).

5. Clarfield published his first book as *Timothy Pickering and American Diplomacy, 1795–1800* (University of Missouri Press, 1969), and followed that with his second and last book, *Timothy Pickering and the American Republic*

(University of Pittsburgh Press, 1980). He also wrote the entry on Pickering for *American National Biography* (Oxford University Press, 1999), replacing the longer and more sympathetic article by William A. Robinson in the predecessor volumes (*Dictionary of American Biography*, 1926–1937). In an empty field, Clarfield has made himself the leading authority on his subject. Others, even fine scholars in their own areas, rely on him as the expert on this little-studied man. Stanley Elkins and Eric McKitrick, for instance, give nothing more than a précis of Clarfield's biography when they are introducing Pickering into their magisterial volume, though they make a very different judgment of him in the one area they look at closely, his Saint Domingue diplomacy as secretary of state. See their *Age of Federalism* (Oxford University Press, 1993), pp. 623–26 and 654–61, and Chapter 2 below.

6. Edward Hake Phillips, "The Public Career of Timothy Pickering, Federalist, 1745–1802" (Harvard, 1950) stops just before Pickering was elected to Congress, and David McLean, "Timothy Pickering and the Age of the American Revolution" (University of Sydney, offprint by Arno Press, 1982) stops in 1795, before Pickering became secretary of state.

7. Hervey Putnam Prentiss, three articles in the *Historical Collections of the Essex Institute*, Jan. 1933, Apr. 1933, Apr. 1934, reprinted as a book by Da Capo Press, *Timothy Pickering as the Leader of New England Federalism, 1800–1815*.

8. McLean, op. cit., p. 9.

9. James Duncan Phillips, *Salem in the Seventeenth Century*, Vol. 1 (Houghton Mifflin, 1933), p. 266.

10. Linda Kerber, *Federalists in Dissent* (Cornell University Press, 1970), p. 64. Wendell Phillips Garrison and Francis Jackson Garrison, *William Lloyd Garrison, 1805–1879*, Vol. 1 (Arno Reprints, 1969), p. 54.

11. McLean (op. cit., pp. 400–401) refutes Clarfield's claim that Pickering was a lukewarm revolutionary.

12. Fischer, op. cit., p. 205.

13. Clarfield treats Pickering as greedy because he pestered Congress for pay raises; but in a time of inflation, when he was denying himself the "perks" of his office, what else could he do? He sold portions of his own land to pay off debts in this period (P 5.280).

14. Compare Pickering's memorandum to Washington, Apr. 22, 1783 (P 5.291–304), with Washington's "Sentiments on a Peace Establishment" (John C. Fitzpatrick, editor, *The Writings of George Washington*, Vol. 26 [U.S. Government Printing Office, 1931–1944], pp. 374–98). McLean (op. cit., p. 424) even calls Washington's text a "blatant plagiarism" of Pickering.

15. McLean, op. cit., p. 188. See as well Phillips, op. cit., p. 41, on this "liberal plan — too liberal to be adopted."

16. David Brion Davis, *The Problem of Slavery in the Age of Revolution, 1770–1823* (Cornell University Press, 1975), p. 174.

17. Paul Finkelman, *Slavery and the Founders*, second edition (M. E. Sharpe, 2001), p. 44.

18. Peter S. Onuf, *Statehood and Union: A History of the Northwest Ordinance* (Indiana University Press, 1987), p. 110.

19. Charles R. King, editor, *Life and Correspondence of Rufus King*, Vol. 1 (G. P. Putnam's Sons, 1894), pp. 122–29.

20. Don E. Fehrenbacher, *The Slaveholding Republic* (Oxford University Press, 2001), pp. 256–60.

21. Finkelman, op. cit., pp. 52–53.

22. Jefferson to John Holmes, Apr. 22, 1820.

23. Robert J. Taylor, "Trial at Trenton," *William and Mary Quarterly*, 1969, pp. 521–47.

24. Merrill Jensen, *The New Nation: A History of the United States During the Confederation, 1781–1789* (Alfred A. Knopf, 1967), p. 335.

25. McLean, op. cit., p. 212.

26. James R. Williamson and Linda A. Fossler, *Zebulon Butler* (Greenwood Press, 1995), pp. 127–29.

27. Lodge (op. cit., p. 217) rightly said of Pickering: "He was a man of the most reckless courage, physical as well as moral, and there was nothing which so strongly moved his contempt as wavering or hesitation."

28. Merrill Jensen, editor, *Documentary History of the Ratification of the Constitution: Ratification of the Constitution by the States*, Vol. 2, *Pennsylvania* (State Historical Society of Wisconsin, 1976), p. 445.

29. Anthony F. C. Wallace, *Jefferson and the Indians* (Harvard University Press, 1999), pp. 239–40.

30. Phillips, op. cit., p. 410.

31. Isabel Thompson Kelsay, *Joseph Brant, 1743–1807: Man of Two Worlds* (Syracuse University Press, 1984), pp. 464–74.

32. Ibid., pp. 494–97.

33. Reginald Horsman, *Expansion and American Indian Policy, 1783–1812* (University of Oklahoma Press, 1967), pp. 99–101.

2. Pickering vs. Jefferson: Toussaint

1. Clarfield (C 161–62) accuses Pickering of inventing an ambiguous quote from Randolph, though he concedes that the remark may have been made and was ambiguous. If Pickering were inventing the words, why would he have made them so vague? The most economical explanation is that the words were genuine and the interpretation a simple mistake.

2. This point is admitted in both the principal articles that defend Randolph and vilify Pickering. Irving Brant, in "Edmund Randolph, Not Guilty!"

(*William and Mary Quarterly,* 1950, p. 193), says that all the first translators erred "with no intent to deceive." Mary K. Bonstrel Tachau, in "George Washington and the Reputation of Edmund Randolph" (*Journal of American History,* 1986, p. 32), says that Randolph's translations were "as poor as Pickering's."

3. Brant, op. cit., p. 190: Washington "was imposed upon by the malevolence of Pickering and Wolcott."

4. Tachau, op. cit., p. 28: "As for the president, however shaken he may have been by the suspicion that this trusted confidant had been disloyal, he was equally disturbed that the French government had been given that kind of information."

5. David Geggus, "The Haitian Revolution," in Franklin W. Knight and Colin A. Palmer, editors, *The Modern Caribbean* (University of North Carolina Press, 1989), pp. 21–23. Carolyn E. Fick, "The French Revolution in Saint Domingue: A Triumph or a Failure?" in David Barry Gaspar and David Patrick Geggus, editors, *A Turbulent Time: The French Revolution and the Greater Caribbean* (Indiana University Press, 1997), p. 55.

6. Timothy M. Matthewson, "George Washington's Policy Toward the Haitian Revolution," *Diplomatic History* 3 (1979), pp. 325–26.

7. Ibid., pp. 324–35.

8. Ibid., p. 328.

9. It should be noted that almost all Americans at that time referred to Saint Domingue by the name of the Spanish part of the island, Santo Domingo.

10. Jefferson to Monroe, July 14, 1795.

11. Rayford W. Logan, *The Diplomatic Relations of the United States with Haiti, 1776–1891* (University of North Carolina Press, 1941), p. 73.

12. Charles Callan Tansill, *The United States and Santo Domingo, 1798–1873* (Johns Hopkins University Press, 1938), p. 15.

13. Ibid., pp. 52–53.

14. Douglas Egerton, "The Empire of Liberty Reconsidered," in James Horn et al., editors, *The Revolution of 1800* (University Press of Virginia, 2002), p. 314.

15. Ibid., p. 315.

16. Jefferson to Madison, Feb. 19, 1799: "a consul general is named to St. Domingo, who may be considered as our minister *to Toussaint*" (emphasis added); Jefferson to Edmund Pendleton, Feb. 19, 1799: "a nomination is before the Senate of a consul general to St. Domingo. It is understood that he will present himself *to Toussaint* as, in fact, our minister *to him*" (emphases added).

17. "Letters of Toussaint Louverture and of Edward Stevens, 1798–1800," *American Historical Review* 16, p. 65.

18. Robert Ernst, *Rufus King: American Federalist* (University of North Carolina Press, 1968), pp. 268–69.

19. Tansill, op. cit., p. 52.

20. Ibid., p. 55.

21. Ibid., p. 56.

22. Stanley Elkins and Eric McKitrick, *The Age of Federalism* (Oxford University Press, 1993), p. 657.

23. John Chester Miller, *The Wolf by the Ears: Thomas Jefferson and Slavery* (Free Press, 1977), pp. 133–35.

24. Logan, op. cit., p. 75; Elkins and McKitrick, op. cit., p. 657.

25. Jefferson to Madison, Feb. 5, 1799.

26. Jefferson to Madison, Feb. 12, 1799.

27. Ibid.; Tansill, op. cit., p. 17.

28. Logan, op. cit., p. 104.

29. Ibid., p. 105.

30. Ibid., p. 109.

31. Tansill, op. cit., p. 81.

32. Logan, op. cit., p. 114.

33. Paul Finkelman, "The Politics of Slavery in the Age of Federalism," in Doron Ben-Atar and Barbara B. Olberg, editors, *Federalists Reconsidered* (University Press of Virginia, 1998), p. 151.

34. For Lear's help in smuggling Washington's slaves out of Philadelphia before they could be manumitted, see Chapter 15 below.

35. Ray Brighton, *The Checkered Career of Tobias Lear* (Portsmouth Marine Society, 1985), pp. 178–79, 185.

36. Tansill, op. cit., p. 82.

37. Carl Ludwig Lokke, "Jefferson and the Leclerc Expedition," *American Historical Review* 33 (1928), p. 324.

38. Jefferson to Rufus King, July 13, 1802.

39. This was a double standard shared by Jeffersonians in general. The Democratic-Republican Societies set up in response to the French Revolution were a kind of proto–Republican party, and Philip Foner notes of them: "Although there were scores of resolutions adopted by the popular societies hailing and supporting the French Revolution, not one was passed supporting another revolution occurring at the same time — the black revolution of slaves in the French West Indies." Foner, *Democrat-Republican Societies, 1790–1800* (Greenwood Press, 1976), p. 13.

40. Clarfield, *Timothy Pickering and American Diplomacy, 1795–1800* (University of Missouri Press, 1969), p. 147. The not-quite-two pages on Saint Domingue straddle pages 147–49.

41. Stephen R. Egerton, "The Empire of Liberty Reconsidered," in Horn, et al., op. cit., p. 326.

42. James Sidbury, "Saint Domingue in Virginia: Ideology, Local Meanings, and Resistance to Slavery, 1790–1800," *Journal of Southern History* 63 (1997).

43. Franklin W. Knight, "The Haitian Revolution," *American Historical Review* (Feb. 2000), pp. 103, 105.
44. Anthony O. Maingot, "Haiti and the Terrified Consciousness of the Caribbean," in Gert Oostindie, editor, *Ethnicity in the Caribbean* (Macmillan Caribbean, 1996), pp. 53–80.

3. 1800: Why Were Slaves Counted?

1. Draft of Articles of Confederation, July 12, 1776, Article XI, in *The Documentary History of the Ratification of the Constitution*, Vol. 1, edited by Merrill Jensen (State Historical Society of Wisconsin), p. 80.
2. Clinton Rossiter, *The Grand Convention* (Macmillan, 1966), p. 173.
3. Northerners against counting slaves included Elbridge Gerry and Gouverneur Morris (F 1.206, 222). Southerners for counting them fully included Pierce Butler and Charles Pinckney (F 1.542, 580, 596).
4. This was Madison's count (F 2.10), though Delaware was sometimes counted a slave state.
5. Donald L. Robinson, *Slavery in the Structure of American Politics, 1765–1820* (Harcourt Brace Jovanovich, 1971), pp. 179–80.
6. The South claimed that it would pay extra taxes because of its extra representation, since Article I, Section 2 of the Constitution said that all direct taxes shall be required from the states according to their population. But the revenue of the early government was almost entirely from indirect taxes (on goods, imported or domestic), so this "balancing" provision never had real impact — a point Gouverneur Morris had predicted. The pinning of the three-fifths clause to the tax rate came after the ratio debate had been shaped in terms of regionalism (see Paul Finkelman, *Slavery and the Founders*, second edition [M.E. Sharpe, 2001], pp. 12–13).
7. Howard A. Ohline argues that the three-fifths measure was not the crucial issue as regards representation. *Proportional* representation was the key matter — and in easing *its* passage, the three-fifths count actually promoted republicanism. But it was presumed that one house at least would be proportional (Madison was hoping that both would be), and arguments for and against the three-fifths measure concerned regional balance under that presumption. See Ohline's "Republicanism and Slavery: Origins of the Three-Fifths Clause in the United States Constitution," *William and Mary Quarterly*, 1971, pp. 563–84. One wonders what records he could have been reading when he wrote: "The evidence, while admittedly impressionistic, suggests that in 1787 the counting of slaves for purposes of representation was not viewed as a specific endorsement of slavery" (p. 583).
8. John P. Kaminski et al., editors, *The Documentary History of the Ratification*

of the Constitution, Vol. 9 (State Historical Society of Wisconsin, 1990), pp. 1002–3.

9. Lance Banning, "Virginia: Sectionalism and the General Good," in Michael Allen Gillespie and Michael Lienesch, editors, *Ratifying the Constitution* (University Press of Kansas, 1989), p. 265.

10. Pinckney boasted back home of the stand he had taken on the slave trade: "While there remained one acre of swampland uncleared of South Carolina, I would raise my voice against restricting the importation of Negroes . . . without them South Carolina would soon be a desert waste" (F 3.254).

11. Speech of Elias Boudinot in the House of Representatives, *Annals of the Congress of the United States* (Gales and Seaton, 1849), Nov. 1791, col. 203.

4. 1800: The Negro-Burr Election

1. Troup cited in Milton Lomask, *Aaron Burr: The Years from Princeton to Vice President, 1756–1805* (Farrar, Straus & Giroux, 1979), p. 151.

2. Jefferson to Monroe, Apr. 13, 1800.

3. Stephen Kurtz, *The Presidency of John Adams: The Collapse of Federalism, 1795–1800* (University of Pennsylvania Press, 1957), pp. 412–14.

4. Jefferson to Madison, Mar. 4, 1800.

5. Noble Cunningham, "Election of 1800," in Arthur M. Schlesinger, Jr., et al., editors, *The Coming to Power: Critical Presidential Elections in American History* (McGraw-Hill, 1971), pp. 36–37.

6. Jefferson to Monroe, Jan. 12, 1800.

7. *Virginia Federalist*, Mar. 19, 1800.

8. Cunningham, op. cit., p. 40.

9. Jefferson to Monroe, Feb. 11, 1799; Jefferson to Archibald Stuart, Feb. 13, 1799.

10. Jefferson to Madison, Mar. 4, 1800.

11. Charles R. King, editor, *Life and Correspondence of Rufus King*, Vol. 3 (G. P. Putnam's Sons, 1894), p. 14.

12. Matthew Davis, *Memoirs of Aaron Burr*, Vol. 1 (Harper & Brothers, 1838), pp. 434–45.

13. Lomask, op. cit., p. 244.

14. *The Papers of Alexander Hamilton*, Vol. 24 (Columbia University Press, 1961), pp. 444–53.

15. Forrest McDonald, *Alexander Hamilton* (W. W. Norton, 1979), p. 352.

5. 1801: Jefferson or Burr?

1. For Burr as "willing to play the spoiler," see most recently Joyce Appleby, *Thomas Jefferson* (Henry Holt, 2003), p. 10.
2. Ibid., p. 11.
3. Ibid., p. 7: Adams "decamped earlier that morning in high dudgeon."
4. Stephen Kurtz, *The Presidency of John Adams* (University of Pennsylvania Press, 1957), pp. 412–14.
5. Jefferson to Joseph Priestley, Mar. 21, 1801.
6. Jefferson draft letter to Adams, Dec. 28, 1801.
7. Jefferson to Madison, Jan. 1, 1797. Madison warned against putting in writing a desire to serve with Adams, since that might be used later against Jefferson (M 16.455–57). Other Republicans would not welcome such a coalition effort — which does not blunt the fact that Jefferson thought it might be for "the common good." Madison, too, accepted "the duty and policy of cultivating Mr. Adams's favorable disposition, and giving a fair start to his executive career" (M 16.456). He was opposed only to *saying* anything about it, not to doing it. In fact, when Jefferson did express a desire for cooperation once he assumed the office of vice president, Madison was proved prescient, since that upset some Republicans. George Clinton fumed in New York: "He was elected vice president. What did he do? His first act in the Senate was to make a damned time-serving trimming speech, in which he declared that it was a great pleasure to him to have an opportunity of serving his country under such a tried patriot as John Adams, which was saying to his friends, 'I am in; kiss my ass, and go to hell.'" Memorandum to Matthew Davis, May 30, 1830, cited in Joanne B. Freeman, *Affairs of Honor* (Yale University Press, 2001), pp. 235–36.
8. Marvin R. Zahniser, *Charles Cotesworth Pinckney* (University of North Carolina Press, 1967), pp. 234–35.
9. Matthew L. Davis, *Memoirs of Aaron Burr,* Vol. 2 (Harper & Brothers, 1837), pp. 58–59.
10. Edward Thornton to Lord Grenville, Dec. 27, 1800.
11. Anne Cary Morris, editor, *The Diary and Writings of Gouverneur Morris,* Vol. 2 (Scribner's, 1888), p. 396.
12. Bayard testifying under oath in 1805: Davis, op. cit., p. 124.
13. *The Writings of Albert Gallatin,* Vol. 1, edited by Henry Adams (J. B. Lippincott, 1879), p. 51.
14. Bayard cited in Davis, op. cit., p. 127.
15. An important new study of Burr's concept of honor is in Freeman, op. cit.
16. Gallatin, op. cit., p. 23.
17. Jefferson, *Anas,* in Merrill D. Peterson, editor, *Thomas Jefferson: Writings* (Library of America, 1984), p. 695.

18. Harry Ammon, *James Monroe* (University Press of Virginia, 1990), p. 193: "In agreeing to call the Assembly into special session, he was certainly aware that measures of resistance might be undertaken . . . The Governor was evidently prepared for drastic measures should they prove necessary."

19. James E. Lewis, Jr., "What Is to Become of Our Government?" in James Horn et al., editors, *The Revolution of 1800* (University of Virginia Press, 2002), p. 20.

20. Thomas McKean to Jefferson, Mar. 21, 1801, cited in Dumas Malone, *Jefferson the President: First Term, 1801–1805* (Little, Brown, 1970), pp. 10–11.

21. Lewis, op. cit., p. 16.

22. William Cobbett, *Porcupine's Works*, Vol. 13 (Cobbett and Morgan, 1801), p. 175.

23. Gallatin, "Plan at Time of Balloting," *Writings*, Vol. 1, pp. 18–23.

24. Tyler to Monroe, Feb. 21, 1801, cited in Daniel Sisson, *The American Revolution of 1800* (Alfred A. Knopf, 1974), p. 426.

25. George Mifflin, *Life and Writings of Alexander James Dallas* (1871), pp. 112–13.

26. Jefferson, *Anas*, p. 695.

27. Jefferson to Joseph Priestly, Mar. 21, 1801: "There was no idea of force." Malone, always Jefferson's defender, has to admit that he here "presented a half-truth [sic] to a lover of peace" (Malone, op. cit., p. 9). Jefferson to Madison, Feb. 18, 1801: the Federalists acted only after "being alarmed with the danger of a dissolution of the government."

28. Bayard cited in Davis, op. cit., p. 125. William B. Hatcher, *Edward Livingston* (Louisiana State University Press, 1940), pp. 69–70, 91.

29. Jefferson, *Anas*, pp. 694–95.

30. Smith cited in Davis, op. cit., pp. 134–35.

31. Bayard cited in Davis, op. cit., p. 132.

32. Freeman, op. cit., pp. 252–53.

33. Stanley Elkins and Eric McKitrick, *The Age of Federalism* (Oxford University Press, 1993), p. 746.

6. 1801 Aftermath: Turning Out the Federalists

1. Jefferson to Levi Lincoln, Aug. 26, 1901.

2. For the republican ideology's condemnation of "place," see J.G.A. Pocock, *The Machiavellian Moment* (Princeton University Press, 1975), pp. 406–9.

3. David Hume, "Of the Independency of Parliament," in Eugene F. Miller, editor, *Essays Moral, Political, and Literary* (Liberty Classics, 1985), p. 45.

4. Lord Byron, *Don Juan*, Canto XVI, verse 73: "As for his place, he could but say of it / That the fatigue was greater than the profit."

5. Ibid., verse 75.
6. Gordon Wood, *The Creation of the American Republic, 1776–1787* (University of North Carolina Press, 1969), p. 78.
7. Ibid., p. 41.
8. Ibid., p. 49.
9. Milton Lomask, *Aaron Burr: The Years from Princeton to Vice President, 1756–1805* (Farrar, Straus & Giroux, 1979), pp. 307–8.
10. Joyce Appleby, *Thomas Jefferson* (Henry Holt, 2003), p. 62.
11. Lomask, op. cit., p. 310.
12. Richard B. Ellis, *The Jeffersonian Crisis* (W. W. Norton, 1971), p. 45.
13. Ibid., pp. 102–3.
14. Ibid., p. 51.
15. Jefferson to Thomas Mann Randolph, Jan. 9, 1802.
16. Ellis, op. cit., p. 49.
17. Ibid., pp. 59–60.
18. Ibid., pp. 62–64.
19. Pocock, op. cit., p. 409.
20. After the election, Robert Livingston preferred appointment as minister to France over being secretary of the navy.
21. William B. Hatcher, *Edward Livingston* (Louisiana State University Press, 1940), pp. 69–70, 91–92.
22. Marvin R. Zahniser, *Charles Cotesworth Pinckney* (University of North Carolina Press, 1967), pp. 222–33, 237.
23. Annals of the Seventh Congress, first session, pp. 640–41.
24. Dumas Malone, *Jefferson the President: First Term, 1801–1805* (Little, Brown, 1970), p. 142.
25. Henry Cabot Lodge, "Timothy Pickering," in *Studies in History* (Houghton Mifflin, 1884), p. 202.
26. Giles to Jefferson, Mar. 16, 1801, cited in Malone, op. cit., p. 72.
27. Henry Adams, *The Life of Albert Gallatin* (Peter Smith, 1943), pp. 278–79.
28. Jefferson to Gallatin, July 26, 1801.
29. Ibid.
30. Jefferson to Elias Shipman, July 12, 1801.
31. Jefferson to Levi Lincoln, June 1, 1803. Jefferson enclosed an article he had written for which Lincoln was to arrange publication without revealing its source.
32. Robert M. Johnstone, Jr., *Jefferson and the Presidency* (Cornell University Press, 1978), p. 110.
33. Lynn W. Turner, *William Plumer of New Hampshire, 1759–1850* (University of North Carolina Press, 1962), pp. 128–29.
34. Ibid., p. 131.

7. 1803: The Twelfth Amendment

1. Gallatin to Jefferson, Sept. 14, 1801; Jefferson to Gallatin, Sept. 18, 1801, in Henry Adams, editor, *The Writings of Albert Gallatin,* Vol. 1 (J. B. Lippincott, 1879), pp. 51–55.

2. Annals of the Eighth Congress, first session, pp. 16–17, 21–26, 78–84.

3. Lynn W. Turner, *William Plumer of New Hampshire, 1750–1805* (University of North Carolina Press, 1962), p. 120.

4. Annals of the Eighth Congress, second session, p. 751.

5. Pickering cited in Charles W. Upham, *The Life of Timothy Pickering,* Vol. 4 (Little, Brown, 1873), p. 60.

6. Ibid.

7. Tadahisa Kuroda, *The Origins of the Twelfth Amendment* (Greenwood Press, 1994), pp. 130–31, 137–38.

8. Only three presidents (W. H. Harrison, Taylor, F. Roosevelt) have died in office of natural causes, and one of those only because he stretched his tenure into a fourth term. But four presidents (Lincoln, Garfield, McKinley, Kennedy) and one presidential candidate (R. Kennedy) have been assassinated, and attempts were made to kill five presidents (Jackson, Truman, Nixon, Ford, Reagan), one president-elect (F. Roosevelt), and two presidential candidates (T. Roosevelt, G. Wallace). No one has considered a vice president or vice presidential candidate important enough to make an attempt on his life.

9. Leonard L. Richards, *The Slave Power* (Louisiana State University Press, 2000), p. 62.

10. Charles M. Wiltse, *John C. Calhoun, Nationalist, 1782–1828* (Bobbs-Merrill, 1944), pp. 299–301.

11. Some well-qualified men have been nominated in more recent years, partly because ideological spread has been considered along with regional representation, giving the vice president more to do in patching together party forces after he is elected. Northern liberals have run with southern conservatives — Roosevelt with John Garner, Truman with Alben Barkley, Adlai Stevenson with John Sparkman one time and Estes Kefauver the second time, Kennedy with Lyndon Johnson. Or one perceived as a southern conservative has run with a northern liberal — Johnson with Humphrey, Carter with Mondale. Or eastern moderates have run with western conservatives — Dewey with Earl Warren, Eisenhower with Nixon. Or a western conservative with an (apparently) eastern moderate — Nixon with Agnew and then with Ford, Reagan with Bush.

8. *1803: Louisiana*

1. E. Wilson Lyon, *Louisiana in French Diploma*cy (University of Oklahoma Press, 1934), p. 194.
2. Jefferson to Robert Smith, with proposed amendment, early July, 1803.
3. Jefferson to John Dickinson, Aug. 9, 1803.
4. Thomas J. Farnham, "The Federal-State Issue and the Louisiana Purchase," in Dolores Egger Labbe, editor, *The Louisiana Purchase and Its Aftermath, 1800–1830* (University of Southwestern Louisiana Press, 1998), p. 179.
5. Ibid., p. 178.
6. William Parker Cutler and Julia Perkins Cutler, *Life, Journals and Correspondence of Rev. Manasseh Cutler,* Vol. 2 (R. Clarke, 1888), p. 138.
7. Annals of the Eighth Congress, first session, pp. 83–85.
8. Joyce Appleby, *Thomas Jefferson* (Henry Holt, 2003), p. 62.
9. Ibid., p. 65.
10. Jefferson to Wilson Carey Nicholas, Sept. 7, 1803.
11. Lowell H. Harrison, "John Breckinridge and the Acquisition of Louisiana," in Labbe, op. cit., pp. 138–55.
12. Jefferson to Wilson Cary Nicholas, Sept. 7, 1803.
13. Senate debate over the territorial act is not reported in the Annals of Congress — a lack Henry Adams called a serious deficiency: *History of the United States During the Administrations of Thomas Jefferson* (Library of America, 1986), p. 384. Adams did not (could not) know that William Plumer kept a set of notes on this Senate session, part of what is known as his *Memorandum,* which was not published until 1917 in *American Historical Review* (Vol. 22, pp. 340–64). The whole *Memorandum* was not published (by Macmillan) until 1922.
14. Cutler, op. cit., p. 148.
15. Jefferson to William Smith, May 4, 1806.
16. William Plumer, *Register,* Apr. 3, 1806. The *Register* is actually a third volume of the *Memorandum,* but published separately and under a different title.
17. Jefferson to John Dickinson, Jan. 13, 1807.
18. Plumer, *Register,* Apr. 3, 1806.
19. Representative James Sloan of New Jersey made the same motion in the House that Hillhouse and Plumer were making in the Senate. Annals of the Eighth Congress, first session, pp. 1185–86.
20. In their Memorial to Congress, the leaders of the opposition in New Orleans asked for what would later be called (by Stephen A. Douglas and others) popular sovereignty: "We only ask the right of deciding it ourselves, and of being placed in this respect on an equal footing with other states" (Everett S. Brown, *The Constitutional History of the Louisiana Purchase, 1803–1812* [A. M. Kelley, 1972], p. 159).
21. Jefferson to John W. Eppes, June 30, 1920: "I consider a woman who brings a

child every two years as more profitable than the best man of the farm. What she produces is an addition to the capital, while his labors disappear in mere consumption."

22. Michael Tadman, *Speculators and Slaves: Masters, Traders, and Slaves in the Old South* (University of Wisconsin Press, 1989), p. 12. The sales outward from Virginia went from 22,727 in the 1790s to 41,097 in the first decade of the century. That number was doubled again in the 1820s, and it reached 118,474 in the 1830s, when Virginia was furnishing the cotton states with their slaves.

23. Ibid., pp. 196–97. Other prominent Virginians who traded in slaves were Floyd L. Whitehead and W.A.J. Finney.

24. Lucia Stanton, "Those Who Labor for My Happiness," in Peter S. Onuf, editor, *Jeffersonian Legacies* (University Press of Virginia, 1993), p. 172.

25. Jefferson to Christopher Ellery, May 19, 1803. Late in Jefferson's life, when he was in danger of losing all his possessions to creditors, he came up with a scheme for a lottery, the winner to get all his property and he to get the total sum paid for tickets to the lottery. His grandson tried to sell the tickets nationwide, which would have put all his slaves at the disposal of whoever won the lottery, whatever his attitude toward blacks. The slaves could be sold, or their families broken up, at his discretion. See Dumas Malone, *The Sage of Monticello* (Little, Brown, 1981), pp. 473 ff.

26. Ely, a Yale-educated lawyer from Springfield, would come down to Washington the very next year, to serve the first of five terms in the House of Representatives. *Biographical Directory of the American Congresses, 1774–1996* (Congressional Quarterly Publications, 1997), p. 997.

27. Pickering cited in Charles W. Upham, *The Life of Timothy Pickering*, Vol. 4 (Little, Brown, 1873), p. 64.

28. William Plumer, Jr., *Life of William Plumer* (Phillips, Sampson, 1856), p. 328.

29. Josiah Quincy, *Political Sermon Addressed to the Electors of Middlesex* (1803), p. 29.

30. Annals of the Eighth Congress, first session, pp. 58–65. Henry Adams, *History of the United States of America During the First Administration of Thomas Jefferson, 1801–1805* (Library of America, 1986), p. 374.

31. Edmund Quincy, *Life of Josiah Quincy* (Ticknor and Fields, 1868), pp. 89–91, 95.

32. Annals of the Eighth Congress, second session, p. 469.

33. Upham, op. cit., p. 79.

9. 1804: Pickering and Burr

1. The flare-up of the matter in 1828 occurred in complex and circuitous ways. The aging senator William Branch Giles of Virginia, to promote the presi-

dential campaign of Andrew Jackson, attacked President John Quincy Adams by publishing a letter that purported to show Jefferson's disapproval of Adams. A side issue in this matter, chronologically confused in the telling, was John Adams's report to Jefferson in 1807 that New Englanders were considering secession. This became, for Henry Adams, the main issue (though Pickering's agitation for secession was in 1804).

2. Adams to Charles W. Eliot, president of Harvard: "I propose that Mr. Lodge should have a course in U.S. history coterminous with mine. His views, being federalist and conservative, have as good a right to expression in the college as mine, which tend to democracy and radicalism." J. C. Levenson et al., editors, *The Letters of Henry Adams*, Vol. 2 (Harvard University Press, 1982), p. 300.

3. Ibid., p. 319.

4. [Henry Adams], "Lodge's Cabot," *The Nation*, July 5, 1877, and [Henry Cabot Lodge], "New England Federalism," *The Nation*, Jan. 3, 1878. They gently tweaked each other on only one point per person. Adams said that Lodge put the best case for his grandfather; Lodge said that Adams omitted one of his grandfather's intemperate attacks on Harrison Gray Otis — though Lodge clearly knew that Henry was deferring in this to Charles Francis Adams, who had qualms about seeing John Adams's screed published.

5. Adams wrote his brother Brooks on Feb. 18, 1909: "I can't forgive him his vote for the Embargo or his defense of Andrew Jackson. He was not punished half enough for either." Levenson, op cit., Vol. 6 (1988), p. 228.

6. David H. Fischer, "The Myth of the Essex Junto," *William and Mary Quarterly* 21 (1964), pp. 191–235.

7. [Henry Adams], "Lodge's Cabot," p. 13.

8. Henry Adams, *History of the United States of America under the First Administration of Thomas Jefferson, 1801–1805* (Library of America, 1986), p. 416.

9. Milton Lomask, *Aaron Burr: The Years from Princeton to Vice President, 1756–1805* (Farrar, Straus & Giroux, 1979), pp. 341–42.

10. [Henry Adams], "Lodge's Cabot," p. 13.

11. Adams, *The First Administration of Thomas Jefferson*, pp. 426–28.

12. Timothy Pickering, *Interesting Correspondence Between His Excellency Governour Sullivan and Col. Pickering* (Greenough and Stebbins, 1808), p. 15. That Pickering's detestation of the "desperate" Catiline was not just a public pose can be seen from his comments in private correspondence (P 3.52).

13. In Twain, "Senator Balloon" franks home his luggage full of clothes by stamping "Public Documents" on the crate. *The Gilded Age* (Oxford University Press, 1996), pp. 323–24.

14. Pickering, op. cit., p. 16.

15. John Quincy Adams, *Reply to the Appeal of the Massachusetts Federalists*, in

Henry Adams, *Documents Relating to New-England Federalism, 1800–1815* (Little, Brown, 1905), p. 52.

16. Jefferson to William Branch Giles, Dec. 26, 1825, in Adams, *Documents*, p. 8.

17. Leonard W. Levy, *Jefferson and Civil Liberties: The Darker Side* (Harvard University Press, 1963), pp. 70–92. Jefferson defended the many illegal acts of his agent in the matter, James Wilkinson, with these words: "A strict observance of the written law is doubtless one of the high duties of a good citizen; but it is not the highest. The laws of necessity, of self-preservation, of saving our country when in danger, are of higher obligation. To lose our country by a scrupulous adherence to written law, would be to lose the law itself, with life, liberty, property, and all those who are enjoying them with us; thus absurdly sacrificing the end to the means . . . on this superior ground he [a man like Wilkinson] does indeed risk himself on the justice of the controlling powers of the Constitution, and his station makes it his duty to incur that risk. But those controlling powers, and his fellow citizens generally, are bound to judge according to the circumstances under which he acted." Jefferson to J. B. Colvin, Sept. 20, 1810.

18. Jefferson wanted to indict one of Burr's lawyers *in terrorem*, in a way that would make defending an accused man a crime: "Shall we move to commit L. M. [Luther Martin] as *particeps criminis* with Burr? Greybill will fix upon him misprision of treason at least. And at any rate his evidence will put down this unprincipled and impudent Federal bulldog, and add another proof that the most clamorous defenders of Burr are all his accomplices." Jefferson to George Hay, June 19, 1807.

19. Leonard Baker, *John Marshall: A Life in Law* (Macmillan, 1974), p. 517. The message to Congress was dated Oct. 27, 1807.

20. Jefferson, *Notes on the State of Virginia*, Query XVIII: "The whole commerce between master and slave is a perpetual exercise of the most boisterous passions, the most unremitting despotism on the one part, and degrading submissions on the other. Our children see this, and learn to imitate it . . . The parent storms, the child looks on, catches the lineaments of wrath, puts on the same airs in the circle of smaller slaves, gives a loose to his worst of passions, and thus nursed, educated, and daily exercised in tyranny, cannot but be stamped by it with odious peculiarities. The man must be a prodigy who can retain his manners and morals undepraved in such circumstances."

10. 1804–1805: Impeachments

1. Giles to Jefferson, June, 1801, cited in Richard E. Ellis, *The Jeffersonian Crisis* (W. W. Norton, 1971), pp. 20–21.

2. The most complete account of the trial of Pickering is in Plumer's *Memo-*

randum (pp. 147–79). Though Plumer was a friend of Judge Pickering, the accuracy of his account has not been challenged.

3. Worthington C. Ford, *Writings of John Quincy Adams,* Vol. 3 (Macmillan, 1913–1917), pp. 106–14.

4. Jeremiah Smith to William Plumer, Jan. 7, 1805, in Lynn W. Turner, *William Plumer of New Hampshire, 1750–1850* (University of North Carolina Press, 1962), p. 155.

5. Milton Lomask, *Aaron Burr: The Years from Princeton to Vice President, 1756–1805* (Farrar, Straus & Giroux, 1979), p. 364.

6. Annals of the Eighth Congress, second session, pp. 291–96.

11. 1808: Embargo

1. Burton Spivak, *Jefferson's English Crisis: Commerce, Embargo, and the Republican Revolution* (University Press of Virginia, 1979), pp. 73–85. Dumas Malone makes only oblique reference to these preparations for war, *Jefferson the President: Second Term, 1805–1809* (Little, Brown, 1974), p. 435.

2. Gallatin to Jefferson, July 15, 1807, in Henry Adams, editor, *The Writings of Albert Gallatin,* Vol. 1 (J. B. Lippincott, 1879), p. 341.

3. Ibid., Feb. 8, 1807, pp. 328–35.

4. Spivak, op. cit., pp. 68–69.

5. Merrill D. Peterson, *Thomas Jefferson and the New Nation* (Oxford University Press, 1970), p. 884.

6. Spivak, op. cit., pp. 107–10.

7. Gallatin to Jefferson, Dec. 18, 1807, *Writings,* Vol. 1, p. 368.

8. Ibid.

9. James M. Banner, Jr., "Sullivan, James," in *American National Biography,* Vol. 21 (Oxford University Press, 1999), p. 110.

10. James Sullivan to Jefferson, Jan. 7, 1808, cited in Louis Martin Sears, *Jefferson and the Embargo* (Octagon Books, 1966), p. 58.

11. Malone, op. cit., pp. 598–99.

12. Jefferson to Dearborn, Aug. 9, 1808.

13. Gallatin to Jefferson, May 23, 1808, *Writings,* Vol. 1, p. 390.

14. James Sullivan to Jefferson, July 23, 1808, cited in Sears, op. cit., p. 83.

15. Peterson, op. cit., p. 889.

16. Jefferson to Gallatin, May 18, 1808.

17. Jefferson to Gallatin, Nov. 13, 1808.

18. Jefferson to Levi Lincoln, Nov. 13, 1808.

19. Gallatin to Jefferson, July 19, 1808, *Writings,* Vol. 1, p. 200.

20. Jefferson to Gallatin, Aug. 11, 1808, *Writings,* Vol. 5, p. 336.

21. Leonard Levy, *Jefferson and Civil Liberties: The Dark Side* (Harvard University Press, 1927), p. 162.

22. Ibid., pp. 137, 139.
23. Jefferson to Gallatin, Sept. 9, 1808.
24. Charles Francis Adams, editor, *Works of John Adams,* Vol. 9 (Little, Brown, 1856), p. 58.
25. Spivak, op. cit., pp. 24, 77.
26. Peterson, op. cit., p. 807.
27. Jefferson to Abraham Bishop, Nov. 13, 1808. His conversion to manufactures — like his animosity to commerce — was lasting. He would support the protective tariff in 1816: "Experience has taught me that manufactures are now as necessary to our independence as to our comfort" (Jefferson to Benjamin Austin, Jan. 9, 1816).
28. Jefferson to Benjamin Stoddert, Feb. 18, 1808.
29. Spivak, op. cit., p. 207.
30. Gallatin to Jefferson, Nov. 2, 1808, *Writings,* Vol. 1, p. 423.
31. Spivak, op. cit., p. 122.
32. Ibid., pp. 10–11.
33. Annals of the Ninth Congress, first session, pp. 549–52.
34. Henry Adams, *History of the United States During the Second Administration of Thomas Jefferson, 1805–1809* (Library of America, 1986), p. 1121.
35. John Armstrong to Madison, Aug. 30, 1808, cited in Sears, op. cit., p. 316.
36. Henry Cabot Lodge, *Life and Letters of George Cabot* (Little, Brown, 1878), pp. 473–74.
37. Jefferson to W. H. Crawford, June 10, 1816.
38. Jefferson to the Republicans of Essex County, Feb. 20, 1809.

12. *1808: Pickering and Governor Sullivan*

1. Jefferson to Leonard Levi, Mar. 23, 1808.
2. Henry Adams, *History of the United States of America During the Second Administration of Thomas Jefferson, 1805–1809* (Library of America, 1986), p. 1091.
3. Henry Cabot Lodge, *Life and Letters of George Cabot* (Little, Brown, 1878), p. 380.
4. Charles W. Upham, *The Life of Timothy Pickering,* Vol. 4 (Little, Brown, 1873), p. 133.
5. Ibid.
6. Gerard Clarfield speculates (C 236–37) that George Rose helped Pickering in planning, or even in composing, his letter to Governor Sullivan, but the correspondence of the two men precludes that possibility (D 369).
7. Irving Brant, *James Madison, Secretary of State* (Bobbs-Merrill, 1953), p. 450.
8. Levi Lincoln to J. Q. Adams, Apr. 18, 1808.
9. Jefferson to Levi Lincoln, Mar. 23, 1808.

10. Upham, op. cit., p. 135.
11. Burton Spivak, *Jefferson's English Crisis: Commerce, Embargo, and the Republican Revolution* (University Press of Virginia, 1979), p. 65.
12. Madison to Jefferson, Apr. 13, 1807.
13. Jefferson to Madison, Apr. 21, 1807.
14. Lodge, op. cit., p. 470.
15. I use the pagination of the letter in the edition printed by William Treadwell (1808).
16. Brant, op. cit., p. 441.
17. Lodge, op. cit., p. 401.
18. Louis Martin Sears, *Jefferson and the Embargo* (Octagon Books, 1966), p. 317.
19. Ibid.

13. *1808: Pickering and J. Q. Adams*

1. Henry Adams, *History of the United States of America During the Second Administration of Thomas Jefferson* (Library of America, 1986), p. 376.
2. I use the pagination of Adams's pamphlet in the edition printed by J. McKown (1808).
3. For the grandson's judgment, see Henry Adams to Brooks Adams, Mar. 13, 1909, in J. C. Levenson et al., editors, *The Letters of Henry Adams,* Vol. 6 (Harvard University Press, 1968), p. 242.
4. Henry Cabot Lodge, *Life and Letters of George Cabot* (Little, Brown, 1878), p. 476.
5. Ibid., p. 471.
6. Henry Adams, *History,* p. 1043.
7. I use the pagination of Pickering's second pamphlet in the edition printed by Greenough and Stebbins (1808).
8. Henry Adams, *History,* p. 1045.
9. Lodge, op. cit., p. 425.
10. Paul Nagle, *John Quincy Adams* (Harvard University Press, 1997), p. 179.
11. Ibid.
12. Henry Adams, *History,* p. 1203.

14. *1809–1815: Pickering and Madison*

1. Merrill D. Peterson, *Thomas Jefferson and the New Nation* (Oxford University Press, 1970), p. 913.
2. Ibid.
3. Henry Adams, *History of the United States During the Second Administration of Thomas Jefferson* (Library of America, 1986), pp. 1209–13.

4. Ibid., p. 108.
5. Levi Lincoln to Jefferson, Feb. 23, 1809.
6. Jefferson to Henry Dearborn, July 16, 1810.
7. Peterson, op. cit., p. 917.
8. Ibid.
9. Jefferson to Thomas Leiper, June 12, 1815.
10. Robert W. Patrick, *Florida Fiasco* (University of Georgia Press, 1954), p. 10.
11. Samuel Eliot Morison, *Harrison Gray Otis,* Vol. 2 (Houghton Mifflin, 1912), pp. 64–65.
12. J.C.A. Stagg, *Mr. Madison's War* (Princeton University Press, 1983), p. 477.
13. Madison to Wilson Cary Nicholas, Nov. 25, 1814.
14. Henry Cabot Lodge, *Life and Letters of George Cabot* (Little, Brown, 1878), p. 542.

IV. The Pickering Legacy

1. Edward Waldo Emerson and Waldo Emerson Forbes, *The Journals of Ralph Waldo Emerson,* Vol. 6 (Houghton Mifflin, 1911), pp. 349–50.
2. Robert P. Ludlum, "The Antislavery 'Gag Rule': History and Argument," *Journal of Negro History* 26 (1941), p. 236.
3. Madeline House et al., editors, *The Letters of Charles Dickens,* Vol. 3 (Oxford University Press, 1974), p. 135.
4. J. C. Levenson et al., editors, *The Letters of Henry Adams,* Vol. 2 (Harvard University Press, 1982), p. 323.

15. J. Q. Adams: The Federal (Slave) District

1. William W. Freehling, *The Road to Disunion,* Vol. 1, *Secessionists at Bay, 1776–1854* (Oxford University Press, 1990), p. 342.
2. Wendell P. and Francis J. Garrison, *William Lloyd Garrison, 1805–1879,* Vol. 3 (Negro Universities Press, 1969), pp. 97–98.
3. Leonard L. Richards, *The Life and Times of Congressman John Quincy Adams* (Oxford University Press, 1986), p. 105.
4. Don E. Fehrenbacher, *The Slaveholding Republic* (Oxford University Press, 2001), p. 72.
5. The best treatments of this reign of terror are Chapter 5, "The Reign of Mob Law," in Russel B. Nye, *Freedom's Fetters: Civil Liberties and the Slavery Controversy, 1830–1860* (Michigan State College Press, 1949), pp. 139–76, and Chapter 6, "Democrats as Lynchers," in Freehling, op. cit., pp. 98–118.

6. Robert V. Remini, *Andrew Jackson*, Vol. 3 (Johns Hopkins University Press, 1984), p. 259.
7. Freehling, op. cit., p. 291.
8. William Lee Miller, *Arguing about Slavery: John Quincy Adams and the Great Battle in the United States Congress* (Viking Press, 1998), pp. 95–96.
9. Remini, op. cit., p. 260.
10. Ibid., p. 261.
11. Richards, op. cit., p. 15.
12. Freehling, op. cit., p. 342.
13. Miller, op. cit., p. 123.
14. Ibid., pp. 306–7.
15. Ibid., pp. 251, 255.
16. Freehling, op. cit., p. 335.
17. Miller, op. cit., p. 30.
18. Ibid., p. 39.
19. Ibid., p. 38.
20. Ludlum, op. cit., p. 210.
21. Ibid., p. 219.
22. Miller, op. cit., pp. 421–22.
23. Ludlum, op. cit., p. 226.
24. Ibid., p. 237.
25. Ibid., p. 223.
26. Fehrenbacher, op. cit., p. 70.
27. Ibid., p. 60.
28. Ibid., p. 73.
29. Ibid., p. 78.
30. Ibid., p. 79.
31. C. M. Harris, "Washington's Gamble, L'Enfant's Dream: Politics, Design, and the Founding of the National Capital," *William and Mary Quarterly*, 1999, p. 527.
32. Edgar S. Maclay, editor, *The Journal of William Maclay* (Albert and Charles Boni, 1927), p. 304.
33. Kenneth R. Bowling, *The Creation of Washington, D.C.: The Idea and Location of the American Capital* (George Mason University Press, 1991), p. 182.
34. Norman K. Risjord, "The Compromise of 1790: New Evidence on the Dinner Table Bargain," *William and Mary Quarterly*, 1976, pp. 309–14.
35. Bowling, op. cit., pp. 179–85.
36. Harris, op. cit., p. 536.
37. Bowling, op cit., p. 213.
38. Harris, op. cit., p. 547. Joseph Ellis, *Founding Brothers* (Alfred A. Knopf, 2001), pp. 79–80. Jefferson wrote that the new seat of government "will vivify our agriculture and commerce by circulating through our state an additional sum every year of half a million of dollars" (J 16.575).

39. The fugitive slave provision in the Constitution is Article IV, Section 2, Clause 3: "No person held to service or labor in one state, under the laws thereof, escaping into another, shall, in consequence of any law or regulation therein, be discharged from such service or labor, but shall be delivered up on claim of the party to whom such service or labor may be due."

40. John E. Fitzpatrick, *Writings of George Washington* (Government Printing Office, 1931–1944), 34.476.

41. James Thomas Flexner, *George Washington: Anguish and Farewell, 1793–1799* (Little, Brown, 1969), p. 432.

42. Fitzpatrick, op. cit., 35.201–2, 296–98.

43. Ibid., 36.122–23, 148–49.

44. George S. Brookes, *Friend Anthony Benezet* (University of Pennsylvania Press, 1937), p. 321.

45. Ibid., 37.573–74.

46. Paul Finkelman, "Jefferson and Slavery," in Peter Onuf, editor, *Jeffersonian Legacies* (University Press of Virginia, 1993), p. 205.

47. Edwin Morris Betts, editor, *Thomas Jefferson's Farm Book* (University Press of Virginia, 1987), p. 15.

48. Fehrenbacher, op. cit., pp. 54–55, 58.

49. Maclay, op. cit., p. 217.

50. Fitzpatrick, op. cit., 31.30.

51. Bowling, op. cit., pp. 212–13.

52. Ibid., p. 213.

53. Ibid., p. 216.

54. Fehrenbacher, op. cit., p. 60.

55. Ibid., pp. 66–67.

56. Leonard L. Richards, *The Slave Power* (Louisiana State University Press, 2000), p. 70.

16. J. Q. Adams: Petition Battles

1. Don E. Fehrenbacher, *The Slaveholding Republic* (Oxford University Press, 2001), p. 72.

2. Russel B. Nye, *Fettered Freedom: Civil Liberties and the Slavery Controversy, 1830–1860* (Michigan State College Press, 1949), p. 34.

3. William W. Freehling, *The Road to Disunion*, Vol. 1, *Secessionists at Bay, 1777–1854* (Oxford University Press, 1990), p. 412.

4. Ibid., p. 326.

5. Ibid., pp. 326–27.

6. Robert P. Ludlum, "The Antislavery 'Gag Rule': History and Argument," *Journal of Negro History* 26 (1941), p. 211.

7. Ibid., p. 213.

8. William Lee Miller, *Arguing about Slavery: John Quincy Adams and the Great Battle in the United States Congress* (Viking Press, 1998), pp. 227–29.
9. Leonard L. Richards, *The Life and Times of John Quincy Adams* (Oxford University Press, 1986), p. 130.
10. Freehling, op. cit., p. 344.
11. Miller, op. cit., p. 251.
12. Ibid., p. 255.
13. Ibid., p. 272.
14. Freehling, op. cit., p. 349.
15. Miller, op. cit., p. 423.
16. Richards, op. cit., pp. 139–41.
17. The Haverhill petition may have been drafted by the abolitionist poet John Greenleaf Whittier (Nye, op. cit., p. 41).
18. Ludlum, op. cit., p. 218.
19. Miller, op. cit., p. 434.
20. Ibid., pp. 437–38.
21. Richards, op. cit., p. 157.
22. Yanek Mieczkowski, *The Routledge Historical Atlas of Presidential Elections* (Routledge, 2001), p. 43.
23. Ibid., p. 161.
24. Richards, op. cit., p. 166.
25. Freehling, op. cit., p. 383.
26. Richards, op. cit., p. 181.
27. Ulysses S. Grant, *Personal Memoirs* (Library of America, 1990), pp. 41–42.
28. Freehling, op. cit., p. 559.

Epilogue: Farewell to Pickering

1. Madison was reported to have said this, before witnesses, on becoming Pickering's successor as secretary of state (P 54.146).
2. William W. Freehling, *The Road to Disunion*, Vol. 1, *Secessionists at Bay, 1776–1854* (Oxford University Press, 1990), p. 342.
3. William A. Robinson, "Pickering, John," *Dictionary of American Biography*, Vol. 14 (Charles Scribner's Sons, 1937), pp. 565–68.
4. Anthony F. C. Wallace, *Jefferson and the Indians* (Harvard University Press, 1999), pp. 322–23.
5. F. Estelle Welles, "Pickering, Charles," op. cit., p. 562.
6. Edward Hake Phillips, "The Public Career of Timothy Pickering, Federalist, 1745–1802" (diss., Harvard, 1950), p. 410.

Acknowledgments

THIS BOOK is an expansion of the three Julius Rosenthal Lectures I delivered at the Northwestern School of Law in the spring of 2002. Individual titles for the lectures were "Louisiana and the Slave Power," "Burr and the Slave Power," and "The Embargo and the Slave Power." I thank David Van Zandt, the law school's dean, for his hospitality while I was delivering the talks, and the Rosenthal Lectures Committee that invited me, especially Steven Lubet. I am particularly proud of the invitation since it was the first time a member of the Northwestern College of Arts and Sciences was asked to give them at our School of Law.

In consulting the papers of Timothy Pickering and the diary of John Quincy Adams, I had the pleasure of working with the superb staff of the Massachusetts Historical Society, and especially with its research librarian Peter Drummey. I quote from the Pickering and Adams papers by permission of the society. I thank the director, William Fowler, for this courtesies, and I am grateful to the previous director, Louis Tucker, under whose tenure I became a member of the society.

I was also greatly helped by the corrections and suggestions of the scholars who read the manuscript — William Freehling, James Oakes, Leonard Richards, and Douglas Wilson.

I received the warm support of my editor Eric Chinski, my agent Andrew Wylie, my publicist Walter Vatter, and the skilled staffs at Houghton Mifflin and the Wylie Agency. As for Natalie, nothing I can say would be adequate.

Index

Abolitionist(s): Burr as, 77; Haitian revolution's impact on, 45; J. Q. Adams as, 197–98, 200–225; in northern universities, 9; petitions of, 200–204, 214–25; Pickering as, 17, 22, 24–25, 105, 186–87, 191–92, 219, 227; Pickering's father as, 17, 19; Pickering's influence on, 20, 105, 192, 197; rights of women, 201; South's marginalizing of, 10–12, 201; and Texas's annexation, 222–25; on three-fifths clause, 8. *See also* Slavery

Adams, Abigail, 228

Adams, Charles Francis (Henry Adams's father), 130, 249n4

Adams, Charles Francis, Jr., 18

Adams, Henry, 247n13; at Harvard, 127–28, 169; on Jefferson, 113, 226; on Jefferson's Embargo, 157; on J. Q. Adams, 173, 249n5; on Pickering, 18, 127–30, 133, 135–36, 159, 189; on Pickering's feud with J. Q. Adams, 171, 180, 181, 198–99

Adams, John: biographers and historians of, 4, 44–45, 234n11; civil service under, 7; compared to Pickering, 227–28, 230; on counting population, 52; in election of 1800, 1–2, 4, 71, 74,

82, 83, 85, 86, 89, 233n2; franking privileges of, 137; Jefferson on, 75–76; Jefferson's service under, 17, 110, 243n7; Pickering's firing by, 105, 106, 129, 172, 185; Pickering's service under, 2, 17, 18, 34, 39–40, 42; as president, 38, 65, 92, 110, 140–41, 151, 153, 163; as vice president, 212

Adams, John Quincy: as abolitionist, 197–98, 200–225; as congressman, 197–98, 200–225; death of, 225; and efforts to repeal three-fifths clause, 122; in 1802 House election, 106–7; Henry Adams on, 173, 249n5; on Jefferson's presidential election, 1; and Judge Pickering's impeachment, 141, 142; and Louisiana Purchase, 117–20, 125, 172, 200; on northern secession, 127–29, 138–39, 174, 197, 220–21, 223; and Pickering's letter on Jefferson's Embargo, 159–60, 162, 163, 171–81; as secretary of state under Monroe, 198, 200; in Senate, 106–7, 117–20, 128–29, 141, 147, 171–81, 183; shifting views of slavery of, 200–225; on slaveholders' power over government, 8, 11, 105; southern cabinet of, 7; as vice president, 113